Also by Phil Mason
Would You Believe It?
Nothing Good Will Ever Come of It
Napoleon's Haemorrhoids
What Needled Cleopatra
Kent Chronicles of Catastrophe and Disaster
Dead Man Wins Election

With Matthew Parris
Read My Lips
Mission Accomplished

One in the Eye for Harold

One in the Eye for Harold

Why everything you thought you knew about history is wrong

Phil Mason

The Robson Press

First published in Great Britain in 2011 by
The Robson Press
An imprint of Biteback Publishing Ltd
Westminster Tower
3 Albert Embankment
London
SE1 7SP

ISBN 978-1-84954-160-2

10 9 8 7 6 5 4 3 2 1

A CIP catalogue record for this book is available from the British Library.

Set in Adobe Caslon Pro by Namkwan Cho
Cover design by Namkwan Cho

Printed and bound in Great Britain by
CPI Group (UK) Ltd, Croydon, CR0 4YY

Contents

Myths of the Second World War – The Blitz – D-Day Deception – Enigma – Trial of Lord Haw Haw – Trial of Mata Hari – Falklands mythology – Planning for Nuclear War

Introduction

The problem with understanding the past is not what we don't know; it's what we 'know' that isn't actually so.

Most of us don't think about it, but we live our daily lives through our past. The past shapes the environment that we, the current edition of humanity, temporarily occupy. It does so through historic buildings, statues of great heroes, places sanctified with historical significance. The past is all around us. It frames our view wherever we look. But the past also colours the way we think about ourselves, about our fellow countryfolk, and about other countries' folk. The past gives structure to our minds.

How often do we find society collectively defining the 'us' living in the here and now in terms of a commonly held stereotype of the past? We self-satisfyingly declare how progressive we are, being more liberated than those prudish Victorians. We express secret and silent gratitude at not having been born at the time of the First World War, and not to have been one of that 'lost generation' who evaporated in the mud of Flanders before they could fulfil themselves. We piously please ourselves that we today do not need to gain our wealth by the callous exploitation that our predecessors resorted to when they created the British Empire.

But what if all these perceptions of the past are wrong? How secure would we feel about ourselves if much of what we have been led to believe about our past is actually not true?

Each of the above views of the past *is* wrong.

And there are more. Lots more. In fact, swathes of commonly held views of our past turn out to be wrong.

What you are about to read will turn the foundations of the history you know upside down.

☞

One in the Eye for Harold shows just how much of the history that generations have absorbed from their history books, teachers and the power of collective belief, is actually wrong. Some of the most familiar tales that we have grown up with from childhood are in fact myths.

So for starters: the Victorians were not, in fact, prudes (nor, for that matter, were they unduly pious, or crime-ridden, attributes they are also often saddled with). The First World War did not create a 'lost generation' in Britain – in fact 86 per cent of military-aged men returned (and most soldiers were at the front for only four days in every month: their strongest memories were of boredom, not fighting). And the Empire, long pilloried for being a mercenary operation of grand plunder, did not, in fact, generate as much wealth and prosperity for Britain as the modern, politically correct, guilt trip makes out (indeed, one line of argument suggests it may even have hindered Britain's development).

Many of the long-cherished building blocks of our culture, encoded into our core beliefs from our schooldays, turn out to be false:

- Harold was not shot in the eye by an arrow at the Battle of Hastings.
- Our traditional view of the origins of the British – Angles, Saxons and Jutes invading from Europe and pushing the ancient Britons to the hills to become Scots and Welsh – is now shown by DNA evidence to be wrong. We all turn out to be from the same genetic stock.

- The Great Depression of the 1930s was not a period of overall economic decline as commonly presented: living standards in Britain actually rose.
- The much-touted Normandy invasion deception scheme did not trick the Germans into thinking the Allies would land somewhere else on D-Day.
- Magna Carta is not the great bedrock of Britain's political rights we assume it to be. The vast majority of the sixty-two clauses actually dealt with barons settling individual scores with the King, not setting a grand new political order.

Some mistakes in the reading of history come from ignorance (the story of the arrow in the eye turns out to be more a coded message to contemporaries than a recording of historical fact for posterity).

Sometimes the falsity comes from folklore stories passing down from the mists of time which only modern methods can unpick (only through DNA sampling have the true origins of the British races emerged).

Others derive from perspectives formed in the moment becoming fixed and simply too 'sticky' to shift even when later evidence suggests an alternative picture (the image of the 1930s as poverty-wracked is iconic, conveniently straightforward and easy to understand).

Some myths become part of the national memory for more questionable reasons, because they make us feel proud, clever or superior, especially in times of stress (the D-Day legend of tricking the Germans is one of the core success stories of the Second World War) or because there is a deep-down collective desire to believe that the myth is true because doing so serves a valuable function in the present (Magna Carta lies at the heart of the British consciousness of the longevity of its legal and constitutional traditions, and thus reinforces a public belief in the depth and solidity of the nation's values.)

One of the best examples of how mythologising about the

past helps the present is the American foundation story. The commonly accepted view of the rebellion of the American colonies from Britain in the 1770s is that the Americans wanted to form their own new nation. That belief creates a shared story that binds the Americans together even today. But it is wrong.

The American War of Independence is now cherished in US folklore as the story of a concerted struggle of oppressed colonials to form their own union. But it was not, in fact, fought with the intention of creating a new unified country. The War was neither a mass popular uprising – only a third at most wanted independence – nor was the preconceived aim to form a united state. A portion of the colonials may have wanted to throw out British rule, but that did not mean they necessarily wanted to join together in a new combined community which we casually assume today was the motivation, and which any modern American would have us believe, because they sincerely believe it too. The journey from the Thirteen Colonies to the United States of America was a rocky, tortured one, and took a generation.

To hear it told today, one would believe it was a tale of a people acting in unison with a clear vision of the objective and achieving their goal with arrow-straight application of purpose. The truth lies far from that, but it is how history tends to remember it, and it remains a powerful narrative that helps hold a heterogeneous collection of people together. The story of the formation of the USA is far from this simple one we have all come to believe, and which American patriotic theology drums into its citizens.

Neither was the other great event in American history – the Civil War – as clear cut as popularly assumed. Surely, it was a war to end slavery? Not so. Abraham Lincoln, revered by history as the friend of the slave, the Great Emancipator, actually never freed the slaves despite his Proclamation which purported to do just that. Nor was Lincoln primarily concerned about slavery. Of greater importance was the Union. The Civil War was fought to preserve the Union, not eradicate slavery. If the battle against slavery got in the way, Lincoln would sacrifice it, and he did.

Sometimes, it seems, we just want to believe a viewpoint even though the facts tell a different story, so we tend to bury the inconvenient facts. The American Civil War is a good example of how one interpretation – some would argue a higher and more moral explanation of the war – has triumphed over the other, rather more practical motivation.

Another is one of the most colourful 'facts' about the most colourful British politician of the 20th century – that Winston Churchill was one sixteenth Iroquois Indian.[1] The story has persevered over the years and has been trotted out in popular histories, even thought the facts were well known a long time ago.

The lineage was said to come through his American mother, Jennie Jerome, whose great-great-grandmother – New Englander Anna Baker – was, the family genealogies asserted, a native Indian. As late as 1999, Churchill's politician grandson, also Winston, was visiting the United States attempting to substantiate the longstanding claim. 'She's got Red Indian written all over her face,' he told reporters covering the trip.[2] He need not have bothered, and should have known better, according to American genealogists.

The story of Churchill's Red Indian ancestry, which supposedly kept its legs because there was a complete absence of information on the Baker family, had, in fact, been known to have no foundation since the 1950s. According to Gary Roberts, senior scholar at the New England Historic Genealogical Society, two researchers there uncovered the family tree of the Baker family in 1951.[3] This showed her full ancestry, revealing that she had been born of English-descended parents – Rhode Islander Joseph Baker and

Experience Martin, a Massachusetts woman.[4] 'I am afraid it is one of those false traditions that somehow grow up in families, but it is simply not the case,' said Roberts. 'There is not a trace of Indian blood.' But history did not want to give up believing so easily.

☞

One in the Eye for Harold is the story of how history gets misused and misremembered, for all sorts of reasons. This is not a book about historical controversies, of which history remains full. It is about the history that we assume to be settled, agreed upon, known and accepted by all – but in fact isn't as we believe.

The phenomenon of 'Bad History' is far more dangerous and pernicious to understanding than plain ignorance. We delve into those 'truths' we commonly 'know' to show how far from the real truth they actually are.

As much of what follows is likely to run counter to what is usually believed, we have taken care to provide the sources for the different view of history presented here. Perhaps the most worrying aspect of the material is how old many of the references are that show the errors of our beliefs. Many of the falsehoods have been known for decades. It has not been that the knowledge is not there. It is that it is buried, often wilfully and consciously, in favour of comfortable stories that explain our past more simply. We hang on to treasured myths with great tenacity. Despite the truth being out there, we prefer the conspiracy of Bad History.

We range across the spectrum of history's themes – war, politics, social history, religion, science, popular culture. We span the globally significant ...

- There is no contemporary evidence that St Peter was the original Pope, or Bishop of Rome. He only appears in the Papal records 300 years after the founding of the Church of Rome.

... to what some would see as trivial:

- The kilt is not an ancient Scottish dress, but invented by an Englishman only in 1727.

We find facts that will overturn long-held perceptions ...

- Manna from Heaven was a punishment from God, not a relief.
- More Scots fought on the English side at Culloden than with the Scottish army.
- Far from being the cradle of democracy, the political system suggested by the leading thinker of the ancient Greeks was for a eugenics-based dictatorship.
- Far from being a ruthlessly disciplined and organised outfit, the success of the Nazi regime was actually built on chaos and deliberate confusion.

... to those that suggest that much of our vision of the past is of modern manufacture:

- The American Wild West was not actually very wild at all. The most deadly year in Dodge City saw just five violent deaths. Almost all our notions of the Wild West are inventions of Hollywood.
- '*Liberté, Égalité, Fraternité*' was not the motto of the French Revolution. It was only adopted when the revolution was almost over ... and Bastille Day has been celebrated as the French national day only since 1880, 91 years after the event.

We guarantee that you will uncover a truth you did not know in the pages that follow. Many are likely to challenge the deepest certainties you thought you had about history.

If you thought the virtue of the past was that, because it was in the past it was fixed and unchanging, think again. Prepare to be surprised. Prepare to have your faith in the 'historical record' shattered.

Phil Mason

References

1   See for example, genealogy in K. Halle, *The Irrepressible Churchill*, Robson, 1985; R Churchill, *Winston Churchill 1874–1900*, Heinemann, 1966

2   Report, *The Times*, London, 13 October 1999

3   Report, *Daily Telegraph*, 15 October 1999

4   See *www.winstonchurchill.org*

What Every Schoolchild Knows

Some facts are so well 'known' that from our earliest ages at school they formed the ground floor of the scaffolding that built our learning about the past. In this chapter, we look at some of the most firmly entrenched views of the past – that are wrong.

A much maligned race (1) – the Neanderthals
(*humorous* and *derogatory*). Primitive, uncivilised, loutish. (*Oxford English Dictionary*)

The Neanderthals have had a bad press. Their place in the evolutionary road map has long been as the slow-witted, unadapting, cul-de-sac of the early human family tree that flourished across Europe around 300,000 years ago – the archetypal caveman – only to be pushed to extinction by the more advanced version of *Homo sapiens*, our direct ancestors, arriving from Africa some 200,000 years later. Neanderthals disappeared completely from the archaeological record 28,000 years ago, and are portrayed as the dead-end branch, swept aside by their more intelligent African cousins. The term 'Neanderthal' has come to personify characteristics that are uncultured, backward, ignorant.

While modern DNA techniques have indeed confirmed the 'dead-end' theory in regard to where modern mankind hails from, the common image of the Neanderthal's primitivism has lodged fixedly in our minds. Only recently has a very different picture emerged from that which was created when the bones of a distinctly human form were discovered by workmen in the Neander Valley near Dusseldorf in 1856.

The timing of the discovery, according to famed paleoanthropologist Richard Leakey, could not have been worse for the fortunes of the Neanderthal.[1] The interpretation of the find, which was long before the conceptual map of early human development had been pieced together, came at the height of the controversy raging across intellectual circles as to whether Man was descended from the apes (Darwin would publish his theory of evolution just three years later) and when the tide of opinion was forcefully against thinking such thoughts.

As more and more remains turned up across Europe in the decades that followed, the conclusion was inescapable that they represented an ancient race, but the temper of the times encouraged a disparaging approach to reconstructing their existence – both metaphorically and physically. Their fate in our modern minds rests a lot on the attitude taken by the man responsible for putting together the first complete skeleton of a Neanderthal from remains that were found in the Dordogne in southern France in 1908.

Marcellin Boule, a palaeontologist working for the French National Museum of History, had the task of giving shape to the collection of bones discovered. According to Leakey, he followed the preconceptions of the time:

> to emphasise everything that was primitive, brutish and apelike about the skeleton. He even failed to take account of the fact that in this particular specimen the old man clearly had suffered from severe arthritis. Marcellin Boule's reconstruction stooped, with rounded shoulders and dangling arms. He walked on the outer part of his feet and with his knees bent. His big toes diverged from the rest of his toes, as in the apes, and his head was thrust forward in a cretinous and improbable manner. Despite the fact that the skull had room for a brain bigger than a modern human's, Boule deduced from the long, low shape of the skull that the old man had been dimwitted.[2]

When he published his conclusions between 1911 and 1913, the image of the Neanderthal was set, the sub-text being to distance this specimen from humanity as far as possible. 'Brutish', 'clumsy', 'bestial' were some of the terms Boule used to characterise the being. They stuck. The common perception of Neanderthal Man was of a race that was inarticulate, unable to fashion adequate tools (hence their eventual eclipse by more advanced species) and more like an ape than a human.

The reality, it now seems, is quite different. Although the popular image has been incredibly hard to shift, Neanderthals' place in the chain of human development has been improving in the arcane technical journals. As early as 1957 a reappraisal of Boule's work by two anatomists, William Straus and AJE Cave, discovered the arthritis bias and demonstrated that, in fact, the body of Neanderthals were pretty much like modern humans. As they famously put it,

> If he could be reincarnated and placed in a New York subway – provided he were bathed, shaved and dressed in modern clothing – it is doubtful whether he would attract any more attention than some of its other denizens.[3]

Neanderthals turn out to have been one of the most successful species – as any would need to be that managed to survive for a quarter of a million years. Modern evidence shows they used and developed stone tools and weapons, had a clan structure for social organisation and – a practice acknowledged to be symbolic of emerging humanity – buried their dead. Findings published in 2010 by the University of York suggest they even had a conscientious side. Analysis of remains showed that one Neanderthal who had acute disabilities including a withered arm, deformed feet and blindness in one eye, nevertheless lived for up to two decades, implying that he was being looked after by others in his group.[4]

They innovated in making tools, something only later species are traditionally thought to have been capable of. Findings published in 2008 suggested that their tools were just as technologically advanced as the *Homo sapiens* who would out-live them, destroying the accepted explanation that Neanderthals lost out because their rivals surpassed them with better devices.[5] And far from stunted intelligence, their brains were actually slightly larger than modern humans (1,400 cubic centimetres compared to our 1,360)[6]

Research by a team from Duke University, North Carolina, in 1998, suggested that Neanderthals may even have been some of the first humans capable of speech, pushing back the accepted moment for verbal communication from 40,000 years ago to 350,000. They discovered that Neanderthals possessed hypoglossal canals – perforations at the bottom of the skull where the spinal cord connects to the brain – of the same size as modern humans. This implied that they had a nerve structure leading to the tongue identical to modern man, and could in theory be capable of speech. By contrast, most other remains known to scientists had canals equivalent to those of chimpanzees, suggesting they were incapable of articulating sounds.[7] Spanish archaeologists endorsed this view in 2004 after studying Neanderthal ear bone remains in northern Spain which showed that they were attuned to picking up the same frequency as that used in modern speech, and distinctly different from that of monkeys.[8]

The mystery of their eventual demise remains, but it is clear now it was not simply due to them being backward and dim-witted. As Metin Eren, from Exeter University, commented in 2008, 'It is time for archaeologists to start searching for other reasons why Neanderthals became extinct while our ancestors survived.'[9]

☞

A much maligned race (2) – the Philistines

Another put-upon body of people whose reputation has been sullied for three thousand years are the Philistines. Turning once more to the *Oxford English Dictionary*, we find a familiar litany of negativity:

> uneducated, unenlightened; indifferent or hostile to culture; aesthetically unsophisticated.

Their fate perhaps illustrates better than any other the reality that history's winners get to cast history's losers in whatever light they choose. As Churchill famously once quipped to an opponent who threatened that history would prove the war leader wrong: 'History will prove me right – because I will write it'. And he did.

The Philistines, who occupied the strategic coastal strip that extended roughly between modern Ashdod and Gaza, had the bad luck to come up against some of the Bible's most stunning Israelite heroes – Samson, Saul, Samuel and, above all, King David – whose memorialists had the advantage of holding history's pen as the Bible set down for posterity a version of what occurred. The Philistines – believed to have been illiterate and leaving no written record – came off distinctly worse for wear.

According to the Old Testament, they were pagan and devil worshippers, constant invaders of Israelite land and accused of stealing the Ark of the Covenant, the sacred container of the Ten Commandments. They famously bribed Delilah to cut off Samson's hair, the supposed source of his strength, and their champion, the giant Goliath, took up arms against David.

If that was not enough, history has been doubly harsh on them because it appears their modern status as the icon for uncouth barbarianism stems not directly from the Bible references but from the practice of 17th century German students in the university city of Jena of distinguishing between them-selves ('the gown') and 'the town' (that is, ordinary everyday folk) by referring to the uncivilised remainder of the commu-nity as *philisters,* thought to derive from an allusion to 'tall men' (from Goliath), assumed to be a reference to the town guards with whom the students had frequent run-ins. According to tradition, after a particularly vicious confrontation which had caused the death of a student, the university rector used the Biblical quotation from *Judges* 16:9, 'The Philistine be upon thee, Samson' in his funeral sermon. It quickly extended to all townsfolk, and it was this usage that the likes of social critic Matthew Arnold and essayist Thomas Carlyle picked up on when they popularised the term in English as a moniker for uncultured attitudes in mid-Victorian times. It has stuck rigidly in our minds ever since.[10]

But the real truth of the Philistines has only recently been emerging, set off in the early 1990s by a team from Harvard University excavating a site near Ashkelon on Israel's coast. They discovered signs of a high culture unseen in the region at the time and streets ahead of contemporary Israel. The imagery of an uncouth, backward people appears now to be far off the truth. Advanced building styles, exquisitely decorated palaces and altars were uncovered. Elegantly decorated pottery, painted with pictures of fish, birds and complex geometric patterns, was unearthed, richly contrasting with that in use by Israelis of the time who were still making do with crude, unpainted ware. The archaeologists proved that they had not simply been imported from other Mediterranean civilisations by testing their composition. They were shown to be cast from local clay. Even a wine press was found. Scenic wall paint-ings depicting stories from ancient Greek literature showed that the Philistines were a cosmopolitan race. The discovery of imported Greek loom weights proved not only that they engaged in weaving, but that they were also sophisticated international traders.

All a far cry from the vision that has been handed down to us. As one commentary on the revelations remarked, 'History is the official record of the winners. ... The moral of the reputation of the Philistines is not to believe everything you read. And for future reputation, get the scribes on your side.'[11]

☞

The Vikings – more savaged than savaging

The only image we have of the Vikings is of bloodthirsty, horn-helmeted invaders who raped and pillaged their way across Britain in the 8th and 9th centuries.

It is now coming to be accepted by archaeologists that the Vikings did not wear horns or wings on their helmets. These seem to have appeared as distinctly Viking accoutrements only in the 19th century. The usually cited culprit is Swedish illustrator Gustav Malmström who used the motif in an edition of *Frithiof's Saga* (1820–25). He is thought to have taken the idea from headgear used in Norse religious rites. None of the many helmets that have been unearthed from Viking archaeological sites have ever been found to have horns.[12]

It was the English translation of Malmström's edition of the *Saga* that introduced the term 'Viking' into English. (With the exception of three references in the Anglo-Saxon Chronicle, where the reference is to 'robbers' rather than to a race of people, the term is not recorded in English until 1807.)[13] Sir Walter Scott is credited with having popularised it by his 1828 novel *The Pirate*. It was not to become a recognised term for the people or the period until Victorian times, and the concept of the 'Age of the Vikings' seems to have first been invented in Scandinavia to label items in the National Museum in Copenhagen in the 1840s.[14]

Some historians have even doubted the Vikings' famed reputation for violence. An investigation by the BBC

Timewatch series in 1995 poured cold water on the image of the Viking as a deranged pillager. Professor Janet Nelson, a medieval historian at King's College, London, confessed that it was difficult to find evidence of specific raids in contemporary accounts. 'In fact, there isn't a single case of rape,' she told the programme. He was more likely, to be 'a decent, respectable migrant' who was 'a little dull'. They were eventually to settle amidst the English for three hundred years, living side by side in relative harmony.

The history of the Viking experience in Britain, in fact, carries a very odd twist. In contradiction to our normally held memory of the Vikings, it is possible that the greatest episode of violence in the long history of the two races' relations was inflicted *on* the Danes *by* the British. It is one of the darkest days of the country's history, but one that is largely forgotten by the modern Briton: the gruesome St Brice's Day massacre on 13 November 1002. Tens of thousands of Danes who had settled in the country were massacred in a single outburst of pent-up fury.

It was the brainstorm of King Ethelred – famously the Unready (meaning 'ill-advised') – who decided he had had enough of the extortionary Danegeld, the annual protection money paid to the Danish kingdom to dissuade them from military invasion. Paid for by a universally unpopular poll tax, it stumped up sums of up to 24,000 pounds of silver a year to buy peace. (No calculation can give an accurate estimate of what proportion of national wealth this represented. Churchill estimates it may have represented up to two to three years' worth of national income.)[15]

It had had the (to Ethelred) unexpected but not illogical effect of encouraging the Danes to keep pushing up the price of peace. By 1002, his patience exhausted, he suddenly snapped and gave orders for every Dane in the country to be slaughtered.

Among the bizarre atrocities of the day was the flaying

alive of captured Danes and the subsequent nailing of their skins to the doors of churches which the Danes were said to have desecrated. The remnants of skins remained exposed to view at many sites at least into the middle of the 19th century. Tradition asserts that the gates to Minster Abbey in Kent were so decorated for centuries. The great doors of Rochester Cathedral were also still so adorned well into the 17th century. No less an authority than Samuel Pepys' diary records a visit he made to the town in April 1661 and his viewing of the Danish skins.[16]

In the long run, it was a blunder of stupendous proportions. One of the victims was the Danish King's sister and the massacre merely prompted ever greater retribution over the next dozen years which culminated in Ethelred fleeing the throne, leaving the way open for the Danish King's son, Canute, to become King of England in 1016. Three hundred years after first contact, the Danish conquest was complete.

☞

The origins of the English

The English derive their name from the Angles, the ancient Germanic tribe which, according to conventional history, migrated, along with the Saxons and the Jutes, from the continent to the British Isles in the five hundred years following the departure of the Romans at the beginning of the 5th century. From AD 450 they supposedly pushed the ancient Britons, of Celtic origin, to the fringes of the isles, into Wales, Cornwall and Scotland and across to Ireland. It supposedly led to the atavistic differences that persist to this day between the English and their border brethren.

According to modern DNA research, however, all that may be entirely wrong. Two separate projects undertaken in 1997 and 1998 by scientists at Oxford and Sheffield Universities came to the same conclusions using different investigations. At

Oxford, investigators compared the DNA of modern Britons with that of Stone Age skeletons and found that 99 per cent of modern Britons can trace their origins back to a common DNA pool that dates to 10,000 years ago. This suggests that the popular image of waves of foreign invaders settling and pushing out the original inhabitants – the core of the British island story – looks likely to be a myth. At best, it suggests that any migrations were smaller than usually presented and had an insignificant impact on the nation's gene pool.

These conclusions lent strong support to those of the Sheffield project which had reported in 1997 the discovery of a distinctive genetic variant that is prevalent amongst people in Lower Saxony and Schleswig-Holstein, the areas from which the Angles and Saxons supposedly came. Had they swamped the British as history currently has it, remnants of the variant would be showing up in modern Britons' DNA. And there is no sign of it.[17]

The findings seemed to be confirmed in 2001 by another study at University College, London. This found that between 50 and 75 per cent of people DNA-tested in southern England shared the same genetic origins as ancient Britons or Celts, rather than Anglo-Saxons.[18] 'Perhaps the most surprising conclusion,' the report said, 'is the limited continental input in southern England, which appears to be predominantly indigenous and, by some analyses, no more influenced by the continental invaders than is mainland Scotland'.

The stark conclusion is that the English are, at root then, no different genetically from the Welsh or the Scots. All the island 'races' are in fact common. 'The genetic evidence does not support the hypothesis of the widespread destruction or displacement of the native population by invaders from what is now northern Germany,' said Dr Martin Evison, head of the Sheffield project in 1997.

The 'True-Born' Englishman

For some reason, the English have a fixation for parading their lineage as a symbol of national purity. To be 'true-born English', or 'English through and through' conveys a deep-down belief in a single, undiluted identity. As long ago as 1701, Daniel Defoe penned a mocking rebuttal of this eccentric Anglocentrism. This is only a small part:

> The Romans first with Julius Caesar came,
> Including all the nations of that name;
> Gauls, Greeks, and Lombards; and by computation,
> Auxiliaries or slaves of every nation.
> With Hengist, Saxons; Danes with Sueno came,
> In search of pounder, not in search of fame.
> Scots, Picts, and Irish from t'Hibernian shore:
> And Conquering William brought the Normans o're.
> All these their barb'rous offspring left behind,
> The dregs of armies, they of all mankind;
>
> …
>
> From this amphibious ill-born mob began
> That vain ill-natured thing, an Englishman.
>
> …
>
> And lest by length of time it be pretended,
> The climate may this modern breed ha'mended,
> Wise Providence, to keep us where we are,
> Mixes us daily with exceeding care:
> We have been Europe's sink, the jakes where she
> Voids all her offal out-cast progeny.
> From our fifth Henry's time, the strolling bands
> Of banished fugitives from neighb'ring lands,
> Have here a certain sanctuary found.
>
> …
>
> Thick as the locusts which in Egypt swarmed,
> With pride and hungry hopes completely armed:
> With native truth, diseases, and no money,

Plundered our Canaan of the milk and honey.
Here they grew quickly Lords and Gentlemen,
And all their race are True-Born Englishmen.
…

French cooks, Scotch pedlars, and Italian whores,
Were all made Lords, or Lords' progenitors.
Beggars and bastards by this new creation,
Much multiplied the peerage of the nation;
…

Fate jumbled them together, God knows how;
What'er they were, they're True-Born English now.
The wonder which remains is at our pride,
To value that which all wise men deride.
…

A True-Born Englishman's a contradiction,
In speech an irony; in fact a fiction.
A banter made to be a test of fools,
Which those that use it justly ridicules.
A metaphor invented to express
A man akin to all the universe.[19]

☞

The origins of the Irish …

Continuing the unraveling of the British racial myths, the Irish suffered their own knock in 1999 when researchers into the Irish DNA stock confirmed that even the Irish appeared to be all part of the common British gene pool. Far from being a distinctive Celtic strain, Irish DNA was found to be part and parcel of the same genetic makeup as the English, and drawing its origins from the same ancestry of 10,000 years ago, millennia before the supposed Celtic migrations of the 5th or 6th centuries BC. 'The image of the Irish as a genetically Celtic people, in fact the whole idea of a Celtic ethnicity … is a load of complete cock and bull,' said Richard Warner, archaeologist at the Ulster Museum. 'The average Irish person probably has more English genes than Celtic.'[20]

☞

... *the Scots*

Hadrian's Wall started it. Francis Lockier, 18th century Dean of Peterborough, seemed to confirm it:

> In all my travels I never met with any one Scotchman but what was a man of sense: I believe every body of that country that has any, leaves it as fast as they can.[21]

And Byron reinforced it:

> A land of meanness, sophistry and mist.
> Each breeze from foggy mount and marshy plain
> Dilutes with drivel every drizzly brain.[22]

The image of the wilds of Scotland being filled with ignorance and barbarism has been a consistent motif down the centuries. Not so. Archaeological finds in the 1990s have begun to paint a different picture, one of culture and finesse. A team from the National Museums of Scotland reported their conclusions in 1996 that far from the standard view of the island communities being rough and uncivilised, the Lords of the Isles developed between the 13th and 15th centuries a highly cultivated way of life. A six-year dig on the island of Islay had revealed much stronger evidence of a taste for music and the arts than had ever been thought. Previous assumptions, drawn from lowland chroniclers, that they lived a primitive existence in thatched wooden and mud huts were overturned with evidence of stone buildings with slate roofs. The Lord's castle even had a timber sprung floor. The archaeologists also found evidence of ship-building techniques that were the most advanced anywhere in Scotland, along with tuning keys for harps which suggested a far more developed interest in music than they have been given credit for.

'We are uncovering a society with a tremendous tradition of learning,' said the team leader, David Caldwell. As to why they should have been so misrepresented in the past, he put it down to jealousy from those living in less harsh parts of the country. 'It is almost a lowland prejudice about these people.'[23] The emerging picture seemed to show that far from the Isles being tamed by the creep of civilization from the south, it was the relatively uncultured lowlanders who eradicated the more sophisticated lifestyle of their more advanced northern neighbours.

☞

... not to mention the French

In 2002, Gallic pride was also dented when one of France's most respected academics published his contention that the French identity is based on a litany of myths and false history. Christian Goudineau, Professor of History at the respected Collège de France, shocked his countrymen by asserting that the Gallic people never existed in the past as a collective community. The famed warrior nation that formed the supposed roots of what became France was all a combination of administrative casualness and someone else's self-serving propaganda.

It was all the doing of Julius Caesar, who first coined the term Gaul for the people he came across as he extended the Roman Empire's reach northwards between 58 and 51 BC. He conquered vast swathes of what is now France, Germany and the Low Countries, and for ease of future administration simply drew an arbitrary dividing line between the Germanic tribes to the east and those of the west, which he termed

Gaul. According to Goudineau, the occupants of 'Gaul' were not a cohesive society but a disparate array of peoples. By branding them all as a single entity, Caesar manufactured a community that in fact had little in common. He also played up their martial qualities, largely, according to Goudineau, to create a glowing impression of his feat for those back home in having overcome them. In practice, the record showed that many of the tribes had done deals with the invaders and actually hardly put up a fight.[24]

Such was the foundation stone of the Gallic myth – the culture that would set itself apart for its fierce patriotism, proud contempt of outside influence and confidence in its own superiority. And to make matters worse, it was a foundation that was barely built upon until the most recent of times.

Surprisingly to us who have been brought up thinking – albeit mainly by the French themselves – that they are an ancient nation, the concept of 'France' is a very modern concept indeed. While it received an undoubted boost during the Revolution that launched itself on the world in 1789, for the centuries leading up to it, and, in reality, for much of the time that followed, the country was more an agglomeration of self-sufficient – and self-identifying – communities, not a nation. Before the Revolution, to say 'France' meant the small area around Paris, no more.[25] There was no common language even, only a mere fifty-five major dialects and hundreds of local vernaculars.

If no one heard the country as a whole, neither did anyone view it as a whole. The first complete map of France was not produced until 1815, and it had taken seventy years to put it together.[26] It was, in fact, only in the late 19th and early 20th centuries that France finally knitted itself together, through roads, railways and telegraph, into a truly national entity. Until then, it was known as the 'land of the thousand *pays*', this being the strictly local area that extended only so far as the sound of the church bells reached. Not until August 1914 did a piece of news – the declaration of the outbreak of the First World War – reach the entire country on the same day.[27]

This, then, is the France that, in modern times, professes on the world stage the most ancient of lineages, steeped in a common bondage of national fraternity. In historical terms, it is, in truth, a creation of almost contemporary manufacture.

☞

Why we don't live longer than our ancestors

It emerged in 1999 that the commonly accepted view of our ancestors living much shorter lives than modern humans is a myth and has been based all along on a statistical error in the standard method of bone-dating. Scientists from Bradford University published their findings in *New Scientist*, suggesting that the error has led to under-estimating the lengths of our forebears' lives by up to thirty years.

Professor Mark Pollard reported that the traditional approach used by archaeologists to date human remains – taking a large sample of bones of known ages and plotting how the tell-tale signs of wear on joints changes with different ages – and the statistical method used, has led to results that understate the real age of the subjects.

The researchers were led to investigate the technique after datings from sites frequently came up with lifespan estimates which did not accord with other documentary evidence available that suggested people had to be living longer.

One celebrated instance cited by the research was the case of the 7th century Mayan king Hanab Pakal whose bones were examined in the 1950s by the accepted method and assessed as dying in his forties. When the inscription on his tomb was finally deciphered decades later, it recorded that he had died aged nearer eighty.[28]

The orthodox view, for example, of how long Britons lived at the time of the Norman invasion in the 11th century had settled on an estimate of no more than fifty-five years. For years, we have been brought up to see our ancestors living lives that were nasty, brutish and short, and ourselves, by comparison, smugly enjoying the benefits of a more civilised life. By correcting for the error the researchers thought they had found, however, they concluded that the estimated age was between seventy and eighty – the same as modern humans. The entire supposed difference in lifespans had disappeared.

So for all the developments of the last thousand years in civilising living conditions and for all our modern creature comforts, it was perhaps not a little disconcerting to discover that so far as enjoying a longer life, they have counted for absolutely nothing.

☞

Harold, Hastings and the arrow
– another one in the eye for history

As Sellar and Yeatman wrote in their landmark comic history *1066 And All That*,[29] other than 55 BC when Caesar invaded ('the first date in English history'), the only 'memorable date' in the country's past is 1066. Every schoolchild learns of the momentous significance of the year, of the battle of Hastings that changed the course of our island history, and the most famous death of an English King – Harold killed by an arrow in the eye.

Unfortunately for tradition, the tale of the arrow appears to have been an invention created more than a decade after the battle. According to research published in 1998,[30] contemporary Latin accounts written immediately after the battle make no mention of the arrow incident. Indeed, the accounts of those present, such as the one written by William of Poitiers, clearly record Harold being killed by four of William the Conqueror's knights. He even names them:

Eustace of Boulogne, William of Gifford, Guy of Amiens and the son of Guy of Ponthieu. They captured Harold in the melee, beheading and disembowelling him on the battlefield. One cut off his 'leg' – a Norman euphemism for penis – and carried it away as a souvenir.[31]

The story of the arrow in the eye does not appear until fifteen years later, and seems to have been introduced to carry a symbolic message about Harold's death, to be depicted for all time through the Bayeux Tapestry: an arrow in the eye was the existing punishment for perjury. The suggestion is that the Norman invaders regarded Harold as a perjurer for breaking his promise to William to back his claim to the throne when Edward the Confessor died in the first week of 1066, sparking off the dynastic struggle. The Tapestry was intended to blackguard Harold's reputation and be a lesson to anyone else contemplating treachery against the new regime.

The other chief historical remnant of Hastings – the Bayeux Tapestry – also holds a secret that contradicts conventional belief. It was long held to be a Norman French creation, produced by the ladies at the court of William's wife, Queen Mathilde, to celebrate the victory over the English. It had always been assumed that it was made in France as once the conquest had been settled, William chose to spend little time in England. (After 1072, of the 170 months left of his life, he spent 130 in France.[32])

Restoration work carried out in 1984, involving the unstitching of the Tapestry's lining, revealed to experts 'incontestable proof' that it could only have been woven in England. One told press reporters that the complexity of the handiwork made it clear that 'England alone possessed the skilled workers ... able to carry out such a masterpiece'.[33] Even the Tapestry museum in Bayeux now acknowledges that it was most probably embroidered, by monks, in the south of England.[34]

☞

Hastings 2 – the forgotten battle

There is a postscript to the Norman success at Hastings that has resurfaced only in the last twenty years to change the accepted view of that momentous year. Archaeologists from the Museum of London discovered in 1996 evidence of a final battle, right in the heart of London, that was fought before William could finally claim the conquest of England. This 'forgotten' battle was, the theory goes, expunged from the traditional accounts because the Normans wanted to portray their King as a powerful victor who overwhelmed the nation in a single contest. That the reality was rather different has been successfully buried in the standard accounts.

The most cited sources for the autumn of 1066 are the Anglo-Saxon Chronicle and the account mentioned earlier by the faithful Norman, William of Poitiers. The Chronicle records the arrival of the Norman forces into London and the receiving of the surrender of Edgar the Aetheling, the thirteen-year-old who had been elected the new English king, at Berkhamsted to the north west of the capital. And then no more is said. William of Poitiers' account is similarly deceptive. This maintains that the city folk surrendered as soon as the Conqueror appeared, yet we know from the Chronicle that there was some resistance: the invader was rebuffed in his attempt to cross into the city from the south by London Bridge, and had to make his way around the outskirts, and hence his encounter with Edgar at Berkhamsted.

Lesser known accounts speak of a further set of events. A French monk writing in 1071 tells of a momentous battle near Ludgate that was the true determination of the fate of the entire invasion. So critical was this encounter that William de Jumieges devotes as much space in his account to the final battle of London as he does to Hastings itself.[35]

It is believed to have taken place on 20 December. William entered the city using siege engines and battering rams – this was no mopping up operation but a substantial effort against a rebellious populace fighting in their own back garden. He did prevail, causing 'many deaths' and was crowned King five days later on Christmas Day.

A modern authority endorses the view that the final battle of London has tended to be airbrushed out of traditional renderings of the Norman Conquest. Far from it all being over at Hastings, the fate of Britain hung in the balance in the final months of that dramatic year:

> It was a significant encounter. Taking London was crucial to William's conquest of England and was not assured even after Hastings. ... One can speculate whether, if London had held William off long enough, perhaps through winter, another Saxon leader might have emerged to challenge William.[36]

☞

Magna Carta – the great leap forward?

King John, Runnymede, 1215. A monarch forced to come to terms with his underlings. After 1066, it is perhaps the date most drummed into our childhood memories. We enshrine it in our folklore as the first stirring of the common people claiming their rights against authority. What opponent of the establishment down the centuries has not acclaimed Magna Carta (the 'great charter') as the bedrock of their case? The inherent rights of an English individual are pictured as having been born that day by the banks of the Thames near Windsor. In our own time still, and even to non-historians, Magna Carta conjures up that deeply-held sentiment that something fundamental happened here that lives on in our political way of doing things.

That Magna Carta serves such a purpose has, in fact, more to do with how the event was later used than with the actual terms of the agreement that was reached at Runnymede. We like to remember the settlement in our common understanding as a set of high principles of behaviour that would condition for evermore the relationship between monarchy and the commonweal. In fact, this was nothing like the set of issues covered.

Far from the document's purpose centring, as we think it does, on what we now take from it as being important – the right of habeas corpus (the principle that anyone detained by the authorities must be brought before a court in public), the right of trial by jury, and the requirement of the king to consult his people (seen as the origins of our parliamentary system) – Magna Carta dealt with such matters only in passing. Far more central to the purpose of the occasion was to settle individual scores and personal interests.

Of the sixty-two clauses, more than half concerned detailed feudal grievances from individual barons. They were distinctly utilitarian in nature. As one historian has noted:

> Such clauses fixed precise payment for reliefs, protected estates under wardship, granted the widow her dower, saved children from ruin on account of their father's debts owed to Jews, and forbade use of the writ Praecipe which summarily removed cases from feudal courts. Not a line gave protection to the villein [peasant], whose lord, be he King or baron, was left free to tallage [tax] him or increase his service.[37]

Other clauses related to issues clearly of contemporary concern – the right to leave the realm without prejudicing one's allegiance to the king, the return of hostages held by the king, the requirement for all foreign knights and mercenaries (who had been an essential buttress for the King's power) to leave the kingdom, and pardons for those who had rebelled against the king. These were the material, basic axes to grind of those confronting the king: immediate, personal, extractive. They were hardly the concerns of a band of high-thinking nobles bent on remolding the order of things. This was the protecting of calculated interests.

Even where a proposal might seem to be geared to be a challenge to authority, the approach was actually conservative:

> And when the barons demanded that the taxes affecting themselves … should be levied 'by common consent', they defined that consent as the full meeting of tenants-in-chief in the Curia Regis, to which greater barons had long been summoned personally, and lesser men through the sheriff. They meant, in short, to stand upon the ancient ways, for if they asked their own rights, they left to the King his demesnes, boroughs and wardships.[38]

While it would be unfair to cast the whole charter as a self-serving exercise – it did have provisions of wider benefit, such as establishing a common set of weights and measures, securing the rights of foreign traders to enter and leave the country freely (provided they paid their customs dues) and rights regarding access to forests and woodland – what matters for a proper interpretation of history is how the whole affair has been portrayed since. The few themes buried in the charter that eventually became a basis for further chiseling away at royal power assume, in our modern understanding, a prominence they simply did not have at the time.

So how did Magna Carta come to be seen as the bedrock of our constitution? Not surprisingly, it was down to more raw politics. The agreement at Runnymede was almost instantly repudiated by John who got the Pope to rule it null and void. England returned to civil war. The entire episode of Magna Carta might have sunk into the depths of history as a passing episode of no lasting consequence had John not then died just over a year later. It was this turn of events that propelled

Magna Carta back to centre stage, and into its lasting place in history. For John's successor was the nine-year-old Henry III. His mother, Isabella of Angoulême, was both French and unpopular. Add to this that the French Prince Louis, who had been brought over by the English barons to help in their war against John, had a distant claim to the throne, and the peril was clear. A power vacuum beckoned and the now emerging English baronage faced the prospect of a reversal of their fortunes at the hands (again) of French invaders.

Magna Carta suddenly became a useful document to both sides.[39] Henry – or more accurately, William the Marshall, the eighty-year-old courtier who became Regent – could secure vital support to ensure the safety of the young King's reign by abiding by the provisions, and the barons could avoid the threat of losing everything to fresh invaders from across the Channel. Magna Carta became a contract enshrining mutual interests, again of an immediate rather than long-term nature. It was picked back up, dusted down – it was, in fact, reissued three times, in 1216, 1217 and again in 1225, each time with changes reflecting the current live issues of concern – and became a totemic document representing the balance of interests of both sides.

As a political tool for immediate purposes, it served them well. And it is not to deny that deep within the agreement were some nudges towards the shifts of power that would later re-cast the political settlement in Britain. We cherish them still, rightly. But we are wrong to believe, as we tend to do when we revere Magna Carta, that the participants at the time were mainly doing this for the high principled reasons we focus upon today. As one of Britain's most august constitutional historians has noted:

> The Great Charter offers little to reward the historian in search of 'constitutional precedents'. ... It was, indeed, essentially what the king called it, 'a peace between us and

the barons'; it stood, perhaps, for no very deep stirring of the nation, and if John had lived another twenty years it might almost have come to be forgotten.[40]

This was not high constitutionalism. It was instead crude politics at its most mercenary. It was to be the huge irony of history that it was the same politics that would elevate Magna Carta to the esteemed position we hold it in today.

☞

Ratting on us – the Black Death

It is the worst loss of human life from a single event in history. We have always blamed the rat for the Black Death in the 14th century that killed an estimated 75 million people in just four years. Between 1347 and 1351, a third of the population in Britain died. It may have been as high as half. Between 40 and 60 per cent of city dwellers in Italy perished.[41] On average, historians generally agree that between a fifth and a third of Europe was wiped out.[42]

The common brown or black rat was blamed for carrying the fleas that transmitted the bubonic plague bacteria. Poor sanitary conditions expedited the spread of the disease. But medical researchers at the University of Liverpool suggested in 2001 that the evidence suggested that the Black Death was not a rat-borne bacteria but an Ebola-type virus. A study by Professor of Zoology, Christopher Duncan, pointed to some simple evidence in the accounts that had tended to be overlooked in previous interpretations.

Communities found that the only effective way of dealing with the disease was to put the affected individual, or even the entire village, into quarantine. But 'quarantine would not have been effective if the disease was spread by rat fleas', said Duncan. 'Rats don't respect quarantines. This disease was transmitted directly from person to person which suggests an infectious virus.'[43]

The symptoms commonly described – rapid onset of fever, aching and bleeding from internal organs, and red blotches caused by blood under the skin – are all classic signs of Ebola-like illnesses. 'The history books are wrong. Intuitively, the Black Death has all the hallmarks of a viral disease,' concluded Duncan.

The theory appeared to get further support some years later when in 2007 a study of recently discovered court records from Dorset, which were unusually detailed in giving dates of death, showed a pattern that made it highly unlikely they were caused by rats and fleas. The records revealed that an estimated 50 per cent of the 2,000 inhabitants of Gillingham died within four months of the Black Death reaching the town in October 1348. The deaths came at a time of the year when the form of plague spread by rats and fleas would have been dormant.

The Liverpool University team suggested that these records supported their theory that the Black Death was a viral disease. 'Bubonic plague relies on fleas breeding and it is too cold during winter in Britain for this to happen,' commented Susan Scott, a collaborator on the original study.[44]

For so long now we have lived with the comfortable assumption that the Black Death is part of history. It could never return now because of the sanitary defences of modern society. For once, getting history wrong might have more alarming consequences than the mere embarrassment that ignorance of the past usually brings. There is still no known cure for Ebola-type diseases.

There is another aspect of the Black Death that may have a difference resonance for us as a society. It all depends on what historical interpretation we put on the event. The classic view of the pandemic is that it had disastrous consequences for Europe's development. Given the scale of the loss and disruption, how else could it be viewed? Economic historians who have delved closer into the effects of the plague, beyond the health dimension and the personal consequences for the millions of individuals, have ventured a rather less destructive assessment. It turns out that the Black Death may not have been as catastrophic as conventional histories make it out to be.

Surprisingly, economists have found that by around 1375 – a single generation after the disease had swept through Europe – most landlords in England were enjoying revenues that had recovered to pretty near to their pre-plague levels. This is a remarkable achievement against the background of the disaster. Even more stunningly, within another generation or two, prosperity in England had reached its medieval peak.[45] Far from the usual simplistic assessment of the Black Death being one of the greatest moments of ill fortune in human history, in fact it seems to have sparked a veritable leap forward in social progress.

The conclusion becoming accepted now is that prior to the plague, England, and Europe more generally, was suffering from stultifying overpopulation. The sudden step-change in population loss caused by the plague re-balanced affairs. According to one account, it 'led to increased productivity by restoring a more efficient balance between labour, land and capital'.[46] Wages in general rose significantly due to the shortage of people, which encouraged more mobility among workers and better distribution of wealth around the economy. This positive effect has been noted in studies of continental Europe too, where many places enjoyed boom years as a result of the plague.

There was another unexpected and, in the long term, beneficial consequence. In Britain, the death of so many clerics as they ministered to their sick communities led to Latin, the common language of church business, and French, the tongue for transacting official business, a hangover from the

Norman invasion, both losing ground to native English as the choice for conducting the rituals of daily life.[47]

So, far from viewing such episodes as unmitigated disasters, as our history books tend to do, we might just steel ourselves to recognise that such a 'catastrophe' as the Black Death can, upon closer inspection, be seen to have some silver linings for society as a whole. Whether you can be persuaded to approach future episodes in the same vein will, very obviously, depend on whether you are part of the lucky portion who manage to survive the actual obliteration.

☞

To the ends of the Earth?

Perhaps the first false history that most children hear in their lives is the old one about Christopher Columbus thinking that the world was flat. For generations, it has made the story of his journey to the New World in 1492 all the more heroic as young minds wonder in awe at the majesty of his command in taking a crew of ignorant sailors out into the unknown, all with the dread fear of falling off the edge of the world.

But not for two thousand years had man believed the Earth to be flat. From the 5th century BC, the Greeks had mathematically demonstrated that the world was spheroid in shape. They had first thought it was a globe simply for aesthetic reasons: a sphere was the most perfect mathematical form.[48] That was Plato's theory who, as we will see from The Republic in Chapter 3, strove after the ideal that reflected God's creation. Aristotle, whose life (384 BC–322 BC) overlapped with Plato's, took a robust mathematical approach. Although he did not put it in terms of 'gravity', his observations that every body fell towards the centre suggested that the world had to be round as the components of Earth would form a sphere as they came together from all directions.[49] He also made a statement of the plain obvious. When lunar eclipses were observed, the shadow moving across the Moon had a curved edge. 'If the eclipse is due to the interposition of the Earth,' Aristotle conjectured, 'the rounded line results from its spherical shape'.[50]

A successor of Aristotle, Eratosthenes (c.276 BC–c.195 BC), even managed a remarkably accurate estimate of the actual size of the Earth. He did so by measuring the length of the shadow cast by an obelisk at Alexandria at the summer solstice on 21 June when the sun was directly overhead and illuminating the bottom of a well at Aswan, which lies almost on the Tropic of Cancer, the most northerly point that the sun is ever directly overhead. He used simple geometry to show that at that moment the sun at Alexandria was $7°\,14'$ off directly overhead, one fiftieth of a 360 degree circle. He worked out the distance from Alexandria to Aswan from the estimates of camel train drivers that it took fifty days to make the journey travelling at 100 stadia (one stadia was thought to be 600 feet) a day and, multiplying that 5,000 stadia by fifty, got the circumference of the Earth as 28,700 miles. This is just 15 per cent higher than the actual value. The accuracy of his effort was not bettered until modern times.[51]

This knowledge of the ancients began to feed back into European thought during the early 13th century – nearly three hundred years before Columbus set sail – as intellectual re-seeding occurred through the rediscoveries of the Arab translations of the Greek masters that emerged from the 'reconquest' of Arab Spain between the 11th and 13th centuries.

As the thousand year 'Age of Interruption' ended in Europe, knowledge of the world's geography re-exploded on the continent, first in a limited fashion as scholars of Greek were few and far between,[52] but then increasingly rapidly as Greek texts were translated into Latin, the *lingua franca* of scholarship. It was then mixed with the contemporary experiences that accumulated through Venetian travellers' tales from the likes of Marco Polo, whose account of his travels to

China was published in 1298, and Nicolo de' Conti who spent twenty-five years travelling through India and the East Indies (modern Indonesia) before returning to Venice in 1444.[53]

So modern historians are very clear that by Columbus' time no educated person had any doubts about the roundness of the Earth.[54] But there is a twist. It is not correct to say that Columbus was thus using accurate data. In fact, it is further false history that lies at the heart of the Columbus story. It is not so much that Columbus defied contemporary belief about the flatness of the Earth that makes his journey so remarkable. It is that the whole enterprise was thought possible only because of the existence of huge errors in the information that seafarers then had available to them.

The key text that refreshed the European world's knowledge on geography was, not that of Eratosthenes, but of his Roman/Egyptian successor Ptolemy, who lived three hundred years later (AD 90–168). He marshelled the knowledge of others into the first accepted general textbook of geography, including maps of the known world. But he also got his estimates wildly wrong. He disagreed with Eratosthenes' measurements, and thought that each degree of the Earth's circumference was only fifty miles, not seventy. When he drew his maps, he also vastly over-estimated the size of Asia, making it span nearly 180 degrees of the Earth's total, rather than the 130 it is in reality. These errors had the effect of making the distance between Europe and the unknown eastern margins of Asia significantly less than it actually was.

One historian of science has labeled Ptolemy's mistakes 'the most influential miscalculation in history'.[55] How successful, he asked, would Columbus have been in persuading his backers to fund his voyage if the truth had been known about the distances involved, or would he even have tried embarking on the voyage into what he assumed would be entirely empty ocean if he really appreciated how far he would need to travel?

That he bumped into an entirely unknown land mass on the way is one of the great accidents of history. But as he planned it, Columbus sailed out on not one error – there was no straight voyage to the East Indies – but two – his objective was far, far further away than he ever imagined. We remember him for this first mistake, as well as for the presumption about a flat Earth that he never possessed. But we tend not to know of the second, and assume that he knew the dimensions of the task in front of him. In practice, he was as in the dark as every other navigator of his time.

Surprisingly, the origins of the myth that the mediaeval world thought that the Earth was flat actually dates from rather recent times. According to University of California Professor of History Jeffrey Russell, it is less than two hundred years old.[56] He blames two contemporaneous writers, although does not establish any specific link between them. The first was the American author Washington Irving, who wrote a popular history of Columbus in 1828 which portrayed him as a 'simple mariner', appearing before a dark crowd of benighted inquisitors and hooded theologians at a council of Salamanca, all of whom believed, according to Irving, that the Earth was 'flat like a plate'.[57] The second was a French anti-religious zealot, Antoine-Jean Letronne, who made the misrepresentation of early church belief in a flat Earth in his *On the Cosmographical Ideas of the Church Fathers* in 1834.

And it wasn't even America he discovered …

Amidst all the disputing whether Columbus thought the world was round, and whether he was the first to reach America (it is now virtually unchallenged that Norse settlers under Leif Ericsson reached Newfoundland around AD 1000) it seems to be generally forgotten that Columbus never actually set foot on mainland America in any of his four voyages across the Atlantic. His inaugural 1492 trip took him to what is now the Bahamas, his famous first landfall in the New

World now being thought to have been in the Turks and Caicos islands just north of Hispaniola. His second voyage of 1493–96 took him to Dominica in the Caribbean, his third (June–August 1498) even further south to Trinidad and his final visit (May–June 1502) took him back to the Caribbean, to Martinique. He never ventured near what we would now regard as America.

The first person recorded as having done that is Spanish eccentric Juan Ponce de León who landed in Florida in April 1513, over twenty years after the first European venture into the region. He had come to the area as part of Columbus' crew on his second voyage, had stayed and had become a governor on Hispaniola and later on Puerto Rico. His motivation for discovery was far from soundly grounded, however. He was obsessed with finding a famed Fountain of Youth whose waters were reputed to reverse the effects of ageing.[58] According to the stories then circulating, the Fountain existed on an island to the north of Cuba called 'Bimini', hence the general north-westerly direction he took that brought him to what we now know is the mainland of America. When he landed, he believed Florida was an island.[59] He spent two months sailing southwards down the Florida coast, rounded the Keys and explored up the Gulf of Mexico coast enquiring amongst all the Indians he encountered about the Fountain of Youth. None had heard of it. He returned a disappointed man, accidentally discovering Mexico on the way back when he landed in the Yucatan peninsula which he thought was Cuba.

Juan tends to be totally overlooked in histories of American discovery. Perhaps because of his mad motivation; perhaps because he signally failed to achieve his declared objective. But his real achievement was to open up the mainland. He attempted to return in 1521 to lead a permanent settlement, but was killed in a fierce battle with the resisting native Indians.

☞

New England – rocky foundations

Despite its central place in the foundation story of America, it is surprising to discover that the traditional tale of the landing of the *Mayflower* Pilgrims in 1620 on Plymouth Rock in what was to become Massachusetts has just a single source – and that from an account written more than 120 years after the event, and furthermore was mere hearsay. It comes from one Thomas Faunce, town record-keeper in Plymouth, who, in 1741, is recorded as identifying for locals the exact Rock that his father had once pointed out to him as the place where the Pilgrim Fathers came ashore.[60] Not that his father was an obviously reliable witness – he did not arrive in America until three years after the Pilgrims. There is no doubting that they did make landfall at Plymouth, as that is documented in the journal of one of the crew, William Bradford, who wrote an account of the voyage. But curiously, there is no other historical evidence for the story that the now revered Rock was the site.[61] Droves of patriotic Americans visit the Rock every year totally unaware how threadbare is the basis for one of their most venerated national icons.

☞

Historians may be a bit thin on the evidence for how the Pilgrims landed, but at least the new arrivals were responsible for creating America's most cherished national tradition? Bigger than Christmas or Independence Day, the annual celebration of Thanksgiving supposedly commemorates the survival of the new colony amidst their harsh New World, enabling modern America to feel a seamless link with those first forerunners of the nation.

Not so. The celebration of Thanksgiving does not stretch back unbroken to that first post-harvest celebration of 1621.

The modern marking of Thanksgiving as a national event actually goes back only as far as 1863. It was first pronounced as a formal calendar event by Abraham Lincoln who needed some popular and sentiment-steeped symbolism to foster a patriotic spirit amongst citizens at the height of the Civil War. The Pilgrims did not actually feature in the narrative until the 1890s.[62]

☞

The theme at the heart of the deeply cherished and traditional recounting of the Pilgrim story is the small band's heroic search for religious freedom. They travelled across an ocean, in flight from persecution, to set up their new way of life in an idyll of tolerance and respect for their fellow human being. We assume that the patterns of life that unfolded as the early colonies grew were ones of untrammelled religious liberty. Far from it. We tend to forget that the society the Pilgrim Fathers fostered, and strictly controlled, was actually harsher and more rigid than the one they had objected to, and fled from, in England. It was simply that the rules that they now lived by were the ones *they* believed in. In the words of one historian:

> Their little commonwealth was an exclusive oligarchy ruled by the elders of the Church with ferocious intolerance. They had not gone out into the wilderness to indulge freedom of thought but to ensure a rigid uniformity.[63]

The Pilgrims are famed for adopting what is regarded as the first written constitution in the Anglo-Saxon world, the *Mayflower Compact*, that pledged the settlers to 'covenant and combine ourselves together into a civil body politic, for our better ordering and preservation' and to enact laws 'convenient for the general good of the colony, unto which we promise all due submission and obedience'. The agreement did not suggest that the colony was to be a free state – on the contrary.

> As amongst the Pilgrim Fathers, political power was strictly confined to Church members, who were not more than one in five of the adult males. Religious orthodoxy was imposed with far more rigour than in royalist England.[64]
>
> (...)
>
> Religious conformity became the basis of the colony's political life, and the penalty of dissent was to be the loss of civic rights. No man might be a church member unless his opinions satisfied the scrutiny of a very narrow circle of the leasing spirits, who had in their own hands the power of admitting new members to their body and of expelling any who might show signs of independent thought.[65]

This produced a mutually reinforcing process that secured the position of the new leaders. As no one could be admitted to the church without having their belief thoroughly vetted, the leadership eliminated the risk of ungodly rule. And as the number admitted were always small, the dangers of majority rule were also eliminated.[66]

Within ten years, there were 14,000 Puritans in the area of what would become Massachusetts. Life in those early years was shaped regimentally by the church elders.

> They believed in strong government by those qualified to exercise it, and they felt themselves divinely called to establish God's kingdom. Hence the narrowness and aggressiveness of the ruling clique of magistrates and clergy which from the beginning distinguished Massachusetts from other colonies.[67]

Religious persecution of minorities broke out almost at once. Quakers, another band of religious outcasts from England, were a favourite target. They were fined, flogged and banished for their non-conforming beliefs. Between 1659 and 1661, the Massachusetts Elders actually hanged four on Boston Common for defying orders that had expelled them from the colony.[68] Even for the mainstream Puritans, there were strict laws regulating behaviour. Church attendance was compulsory.[69] Smoking was forbidden, and lying incurred a fine.[70] Drunkenness or petty theft warranted jail, and the stocks awaited anyone guilty of 'raillery' near a church.[71] A husband could not kiss his wife in public. A seaman, Captain Kimble, is recorded as having spent two hours in the stocks after kissing his wife on his doorstep after returning home from a three year voyage.[72] Massachusetts' legal code, the Body of Liberties of 1641, prescribed twelve offences punishable by death, including adultery, homosexuality, idolatry and blasphemy.[73]

Early Massachusetts has been described as 'a close and intolerant oligarchy'.[74] One dissentient, Thomas Morton, who had been banished back to England by the Boston magistrates and who unwisely chose to return to the colony, was seized and deported a second time, but only after the authorities burned down his house as a demonstration to any other free thinkers.[75] In 1631, a man named only as Ratcliffe was flogged, lost his ears and was banished from the colony – for 'defaming' the government.[76]

Even Alistair Cooke, the doyen of British Americophiles, could write of this period in his celebrated history of America:

> Looking back on it, I am bound to say that it also bears some striking resemblances to a Communist or other totalitarian government. The Party will tolerate you as a citizen, but you have no say in the government if you are not a Party member. Life ... cannot be sustained by consent but only by a rigid discipline imposed from the top. The rulers direct every function of society – work and worship and play, business and literature, and morals.[77]

Three future states of America – Connecticut and Rhode Island to the south west and New Hampshire to the north – owe their very existence to the intolerance of the Pilgrims. It was the scale of religious bigotry inflicted on non-Puritans that, within a mere fifteen years, forced many to decide to up sticks and trek away from the settled areas around Plymouth and Boston, and to lands beyond the reach of the dogma of the leadership.

☞

The fall Guy?

The most famous plot in British history – Guy Fawkes and his conspirators' attempt to blow up the Houses of Parliament during the State Opening attended by the entire government of the day and the King in 1605 – is set firmly in our cultural landscape as the miraculous 'near miss', the fate of the nation salvaged by breathtaking last-minute fortune. The discovery of the gunpowder stash in the bowels of Parliament just hours before the ceremony has been a staple of our childhood imagery. Guy Fawkes Night on 5 November has been celebrated for four centuries since. Modern research, however, suggests that our understanding of the affair is a lot more simplistic than it actually was. Although we shall probably never know the truth, there are grounds to believe that the plot was likely known to the authorities well in advance. They allowed it to develop almost to fruition in order to maximise the political 'spin' that could be drawn by the spectacular style of its exposure.

Recent research suggests that while the Catholic plot to protest against nearly a century of alienation and discrimination by the English Protestant establishment was genuine enough, the two central themes that lie at the heart of our commonly held version – that the institution of Parliament and the entire government were the target and that the discovery of the plot was a turn of luck – appear to be creatures of fiction.

According one historian, the attack was personal. This was a plot against a person, not the wider establishment. Extremist Catholics were after James I himself. The image of the conspiracy being an attempt to bring down all the pillars of the state in one fell swoop by targeting the moment when King, Lords and Commons were all assembled, was a dimension that only emerged in the re-telling in Victorian times. It was not a feature of the contemporary perspective.[78]

Of the thirteen conspirators in all, fewer than half were responsible for the operation to smuggle the gunpowder into Parliament. On the day of the planned coup, most were in Warwickshire waiting to seize the king's children. Their grievance against James' lack of action on restoring toleration for Catholics burned stronger than hatred against the abstract political system. They had had high expectations of him, this son of Mary Queen of Scots whom Elizabeth I had had executed for her supposed Catholic plotting. One factor said to have counted for much in their calculation was that James had recently signed a peace treaty with Catholic Spain. To the Catholic faithful, this fatally ruled out any hope that the Spanish would come to their rescue, as they had tried to do a generation before with the Armada.[79]

The exposing of the plot is now reckoned to have been a carefully orchestrated denouement. Circumstantial evidence strongly suggests that Robert Cecil, Secretary of State and Keeper of the Privy Seal, the King's senior political adviser and master of one of the most intricate spy networks in British history, knew of the planned assassination, and may even have forged the letter that the orthodox account tells of providing the last minute warning to the government.[80] The modern version now goes that the plot was allowed to develop, safe in the knowledge it was to be interrupted at the most politically convenient moment.

It was, in its duly dramatic fashion that has resonated ever since across four hundred years, one of the seminal episodes of our past that every schoolchild learns. An outraged country rejoiced in what was portrayed as a divine (and Protestant) intervention.

The spin was determined. Eight weeks afterwards Parliament passed the Observance of 5th November Act which laid down the legal requirement for an annual national celebration of thanksgiving for the failure of the plot, described as 'an invention so inhuman, barbarous and cruel, as the like was never before heard of'. While the law remained on the Statute Book until 1859, the imagery has stayed indelibly part of our cultural mindset. As an archly manipulated act of mass public persuasion, Robert Cecil executed a masterstroke. That we still 'remember, remember, the Fifth of November', and not quite know what it is we are actually remembering, is testimony to his craft.

☞

Victoria would be cross

Aside from Florence Nightingale and the Charge of the Light Brigade, the most likely snippet every schoolchild knows about the Crimean War is that every Victoria Cross, the country's highest award for military bravery, is made from the melted down bronze of two Russian cannons captured during the conflict. Sadly, not so. After doubts were raised in the 1970s, the spirit of historical mythbusting seized a dedicated group of scientists in the Royal Armouries in the Tower of London. They spent an astonishing seven years amassing evidence that showed that the old belief about their Russian origins was a myth. The cannon still used to produce the medals were actually of Chinese origin, and whether they were ever in the Crimea at all is entirely unknown.

According to the folklore account, Queen Victoria, who

took a close interest in the design of the medal, opposed initial proposals to make the cross from copper.[81] She suggested bronze, and legend has it that this inspired an aide to think of using metal from captured bronze cannons held at Woolwich Barracks. Two eighteen-pounders were made available, from which it was decided to saw off the cascabels, the large knobs on the end of the breeches. These were said to have been Russian ordnance seized at Sebastopol, but experts in the 1970s pointed out that it was obvious by looking at their markings that they were of Chinese origin.

Starting in 1986, Royal Armoury scientists began locating and testing the metal composition of VCs held across Britain and Australia. To their surprise, in view of the accepted account about the medals all deriving from the same source, they discovered that some had identical matches to the composition of the Chinese cannons, while others differed. They announced in 1993 their conclusions that as many as 800 of the more than 1,350 medals awarded since 1857 were probably made from the Chinese metal. 'We have established that the material used in crosses produced since the time of the First World War is Chinese,' said Brian Gilmour, a metallurgist in the research team.[82] Whatever the source was of the original medals, it is believed it ran out before 1914 and the two Chinese cannons were used as replacements. So two cherished beliefs of British military heritage were demolished by the research – that all VCs originate from a single source, and that that source was Russian.

Subsequent research has failed to find any evidence of where the medals issued before 1914 were sourced from. There is no clear evidence either of how the Chinese guns which remain in the Royal Artillery Museum at Woolwich to this day, came to be there, although research published in 2005 suggested that they were captured after the storming of the Taku Forts in China in 1860.[83]

And if you thought the very first feat for which a VC was

awarded took place in the Crimea – you would be wrong again. Charles Lucas, a twenty-year-old seaman, won it for bravely picking up a live shell and throwing it overboard before it exploded on his ship, the *Hecla*, during an action against Russian forts in the Baltic in June 1854 in the little-known northern sideshow of the war.

☞

Not the edge of the world

The first thought that comes to mind when Hadrian's Wall is mentioned is the remoteness of its location. Our vision of its origins is as a barrier built across a bleak, isolated landscape, thought at the time to be on the very edge of the known world. But recent archaeological work has thrown up a surprising and entirely different picture. Far from the Wall being constructed in the middle of nowhere, it was laid out across a land rich with farms and cultivation.

Researcher Tim Gates reported in *British Archaeology* in November 1999,[84] that aerial photographs showed that throughout the course of the wall there was evidence of farmers working the nearby fields long before the coming of the Romans, since the wall frequently shows signs of cutting across pre-existing farm patterns. During the research, some 200 previously unknown settlements were discovered. The choice of the wall's placement and route appears to have been dictated as much by the proximity of populated settlements as by military consideration. Gates suggested that the myth of isolation was first propounded as recently as the 17th century.

So forget the image of the lonely Roman guard stationed in depressing isolation at the outpost. He would have enjoyed a far more hospitable environment than our schoolbooks have led us to believe.

☞

The bare truth

The cherished ride of Lady Godiva, naked through Coventry market, to protest at the levying of taxes by her husband, the Earl of Mercia, appears to be a highly doubtful historical event. While there is evidence that she did exist around the mid-11th century, there is no contemporary account of the famous ride. The usually reliable Anglo-Saxon Chronicle is silent: the first record surfaces in 1236, nearly 200 years after her death, in the chronicle of one Richard of Wendover.

As with other folkloric tales – Robin Hood is the classic example[85] – the story became encrusted over the centuries with additions. The detail about the ride being in the early morning was added by Ranulf Higden writing in 1364,[86] and the element of Peeping Tom, the voyeur who breached the rules of the demonstration – it was mounted on condition that all the townsfolk should remain indoors with their windows shuttered – only appears in written accounts in 1670.[87] The further notion that he was struck blind as a result was only added 700 years after the event.[88] Once again, as we shall see with the Charge of the Light Brigade in Chapter 4, it was a poem by Tennyson that popularised the final imagery. His *Godiva*, published in 1842, 800 years after the supposed event, finally cemented all the elements into the familiar version we know – and believe – today.

☞

Defender of which faith?

It is one of the commonest (but probably mostly unnoticed) phrases in Britain's cultural life: *Fidei Defensor* – Defender of the Faith. It appears on every coin of the realm, though usually abbreviated to Fid Def (or even F. D. these days). It has been there ever since the title was bestowed on Henry VIII in the 16th century. But ask anyone why Henry was given the title, and chances are they will answer wrongly, for it has one of the most misremembered origins of any of our national traditions.

We remember Henry chiefly for being the King who had the bust up with the Catholic Church over the Pope's refusal to grant an annulment of his marriage to Catherine of Aragon. The consequence was the country's break with Rome and the establishment of the Church of England, with Henry its supreme head. He and all his successors have enjoyed amongst their regal labels the grand title of *Defender of the Faith*. It is often assumed that this title derives from Henry's assumption of the leadership of the new Church of England and that it refers to a defiant stance against the challenge of Papal authority. Not so.

It is largely forgotten today that Henry was awarded the title *by* the Pope – Leo X – in 1521, six years before his dispute broke out.[89] It was a reward for Henry's work in writing a popular tract opposing the emerging ideas of the Protestant reformer Martin Luther. The faith Henry was defending was Catholicism. When he subsequently broke with Rome in 1533, he kept the title, now resonating even more as a symbol of protection of the fledgling national church and rebellion from the old order.

So while modern Britons see the title as reflecting the monarch's leadership of the national church, very, very few remember where its original sentiments actually lay.

☞

The first passenger railway

Ask anyone where Britain's passenger railways began, and you are likely to be told it was the Stockton to Darlington Railway. Actually, not so. While the line did carry passengers on the ceremonial opening day in September 1825, it was never intended primarily as a passenger service. The line was designed to transport coal, which predominated. It did carry passengers once the company had acquired more than the single passenger carriage it owned on the opening day, but for the first eight years, haulage was actually done by horses.[90]

No, the honour for Britain's (and the world's) first regular steam locomotion passenger railway lies with the Canterbury-Whitstable railway which was inaugurated on 3 May, 1830, four months before the more famous Manchester-Liverpool line. That event in Canterbury – a regular service began the following day – marks the real birth of the steam passenger train.

It had come about as Canterbury, then the largest and busiest town in the county, was desperate for good communications with a coastal port. Whitstable lay just six miles to the north over the hump of the Blean, a 200ft high clay plateau. The service which emerged was run with a curious mixture of stationary and mobile steam power.

With the steep gradient up and down the hill, railway pioneer George Stephenson built three locomotives – two were mounted in fixed positions on either side of the crest and pulled the carriages along by a cable and tackle method. The only stretch actually served by a mobile locomotive was the 1¾ mile run down into Whitstable after the negotiation of the hill. This was done by the celebrated Stephenson engine No 24, christened *Invicta*. (When *Invicta* proved incapable of lasting the pace, the whole line was worked by cable for seven years between 1839 and 1846 until more powerful locomotives were available.)

The opening ceremony was a vast public celebration in Canterbury with thousands lining the route to watch the strange spectacle. Twenty carriages and twelve goods vans made the first journey. Travelling on the line was clearly an experience. At the top of the hill, the operation employed a rather alarming practice that could never have been contemplated in today's health-and-safety-conscious world. Passenger carriages were usually uncoupled from the freight wagons and allowed to roll down the hill just by the force of gravity, sometimes as many as three carriages together holding fifty passengers would hurtle free-wheel fashion down the hill – 'hurtle' being employed in its comparative sense: the speeds reached were sometimes up to just 25mph, but a considerable thrill compared with the sedate 12mph behind Invicta.

Although a novelty and successful at first – season tickets (again, the world's first) were introduced in March 1834 – the service was always rather infrequent and slow. It maintained operations but suffered greatly with competition from motor traffic, particularly buses after the First World War. The passenger service was eventually withdrawn at the end of December 1930. Freight continued to run until November 1952 but after that the line was closed and the track gradually taken up.

☞

References

1   R. E. Leakey, *The Making of Mankind*, Abacus, 1981

2   *Ibid.*

3   *Ibid.*

4   *Time & Mind*, report, *Daily Telegraph*, 6 October 2010

5   University of Exeter research, reported *The Times,* London, 26 August 2008

6   Leakey, *op cit.*

7   R. Kay and M. Cartmill, Proceedings of the National Academy of Sciences, April 1998

8   I. Martinez, University of Alcalá, reported by *The Times*, London, 22 June 2004

9   Interview, *Daily Telegraph,* London, 26 August 2008

10   H. Rawson, *A Dictionary of Invective*, Robert Hale, 1991

11   Report, *The Times*, London, 30 September 1992

12   J. D. Richards, The Vikings: A Very Short Introduction, Oxford University Press, 2005

13 *Oxford English Dictionary*, online edition

14 Richards, *op.cit.*

15 Churchill, *A History of the English-Speaking Peoples*, Cassell, 1956

16 Entry for 10 April 1661

17 Report, *Sunday Times*, 20 April 1997

18 Report, *Sunday Times*, 2 December 2001

19 D. Defoe (1660–1731), *The True-Born Englishman*, 1701

20 Report, *Sunday Times*, 14 November 1999

21 Quoted in Joseph Spence, *Anecdotes*, 1820

22 *The Curse of Minerva* (1812)

23 Report, *Sunday Times*, 21 April 1996

24 C. Goudineau, *Par Toutatis*, Avenir Passe, 2002

25 G. Robb, *The Discovery of France*, Picador, 2007

26 *Ibid.*

27 *Ibid.*

28 Report, *Daily Telegraph*, 11 March 1999

29 W. C. Sellar and R. J. Yeatman, *1066 And All That*, Methuen, 1930

30 F. McGlynn, *1066: the Year of Three Battles*, Jonathan Cape, 1998

31 D. Howarth, *1066: The Year of the Conquest*, Viking Press, 1978

32 D. Carpenter, *The Struggle for Mastery: Britain 1066–1284*, Allen Lane, 2003

33 Report, *The Times*, London, 7 July 1984

34 www.tapestry-bayeux.com

35 Report, *Sunday Times*, 29 December 1996

36 Prof. David Bates, Glasgow University, quoted *ibid.*

37 K. Feiling, *A History of England*, Macmillan, 1973

38 *Ibid.*

39 D. Danziger & J. Gillingham, *1215: The Year of Magna Carta*, Hodder, 2003

40 J. E. A. Jolliffee, *The Constitutional History of Medieval England*, A&C Black, 1937

41 P. Ziegler, *The Black Death*, Collins, 1969

42 K. F. Kiple (ed.), *Plague, Pox and Pestilence: Disease in History*, Weidenfeld & Nicolson, 1997

43 Report, *The Independent*, 23 July 2001

44   Report, *The Times*, London, 1 June 2007

45   J. P. McKay, B. D. Hill & J. Buckler, *A History of Western Society*, 4th ed., Houghton Mifflin, 1991

46   J. Hatcher, *Plague, Population and the English Economy*, Macmillan, 1986, cited in J P McKay, B. D. Hill & J. Buckler, *op. cit.*

47   R. Guest & A St George, *History's Turning Points*, Boxtree, 1995

48   D. J. Boorstin, *The Discoverers*, J. M. Dent, 1984

49   *Ibid.*

50   *Ibid.*

51   *Ibid.*

52   *Ibid.*

53   *Ibid.*

54   S. E. Morison, *The European Discovery of America – The Southern Voyages 1492–1616,* Oxford University Press, 1974

55   Boorstin, *op. cit.*

56   D. Noble & J. B. Russell, *Inventing the Flat Earth – Columbus and Modern Historians,* Greenwood Press, 1991

57   Russell, at www.asa3.org/ASA/topics/history/1997Russell.html

58   S. E. Morison, *The European Discovery of America: the Southern Voyages, 1492–1616*, Oxford University Press, 1974

59   *Ibid.*

60   R. Shenkman & K. Reiger, *One-Night Stands with American History*, Quill, 1982

61   T. Morgan, *Wilderness at Dawn*, Touchstone, 1993

62   J. W. Loewen, *op. cit.*

63   C. E. Carrington, *The British Overseas*, Cambridge University Press, 1950

64   *Ibid.*

65   J. A. Williamson, *A Short History of British Expansion*, Macmillan, 1936

66   H. Brogan, History of the United States, Longman, 1985

67   J. H. Rose, A. P. Newton & E. A. Benians (eds), *Cambridge History of the British Empire, Vol I*, Cambridge University Press, 1929

68   N. Canny, *The Origins of Empire: Oxford History of the British Empire, Vol I*, Oxford University Press, 1998

69 D. MacCulloch, *A History of Christianity*, Allen Lane, 2009

70 A. Calder, *Revolutionary Empire*, E. P. Dutton, 1981

71 A. Cooke, *America*, Weidenfeld and Nicolson, 2002

72 H. W. Elson, History of the United States of America, MacMillan Company, 1904; cited in *Puritan Laws and Character* at www. usahistory.info/NewEngland/Puritans.html

73 Listed at www.lonang.com/exlibris/organic/1641-mbl.htm

74 Williamson, *op. cit.*

75 Williamson, *op. cit.*

76 Williamson, *op. cit.*

77 Cooke, *op. cit.*

78 Jonathan Clark, *The Times*, London, 3 November 1990

79 *Ibid.*

80 A. Fraser, *The Gunpowder Plot*, Weidenfeld, 1996

81 J. Percival, *For Valour: The Victoria Cross*, Thames Methuen, 1985

82 Report, *Daily Telegraph*, 13 May 1993

83 J. Glanfield, *Bravest of the Brave*, The History Press, 2005

84 www.britarch.ac.uk

85 See P. Mason, *What Needled Cleopatra ... and other little secrets airbrushed from history*, JR Books, 2009

86 D. Wallechinsky & I. Wallace, *The People's Almanac 2*, Bantam Books, 1978

87 *Ibid.*

88 A. S. E. Ackermann, *Popular Fallacies Explained and Corrected*, The Old Westminster Press, 1923

89 M. Ashley, *British Monarchs*, Robinson Publishing, 1998

90 C. Woolmar, *Fire & Steam: A New History of the Railways in Britain*, Atlantic Books, 2007

2

Gospel Truth

While the Bible today is no longer widely taken to be an actual account of history, it nevertheless continues to cast a powerful influence over many aspects of our lives. As a society, we hold collective perceptions of events that are believed to be grounded in biblical sources: Christmas, for example. By having commonly shared views of biblical characters, we use them in every-day parlance to stand for a particular attitude or trait: Judas as a traitor, for example, or Herod as a mass murderer. Some things we take for granted: that there were Ten, and only Ten, Commandments. Since few of us have actually read the Bible in full ourselves, if we are honest most will confess that the vast majority of one's presumed knowledge of the Bible comes from someone else having told us – our teachers, our vicar or church minister, our more religiously-inclined friends. And therein lies the problem.

In this chapter, we show how there is much in the Bible that departs from the many commonly held assumptions we are likely to hold. And how much that we think is there, actually isn't.

The Nativity – when, where and with whom?

The Christmas story is one of the most artificial creations of our culture. Barely anything of the stock account we take for granted today actually appears in the Bible. For a start, the birth of Jesus is only documented in two of the four Gospels (Matthew and Luke). They conflict on whether he was born in (presumably) a stable or barn, and then laid in a manger (Luke), or whether the birth of Jesus took place in a house (Matthew).

Only Luke mentions the taxation census that had supposedly required Mary and Joseph to travel away from their home to Bethlehem, but this jars with the known historical record – and his own chronology – as the only known exercise of this kind took place in AD 6, ten years after Luke's placing of the birth in the reign of Herod, who died in 4 BC. Neither of the authors mention a crib or a stable – these were invented by St Francis of Assisi in the 13th century when he created history's first Nativity scene, using live figures to create our now traditional montage.

There is no mention of the timing, other than Luke's reference to the shepherds watching their flocks 'by night'. This strongly suggests it was not in deep mid-winter, more likely spring. One astronomical calculation in 1999 on the 'star in the East' points to April as the most likely date.[1]

Church authorities settled on 25 December for marking the birth of Christ only in the 4th century, and it seems to have come from no more than adding nine months onto 25 March, the spring equinox, signifying the notional beginning of new life. The church had long taken the date as that for the Annunciation of the Virgin, the revelation of Mary's conception. St Augustine, writing between 399 and 419, makes one of the earliest assertions of this explanation.[2]

Another, more sophisticated, theory has become ingrained in the mythologizing over dating Christmas – that the celebration of Christ's birth became aligned with the traditional pagan mid-winter festival of Saturnalia, not least as a way to encourage the spread of Christianity. Many scholars in fact doubt that this is likely since it only begins to be mentioned in the 12th century. A marginal note in the wrings of a Syrian biblical commentator is the first reference found, nearly eight hundred years *after* the explanations based on supposed gestation time. It only began to achieve popularity amongst 18th and 19th century biblical scholars, but no early Christian writers actually make the link.[3]

The retinue of 'three Kings' and/or 'three wise men' has become a hopeless confusion, and has no grounding in the Gospel accounts. No mention of any numbers is made at all, and indeed the existence of them (simply as 'wise men') comes in only one of the four Gospels (Matthew). Matthew mentions three gifts – gold, frankincense and myrrh – and it seems it is from this that the later invention of a triad of visitors is taken. It was not always settled on three. Early depictions in Rome's catacombs showed variations between two and six.[4] Their traditional names – Caspar, Melchior and Balthazar – do not appear until the 6th century when they are depicted in a mosaic in a Ravenna church.[5]

There is not a single mention of any animals present either. Almost the entire ensemble – oxen, asses, sheep and stable – that makes up the 'traditional' image of the Nativity appears to come not from the scriptures but from St Francis' imagination over twelve hundred years after the event.

In sum, a journalist encountering this degree of uncorroborated or inconsistent evidence would be deeply hesitant at producing a viable story. Yet it is on such a basis that much of our deeply-held belief about one of the most significant moments in our cultural history rests.

☞

The Crucifixion – embellishing the end

As with the Nativity, while the story told of Jesus' crucifixion is one of the most familiar in our collective memory, suggesting it is grounded in solidly agreed facts, there is actually the same dizzying array of inconsistencies amongst the recorders of Jesus' demise as we found for his birth. The pivotal element of Judas' apparent betrayal of Jesus, which is analysed further below, is only detailed by one of the Gospel authors (Matthew); the others merely mention him almost as if in passing. The traditional image of Jesus' tortuous suffering and struggle under the weight of his cross, and his falling three times on the route to the crucifixion, is entirely a latter-day fiction. It does not in fact appear in any of the four gospels. Indeed, three of them (Matthew, Mark and Luke) all state that the cross was actually thrust upon a passerby, one Simon, a Cyrenian, who had to carry it behind Jesus. Only John maintains that Jesus bore it himself, but is completely silent on how he made it to the place of execution.

And despite its defining resonance in the historic memorialising of Christ's death, it is just one of the four authors (Luke) who records Jesus uttering his homily, 'Father, forgive them for they know not what they do'. And it is just one (John) who has the Virgin Mary present at the scene.

☞

Exodus – a mystery tour

The Old Testament story of the Exodus, the departure of more than two million Jews from slavery in Egypt, led by Moses, to the Promised Land across the Red Sea, has puzzled biblical scholars and archaeologists for centuries. There is absolutely no mention of it in any of the normally thorough records of the Pharaohs, yet it seemed impossible that a population movement of that magnitude would escape at least a record somewhere in the bureaucracy. An answer appeared at hand in 1997 when Professor Colin Humphreys of Cambridge University announced he had identified a numbering error in the translations from ancient Hebrew. In short, instead of 603,550 men over 20 years of age that current translations of the Bible show (which, when wives and families are added, brings the total to the usually accepted 2 million estimate), Humphreys identified a single mistranslation of the word 'lp' ('elep') which is usually taken to mean 1,000 men. It can however mean either 'troop' or 'family'. With the correction in place, Humphrey estimates that no more than 20,000 people may have been involved in the migration, making it a less gargantuan undertaking than historically presented – but at least increasing credibility that it actually occurred at all.[6]

☞

The ten plagues explained

A 1998 study by American doctors claimed to have a rational explanation for the otherwise mystifying series of ten plagues, vividly described in Exodus, that hit Egypt and eventually persuaded the authorities to let the Jews leave. Dr John Marr, former epidemiologist to the New York City department of health, and Curtis Malloy of Columbia University, identified connections between most of the outbreaks, one falling as a consequence of the other. The initial plague – all the fish in the Nile, which turned blood-red – was likely to be an algae, *Pfisteria*. This would have led to the explosion of frogs, the next plague, who sought food away from the poisoned river. Although biologists identified such behaviour as more toadlike than froglike, the authors found that the biblical word used in the original meant both. The epidemics that attacked both humans and animals were likely spread by the tiny *Culicoides* gnat which easily bred in the right conditions. And the animal sicknesses were likely crucibles for glanders disease, which causes the lymph glands to swell, hence the plague of boils. Hail storms, the next 'plague', were not uncommon in Egypt, and the destruction of crops, caused or accentuated by the plague of locusts, reads credibly. The final, and strangest, plague, the deaths of the first born, would have had a logical explanation too. The doctors assumed that families would try to salvage as much crop as possible. Storing it poorly, in damp conditions, would have led to poisonous moulds – mycototoxins – growing. And it was the tradition in ancient Egypt for the eldest son to be sent into the granary to collect the grain. Inhaling the spores was often fatal. And if they survived that, they were also likely to receive double portions of food, standard practice for dealing with famine conditions, so ingesting lethal quantities of contaminants.[7]

☞

No destruction of Jericho

An Israeli archaeological study of settlement patterns in the Jericho area led a Tel Aviv University team to announce in 1992 their conclusion that it was highly unlikely that the story of Joshua's invasion of Canaan and the destruction of Jericho – the first conquest on their arrival in the Promised Land – had happened at all (still less in the way the Book of Joshua famously describes, by circling the city and blowing on trumpets until the walls came tumbling down). The team discovered that ancestors of the Jews had actually been living in the area for centuries, and were actually of Canaanite descent. They were not visible in the archaeological record because they tended to choose a pastoral way of life, living symbiotically with the Canaanite cities on the coast that provided food from their more settled agriculture. That all changed when the coastal communities came under threat after the collapse of the Mycenaean civilization in the Mediterranean around 1250 BC, and became less reliable food sources. The Jews adapted from their wandering life to more settled farming, leading to a sudden upspringing of Jewish settlements in the area. Far from a mass immigration implied by the 'conquest' narrative of the Bible, the Jewish presence was explained by simple changing fortunes of economics. The story of a battle was 'a saga compiled by loyal court poets to flatter later kings'.[8]

☞

King Herod – an overblown reputation

The reputation of King Herod, whom Matthew's gospel has ordering the 'Massacre of the Innocents', the killing of every male child under two years old when rumours of the birth of the Messiah began to circulate, has been partially restored by recent demographic research. In contrast to the centuries-old image as one of history's great tyrants responsible for tens of thousands of deaths in the massacre (the Byzantine liturgy puts the number at 14,000; Syrian calendars quote 64,000), modern estimates presented at a symposium of the American Academy of Religion and the Society of Biblical Literature in San Francisco in November 1992 painted a very different picture.

Biblical scholar Professor Paul Maier from West Michigan University pointed to evidence of already high child mortality occurring naturally in the Bethlehem of the time. With a total population of about 1,000 people, there would not have been likely to be more than around fifteen male babies at any one time. Leaving aside whether he actually killed these or not, the consensus amongst academics now is that the scale of the story about the babies was inflated as a device to raise the status and importance of Jesus. They now believe that the gospel writer wanted to create for Jesus a compelling 'life moment' similar to that of Moses who escaped a similar pogrom of Hebrew child-killing in Egypt by being hidden in the bulrushes. While no angel – he is known to have been a bloodthirsty ruler and killed many adults during his reign – according to Maier, Herod's actions in regard to babies were deliberately exaggerated beyond the point of credibility in order to establish a narrative designed to boost Jesus' historical image.[9]

☞

Judas – not so bad after all

Judas, long portrayed as the arch traitor for betraying Jesus to the Jewish high priests for his 30 pieces of silver, has also come in for scholarly rehabilitation in recent years. Textual expert William Klassen, of the Ecole Biblique in Jerusalem, published a new interpretation of Judas's actions in 1996 that largely exonerated him from deliberate betrayal.[10] Surprisingly, the depth of his research led to many scholars announcing they were persuaded of the case Klassen set out. A critical point in the analysis was Klassen's discovery of what we would in modern times regard as deliberate 'spin' in the telling of the tale. He found that the word in the original New Testament – the Greek *paradidomi* – was translated differently when used in relation to Judas. It is used fifty-nine times in connection with Jesus' death. In twenty-seven instances, when not referring to Judas, it is translated as its more neutral meaning of 'hand over'. In the other thirty-two, when used to describe acts by Judas, it is translated as 'betrayed'. Klassen argues that Judas genuinely believed himself to be on a mission to bring Jesus and the Jewish priestly authorities together, to foster an alliance against Roman rule. 'If Judas believed that, then he was acting honourably, at least in his terms. The fact that he later killed himself suggests he was horrified at what subsequently happened,' says Klassen.

Klassen has not been the only one on the trail. In 1993, Dr Hyam Maccoby, a Jewish scholar from the University of Leeds, published an account of the evolution of Judas's reputation that, while leading to a very different explanation, still radically challenged the orthodoxy of centuries.[11] He established that in the earlier strands of the New Testament, Judas's alleged treachery is not even mentioned. It gets added later, principally Maccoby contends, to fulfil a theological necessity for the future of Christianity: the Christian followers could hardly be seen to have benefited from the salvation granted by God through Jesus' sacrifice if they had been the cause of the sacrifice in the first place. Hence the need for an evil, external figure to assume the responsibility: Judas, and by extension, the Jews. Judas was therefore an essential prerequisite for a successful continuation of Christianity, so his role was invented long after Jesus' death to appear in the final versions of the Gospels as the provider of that essential escape clause.

A further strand of evidence indicating that dark hands have been at play is the fact that St Paul, the earliest Christian writer and a contemporary observer, never mentions Judas at all: an astonishing – but obviously telling – omission given the role he is alleged to have played in the denouement. Judas' part in the Gospels, which are known to have been written up to a century after the events they depicted, becomes clearly suggestive of manipulation of the record for ulterior motives.

Two different explanations, but one common theme – the story we have grown up with, and which continues to serve as a symbol of treachery to this day, may itself have been a betrayal of history by those who needed that history to serve particular purposes of their own.

☞

A humble born Jesus?

Jesus himself may not have been the low-born, humble carpenter that the standard story makes out. According to a leading Vatican theologian, Father Ugo Vanni, who in 1997 published the fruits of twenty years' research into the original scriptural texts, Jesus was more likely to have hailed from a well-off, middle-class family. The original Greek word used to describe his trade – *tékton* – actually denotes, according to Fr Vanni, rather more than the 'carpenter' it is usually translated as. It more accurately signifies a high level of professional craftsmanship and standing in the community, 'more like a surveyor or building engineer'. Bethlehem, the place of his birth, was a 'suspiciously good address', being the birthplace of King David, and Jesus' frequently reported dining engagements with evidently financially comfortable companions, show him to be at ease in a wealthy social environment. 'We are not talking here of about a backward rural milieu,' Vanni asserted, 'Jesus came from a highly cultured background.' Vanni also challenged the orthodox view of Jesus' disciples as poor and simple fishermen. Instead, these were businessmen who ran a serious operation with large boats capable of carrying up to a dozen fishermen and a ton of catch. They were, after all, able to find enough money to keep twelve of them on the road for a prolonged stretch preaching Jesus' message. The father of John and James was wealthy enough to hire servants, while Peter had a house and a boat. These, the historian says, were distinctly middle class accessories.[12]

☞

In the beginning ... confusion
It is sometimes not clear why some beliefs have formed at all. That Adam and Eve were expelled from the Garden of Eden for the offence of eating the forbidden fruit off the Tree of Life is one of them. (Leave aside any talk of the fruit being an apple: nowhere in the Bible is the fruit identified.) The relevant text in Genesis is unequivocal. In Genesis 3:22–23, it is made clear that Adam is cast out of Eden to *prevent* him from taking of the tree, not because of it ('... and now, lest he [Adam] put forth his hand, and take also of the tree of life, and eat, and live for ever; therefore the Lord God sent him forth from the garden of Eden ...').

There is, in fact, no reference to Eve's expulsion, only the deduction of it since the next Chapter of Genesis begins with Adam's 'knowing' of her and the birth of their sons, Cain and Abel[13] along with the almost always forgotten third offspring – Seth,[14] quite important really as, according to Luke, it is from Seth that Jesus was descended.[15]

☞

Not quite the gift

Quite why manna from Heaven has come to be regarded as the unqualified blessing we usually take it to be is unclear. The story, in Numbers 11, is hardly the relief of the Israelites in the wilderness that we commonly think. The appearance of manna comes after the wanderers begin complaining at God at the deprivation they felt they were suffering having left Egypt. Numbers 11:4–5 has the Israelites moaning, 'Who shall give us flesh to eat? We remember the fish, which we did eat in Egypt freely; the cucumbers, and the melon, and the leeks, and the onions, and the garlick.' As for the manna, they complained about its taste and lamented that 'our soul is dried away'.

God is deeply displeased and in Numbers 11:19–20 tells Moses the ungrateful tribes will not eat anything but the manna for a month 'until it come out at your nostrils, and it be loathsome unto you: because you have despised the Lord'. So far from a salvation – the usual way the manna story is told – the action of God appears more like a punishment for their loss of faith or conviction in the exodus from Egypt. Less well known is the coda to the story. At the end of the chapter (11:31–33) God creates a great wind that blows in quails from the sea, so many that they spread a days' walk around their camp in all directions. As the Israelites feasted, God's vengeance was smitten on them through 'a very great plague' that appears to have killed a huge number. So much for what our Sunday school version told us.

☞

How many in the Ark?

The belief that Noah's Ark came to rest specifically on Mount Ararat is similarly misconstrued – how it is unclear – as Genesis 8:4 reads explicitly that it grounded in the *mountains* of Ararat, a region, not a particular mountain top.

And why we believe that the Ark contained only two of each kind of animal is down to careless haste. True, the first part of the story (in Genesis 6:19–20) has God's instruction to Noah that 'and of every living thing of all flesh, two of every sort shalt thou bring into the ark', but readers who persevere into the next chapter find further injunctions: 'Of every clean beast thou shalt take to thee by sevens, the male and his female ... of fowls also of the air by sevens.'[16] As with the Nativity, inconsistencies in the basic text have simply been smoothed over in the telling down the years – and since few actually now read the Bible itself, our collective memory gets re-wired accordingly.

Divorce – no bar
Despite the belief in some streams of Christian faith – Catholicism in particular – that divorce is against God's teaching, there is in fact no direct prohibition of it in the Bible. Two of the Gospels (Mark and Matthew) allow it where the wife commits adultery. The only other reference to divorce, in Deuteronomy, is how to go about it: 'When a man hath taken a wife, and married her, and it come to pass that she find no favour in his eyes, because he hath found some uncleanness in her, then let him write a bill of divorcement, and give it in her hand ...' (24:1). It even allows them both to re-marry (24:2, 24:5).

How many Commandments?
Even God's Commandments get variable treatment. While the traditional rendering of the Ten Commandments is taken from Exodus 20:3–17 or Deuteronomy 5:7–21, there are more references to there being only Six Commandments. The Gospels – supposedly recounting the pronouncements

of Jesus in his lifetime – more frequently cite six than ten Commandments as God's law (and one of the other Gospels has only five). Both Matthew (19:18–19) and Mark (10:19) lay out six, but different ones: Matthew goes for prohibitions against murder, adultery, theft and lying, with the addition of the injunctions to honour one's mother and father and loving one's neighbour. (This leaves out the laws against not having any other gods, making graven images, taking the Lord's name in vain, and for keeping the Sabbath, and slightly modifies the commandment against coveting one's neighbour's goods or wife into one for simply loving them 'as thyself'). Mark has the strictures against murder, adultery, theft and lying, and the honouring of parents, but adds a new one – 'defraud not'. According to Luke (18:20) there are only five Commandments (the ones regarding adultery, killing, theft, lying and the one for honouring parents). The fourth Gospel, John, does not spell them out at all. Romans (13:9) also mentions just six Commandments, but a different permutation again: the usual four against adultery, murder, theft and lying, and then the one against coveting and finally for loving one's neighbour.

So one can be forgiven if there is some confusion about exactly what God meant us to do.

☞

It's all about Satan?

The existence of Satan as the arch opponent of God's good works might be expected to form a central core of the Biblical narrative. Not so. In fact, the familiar depiction of Satan – the fallen angel, Lucifer, who rebelled against God's teachings, was cast out of Heaven, and who ultimately lured Adam and Eve into their own falling from grace – is not Biblical at all, but was developed much later by the early church theologians.[17] In the original Hebrew texts, Satan translates simply as 'adversary' and the name is applied to a range of people who merely are acting against one another. So in I Kings when Hadad the Edomite is an enemy of King Solomon, he is described as a 'satan'.[18] In the book of Zechariah, a 'satan' acts as a prosecutor in the trial of the high priest Joshua.

The ancient Israelites of the Old Testament did not conceptualise a single arch enemy of God.[19] It was the later Jewish translation of the Hebrew scriptures into Greek that introduced the link with the devil. The Greek 'diabolos' was the chosen translation of 'satan', leading to the English 'devil', and the terminology evolved from the indefinite label of 'a satan' and 'a devil' to 'Satan' as a specific individual and 'the' Devil. In later Jewish Talmudic writings, Satan then assumes this more prominent position we are familiar with today as *the* adversary, actually inciting humans to disobey God.[20]

℘

Biblical ideas, but not from the Good Book

Along with the well-known misquotations of Biblical wisdom, such as money being the root of all evil (no, the love of it is: I Timothy 6:10) and pride going before a fall (no, pride 'goeth before destruction, and a haughty spirit before a fall': Proverbs 16:18), there are quotations that we readily assume are Biblical but which are not at all.

Thus 'cleanliness is next to godliness' is often thought to be scriptural, but actually derives from John Wesley in his sermon number 88 'On Dress': 'Let it be observed, that slovenliness is no part of religion; that neither this, nor any text of Scripture, condemns neatness of apparel. Certainly this is a duty, not a sin. "Cleanliness is, indeed, next to godliness."' He is quoting, according to *Brewer's Dictionary of Phrase and Fable*, Phineas ben Yair, a rabbi who lived around AD 150–200, and the sentiment appears in the Jewish Talmud as 'The doctrines of religion are resolved into carefulness ... abstemiousness into cleanliness; cleanliness into godliness.'[21]

'God helps him who helps himself', sounds as if it should be in the Bible, but it isn't. It actually seems to come from an Aesop fable, 'Hercules and the Wagoner', where the phrase 'never more pray to me for help until you have done your best to help yourself', seems to be the original from which the pithier phrase was adapted.[22]

'Spare the rod and spoil the child', is actually from Samuel Butler's poem 'Hudibras', published in 1664: 'What medicine else can cure the fits / Of lovers when they lose their wits? / Love is a boy, by poets styled; / Then spare the rod and spoil the child.' It is a far more memorable rendition of the sentiments that do appear in the Bible, but no more artfully expressed as: 'He that spareth his rod, hateth his child.' (Proverbs 13:24)

☞

St Peter, Rome and the Papacy – another muddle

It is the bedrock of the Christian story that after Jesus' crucifixion, the apostle Peter travelled from the Holy Land to Rome, founded the Christian church there, and became the first Bishop of Rome, and hence the first Pope. From those origins, the modern Roman Catholic church takes its heritage, and all its ecclesiastical power. St Peter's in Rome, the Vatican City, is the centre of the Church, drawing its authority from its ability to trace a lineage all the way back to Christ's chief apostle.

The real historical doubts and uncertainties surrounding this basic foundation story are rarely mentioned. It is a fact, however, that our common assumption that Peter was the first Pope is based on assertions that began to be made only three hundred years after Peter's death. It may surprise adherents to realise that the first reference to Peter being Bishop of Rome only surfaces in the time of Pope Damasus who occupied the Papal seat between 366 and 384. He was the first to promote the claim that Peter not only founded the Christian church in Rome, but took on its leadership too as its first Bishop.[23]

Indeed, the concept of the Papacy was a hazily constructed one at the beginning, and only acquired its present attributes many centuries later. The first lists of the Popes were not created until nearly two centuries after the foundation at Rome, indicating that the centrality that the Bishop of Rome would later assume in the church was not necessarily envisaged at the outset. The practice of referring to the occupant in Rome as 'the' Pope only started after a thousand years of church life. It was not until 1073 that Gregory VII banned Catholics from the commonly held practice of using the form of address ('papa', meaning 'father') to refer to any bishop in the western church.[24]

As for the origins, these are really clouded in a degree of mystery that few prefer to acknowledge today. For example, there is no historical evidence for how long Peter actually spent in Rome. Although the official lists cite Peter as Bishop of Rome (and Pope) for thirty-five years, from AD 32 (shortly after the death of Christ) to AD 67,[25] there is no historical record for this. There are, by contrast, several tantalising curiosities which cast doubt on the role of Peter at the birth of the Roman church.

For example, when in AD 58 Peter's apostolic rival Paul wrote his letter to the Romans, in which he greets by name twenty-nine individuals in the city, he does not mention Peter at all.[26] As sceptics argue, that is surely an astonishing omission if Peter was head of the Church at the time. Other historical records support the contention that he was elsewhere. Eusebius, the recognised father of early church history, records him as preaching across the near east, not Rome, for most of the years after the death of Jesus, only reaching Rome 'about the end of his days'.[27] In all of his extensive writings on the church, he never once mentions him as Bishop of Rome. Modern scholars now tend to accept that Peter might only have spent three or four years in Rome at most.[28]

Even more astonishing, the first lists of the Bishops of Rome that were produced in the late 2nd century also omitted Peter's name entirely. Irenaeus, who produced one of the first lists while serving as Bishop of Lyons between 178 and 200, names Linus the first Bishop of Rome.[29] In the standard church lists of Popes, Linus is traditionally ranked the second Pope, and successor to Peter. Seventy years later, the Apostolic Constitution of 270, a collection of church laws, also cited Linus as the first Bishop. [30]

But if the early origins of the position of Rome in the Church are unclear, murkier still are the later machinations that would cement the Vatican's primacy across the Catholic faith, and its claimed right to speak on behalf of the entire Church. Astonishingly, much of the Papal authority that would form the power base that Rome was to become in the second millennium of the Church, derived from forged documents that have been used to buttress, and in some cases, simply invent, the powers of the Papal office.

When Pope Gregory ascended in 1073, he issued what he asserted was a summary of the authorities of the Pope. These included tenets that were to become fundamental to the operations of the Catholic Church for centuries, such as the absolute power of the Pope to appoint and dismiss Bishops of the Church, the primacy of the Pope on earth, being subject to judgement only by God, the infallibility of the Church, and – importantly for earthly politics – the right to depose kings and emperors. These were a powerful, not to say overwhelming, assertion of the Church's right to a monopoly of spiritual and temporal authority on Earth under God. Gregory claimed they derived from the authorities that had been vested in the Church over the previous thousand years. In fact, most had simply been made up.[31]

A key batch of canon laws, the so-called Pseudo-Isidorian Decretals, consisting of 115 documents which were supposedly put together in the 9th century, and said to be the authorities set down by some of the early Church bishops starting with Clement, the fourth Pope, were actually forgeries. A further 125 documents were tinkered with by adding forged provisions that extended the power of the Pope without any historical provenance or authority.[32]

According to one historian of the Papacy, when the 12th century legal scholar Gratian came to compile his *Decretum*, the Code of Canon Law, which became 'the most influential book ever written by a Catholic', of the 324 passages Gratian cited giving purported authorities from the Popes of the first four centuries, only eleven are genuine statements.[33] Gratian's work would become the foundation for later scholarly works that came to be the essential underpinning of the Papacy, so these falsehoods became neatly embedded in other authorities until no one could tell the difference. And in an era, and subject matter, that rested so much on reference back to 'authorities' the early forgeries became the most powerful asset of the Pope as he competed with kings and emperors for religious and political supremacy.

The sum of these sorry tales is startling. The power of the Vatican, popularly assumed today to be built on the edifice of two thousand years of learned and spiritual undertakings, is more accurately revealed to be the outcome of tawdry political manoeuvrings and, at times, outright deception. And what millions take for granted, and faithfully believe as true statements of the origins of their Church, turn out to have less basis in fact than would be supposed and, perhaps, expected. The implications are enormous. As the Church relies on faith to persuade its adherents about the truth of the *spiritual* message, what should those faithful make of the fact that the supposedly objective *historical* record about the Church turns out to be so shaky?

☞

References

1 M. Molnar, *The Star of Bethlehem: The Legacy of the Magi*, Rutgers University Press, 1999

2 A. McGowan, *How December 25 Became Christmas*, Biblical Archaeology Review, December 2009

3 *Ibid.*

4 W. Januszczak, *Artistic licence or the gospel truth? Sunday Times*, 21 December 1997

5 C. Howse, *The 12 myths of Christmas*, Daily Telegraph, 22 December 2006; www.sacred-destinations.com/italy/ravenna-st-apollinare-nuovo

6 Report, *Sunday Times*, 30 November 1997

7 *Equinox*, Channel 4 TV, 18 August 1998

8 *Archaeology* 45 No 2, May 1992

9 Report, *Daily Telegraph,* London 23 November 1992

10 W. Klassen, *Judas: Betrayer or Friend of Jesus?* SCM Press, 1996

11 H. Maccoby, *Judas Iscariot and the Myth of Jewish Evil*, Peter Halban, 1993

12 Reports, *The Times*, London, 12 November 1997; *Sunday Times* 21 December 1997

13 Genesis 4: 1–2

14 Genesis 4: 25

15 Luke 3: 38

16 Genesis 7:2–3

17 J. Bowden, *Christianity: The Complete Guide*, Continuum, 2005

18 *Ibid.*

19 C. Panati, *Sacred Origins of Profound Things*, Penguin, 1996

20 *Ibid.*

21 N. Rees, *Cassell Companion to Quotations*, Cassell, 1997

22 P. F. Boller & J. George, *They Never Said It*, Oxford University Press, 1989

23 D. MacCulloch, *A History of Christianity*, Allen Lane, 2009

24 J. Bowden (ed.), *Christianity: The Complete Guide*, Continuum, 2005

25 *Catholic Encyclopaedia* at www.newadvent.org/cathen/12272b.htm

26 P. De Rosa, *Vicars of Christ: The Dark Side of the Papacy*, Bantam
    Press, 1988

27 *Ibid.*

28 *Ibid.*

29 *Ibid.*

30 *Ibid.*

31 *Ibid.*

32 *Ibid.*

33 *Ibid.*

3

Political Spins

*Throughout the centuries, politics has been more associated in the
public mind with duplicity and deception than perhaps any other
of its attributes. So it should come as no surprise that many of our
most firmly held beliefs about politics in history turn out to be
rather more complex than we have been led to believe.*

The beginnings of democracy

We might admire the Ancient Greeks for giving us the
concept of democratic government. There is no doubt
of the truth of that. But what we tend not to know is that the
classical age of politics that we casually assume represented
everything Greece was, was in fact a tiny slice of Greek existence: it lasted less than 180 years – a period roughly equivalent to the time between our modern world and the Battle of
Waterloo. It began around 510 BC and lasted until Alexander
the Great's father, Philip of Macedonia, defeated Athens
in 338 BC. For the largest part of ancient Greek 'civilisation',
which began to emerge around 2000–1500 BC, politics was
distinctly undemocratic, and based on the rule of city state
tyrants, in constant warfare with neighbours.

In that brief golden age, though, the Greeks laid down
the foundations of an approach to government that we still
broadly recognise to this day. But behind the story lies another,
darker secret that we all too often like to forget. 'Democratic'
government, the idea that people exercise a direct control
over their leaders and the decisions that are made in their
name, flowered in Athens but grew for one uncomfortable

reason that we prefer not to remember today: slavery. One of the main reasons that democracy was able to develop was that citizens had an army of slaves to do the hard work of normal existence, allowing them to partake in the elevated business of government.

And it was no small army. The structure of Greek society was extreme. While there had always been slavery in the ancient world, the Greeks took it to a new dimension: chattel slavery.

In past civilizations, there had always been master and servant relationships based on historic ties – bonded labour, serfdom, sharecropping. The Greeks went one stage further. In the 6th century BC, the citizens of the island of Chios began acquiring barbarian slaves by simple purchase.[1] This novel approach had two dramatic consequences. It broke the traditional link between slave and their labour: the basis of the relationship between master and servant was now pure commercial ownership, as a bought commodity, a chattel. It also changed a slave's legal position. He or she was, in the eyes of the law, a non-person, possessing no rights.

Chattel slavery spread like wildfire, and revolutionised Greek society. One estimate is that by the time of the emergence of 'democracy' in the fifth and fourth centuries BC, slaves outnumbered free citizens by three or four to one.[2] More conservative estimates put it at two to one. By any measure, it is undisputed that slaves outnumbered free citizens. Athens, for example, in 432 BC, had 45,000 citizens and 110,000 slaves.

As the doyen of the history of government has written, this form of slavery was crucial to the beginnings of participative politics.

> The institution did not just increase the wealth of the Greek cities; it also made possible a class which was leisured enough to participate in the government of the cities. Realizing the potential of 'citizenship' and of a 'forum' polity required the

existence of a subclass of slaves to provide for the (relatively) toil-free citizenry.[3]

Citizens needed all this time to attend the debating assemblies which decided laws in their city state. Politics was direct, not our modern concept of representation (where politicians are elected to act on voters' behalf). All citizens (men only, of course) were entitled, and expected, to take part in the deliberations on laws and the administration of public business. Even courts were 'democratic' in that judgements on public lawsuits were reached by a jury which could number up to 1,000 citizens.

To deter the emergence of tyrants, Greek politics worked on the notion that all posts in government should rotate throughout the citizenry.[4] In Athens, where the political year was divided into ten periods, the population was divided into ten 'tribes' each electing fifty members to the Council. Each tribe took responsibility for managing the Council for one of the periods. Within that, for each day of business, the tribe selected by vote the chairman who would be allowed to serve for that day only. Even the Athenian bureaucracy charged with executing the decisions made by the Council – the magistrates – were elected. Every citizen over thirty could stand, but terms of office were limited to a single year, and re-election was, with a few exceptions, forbidden. They usually comprised a representative of each of the ten tribes, again to limit the prospects of powerful individuals emerging.

The Greek invention was a stunning operation of civic involvement. It changed the way people thought about responsibility for government. Its legacy endures right down to the modern world. But when we admire the transformation of politics that would give us the way of doing things that we enjoy, and laud the Greeks for their imagination and wisdom, spare a thought for the means which enabled them to do it.

☞

A model to follow?

But did the greatest of Greek political minds want successors to follow what the Athenians had created? Although we might assume that this was the direction thinkers of the period took, which is why we hold Greek political philosophy to be the starting point of our journey towards the equitable, democratic politics we have and hold dear today, surprisingly, that is not the case. Far from it. The political theorist of the era who has come to be held in the highest esteem had a very different formula for the ideal society – and it bore little resemblance to what we readily assume the Greeks to have passed down to us as a recommendation for a way of government.

The philosopher in question is Plato. His life (c.428 BC – c.348 BC) spanned the zenith of Athens' political golden age, and he is regarded as the greatest of the ancient thinkers on political theory. It might be expected that he distilled the essence of the Athenian experiment into the model for the future. Not so. Definitively, not so.

In his most famous work, *The Republic*, he set out his recipe for the ideal form of government. But if Plato is assumed to be encapsulating for posterity the tenets of Greek democracy, readers of his treatise are in for a shock. Far from it being the summation of the Athenian method of politics, it turns out to be a startlingly different template and one to send shivers down the spine of any believer in democracy.

Greece's most renowned political thinker came up with an astonishing vision for society. Plato's formula for sound public administration is far removed from what might be assumed to have come from the mind of the age's foremost observer of political life. After his scheme has been examined, the most intriguing question becomes how Plato manages still to retain his historical reputation as a political mastermind.

For Plato's concept of organising society was almost the polar opposite to that practised in his native Athens. Contrary to the ever-fluid and freely chosen civic participation on which politics in the city state depended, Plato foresaw a society working best through the rigid separation of citizens into a three-way division of function: guardians (leaders), defenders (soldiers) and producers (workers). Each had their distinctive role, and at the heart of the success of society was a concept of strict and forcibly exercised control.

At the top, society would rely on an elite of guardians to govern, and supreme power was vested in this leadership. They were supported by a professional soldiery which was loyal to the utmost to the guardians. Underneath this came those who would ensure society prospered – the workers, business owners, farmers and creators of the goods needed by the community to exist. This last category was by far and away the largest section of the population.

So far, so unexceptional. It is how the society operated that puts Plato's ideas on a level of their own. Plato sees the top two classes strictly ruling the third – the majority – and it is this that, to our modern eyes, appears to fix relations into an inflexible straitjacket. There is none of the ever-fluid movement between ruler and ruled that Athens practised through its constant elections for key roles. For Plato, the opposite was the essence of proper government: once you were in one of the three classes, you were there for life. And life for the majority was set to be severe indeed. As one assessment has put it:

> This third class cannot claim a virtue special to itself, as wisdom is the virtue of the first and courage of the second. ... Less noble than the guards, the producers will, like them, obey unquestioningly the commands of the guardians; like them, they will have no part in politics. But they will be content because they will have the wealth that they desire, and they will be doing the job for which they are fitted.[5]

Society rested on 'proper leadership, proper protection, proper provision'.[6] And it rested on the division of men into those fit to rule, those fit to fight and those fit to work. Plato saw this structure as fulfilling the natural order, or 'human excellence' as he termed it. He believed that every man had a predominant character, and only through that character could man excel. Thus, 'human excellence' made the Ideal or Efficient State because 'in it, everybody does only what he is best at'.[7]

For the lowest, and most populous, class, this meant complete subservience to the leadership, so that, in Plato's own words, 'the desires of the vulgar many may be controlled by the desires and wisdom of the cultivated few'.

An even more sinister dimension lay at the core of this concept, since Plato's system 'drafts each to his proper place and seeks to make sure that he stays there'.[8] Plato did not believe in upsetting the order that nature had crafted for each individual. For him the key to society's success was how to ensure that citizens did not move outside the class that nature had placed them in.

The most important instrument for Plato was education – or in practice, the withholding of it. Plato only foresaw education being provided to the guardians and the guards. There would be none for the lowest classes. For the higher echelons, education would be extensive and last beyond youth, the most promising having a ten-year period between the ages of twenty and thirty for rigorous training, and then for the elite of the elite, a further fifteen years of practical experience. This elite would emerge, aged around fifty, ready for the future leadership of the community.

The guardians and guards would live separate existences to the ordinary citizen so as not to be contaminated by the earthly concerns of normal folk. They would be denied any rights to own property to keep them free of personal temptation and would live in communal housing. Described as a 'thorough-going Communism',[9] this extended to family life. Leaders would not marry, but mate annually, the children being taken away for the start of their education treadmill that would produce the next generation of leaders.

> For as history has so clearly shown, family affairs too frequently distort the attention and undermine the integrity of rulers, and it would seem that the only way of ensuring that love of family will not take precedence over love of the State is to abolish the family altogether. Thus deprived of property, of homes, and of family life, nothing can come between them and their service to State.[10]

The key to Plato's vision is thus the biological structuring of society to ensure only the best emerge to rule. In other words, eugenics. It was the duty of guardians and guards to produce future generations of leaders, but in the interests of the State they would not be allowed to do this in an uncontrolled fashion. 'They must beget children when the State directs and with partners whom it chooses.'[11] Plato describes 'an ingenious system of lots' to regulate reproduction. 'Brave men' would be allowed, in his words, to reproduce 'more frequently than others will, and to exercise more than the usual liberty of choice in such matters, so that as many children as possible may be obtained from a father of this character ... No one whom he has a mind to kiss should be permitted to refuse him that satisfaction.' In this way, the State bred itself into self-perpetuation.

So at the heart of Plato's ideal State is regimented control of life, a rigid hierarchy of classes that allows no movement between them, and the complete and utter sacrifice of personal interests to those of the commonalty. For the leadership, that meant the end of family life; for the masses, the absence of any engagement at all in political life.

Historians muse whether Plato ever imagined his State capable of existing in reality. The 20th century did, in fact, on occasions seem to replicate elements of it, in the controlled societies of the most extreme Communist states and in the racial breeding policies of Nazi Germany. But few would have credited the Greeks with coming up with the idea. So when we remember the Greeks, we do so largely for the wrong reasons. We fancy we remember them for their ideas about democracy. But in fact, the legacy they gave us that endured was *how* they did things in everyday practice. What we forget is that the most refined thinker of the time had a completely different concept ready for us. In fact, the Greek idea for political governance was the very stuff of nightmares.

☞

Breaking with the motherland
– the American War of Independence

The 'loss of the colonies' and the battle for the creation of the United States in the years between the Declaration of Independence in 1776 and victory in war over the British in 1781 is a watershed moment in world history. Americans are quick to note that it was the first occasion in modern history of a colonial people throwing off their shackles and throwing their 'oppressors' out of their country.

The case on which America declared, and then fought for, a new political relationship with the mother country was from the beginning cast in deeply moralising terms and sentiments of the highest order. These endure as the main themes in the popular picture that comes down to us today.

The founding of an independent America is revered, by Americans at least, as the embodiment of a people's entitlement to, in the words of the Declaration of Independence, 'life, liberty and the pursuit of happiness'. The movement for overthrowing the shackles of a colonial power has been seen by generations since as the flowering of a philosophy of self-evident justice concerning the fundamental rights of a nation to its freedom in the face of an imposed tyranny. The common perception of the America Revolution is one of a community arguing as one, rising as one, and rebelling as one for their right to be a nation.

It is a long way from being accurate.

Far from being an overwhelming national spirit, the revolt against British rule was an enterprise launched and led by a relatively small band of loquacious political agitators. They created a sophisticated and highly effective network of clandestine correspondence clubs to circulate their ideas around the colonies and feed off each other's increasingly extreme ideas. As friction grew on issues of taxation, commercial rights and political representation between the colonies and London in the 1760s and 1770s, most colonies were divided for most of the time on most of the questions, between conservatives who sought moderation of the impositions from the British within the existing political framework, and radicals backing a more fundamental rupture.[12] The radicals may have ended up winning the day, but it is a fiction that the Revolution was a unanimous revolt of discontent with the prevailing political settlement.

The myth that America was a nation yearning to breathe free in the mid-18th century is a construct of hindsight. Alistair Cooke, in his magisterial survey of America, noted that most of the colonials, if they had visited each other much, would have felt themselves to be in a foreign land.[13] There had never been a sense of unity amongst the colonies as they slowly developed inland from their coastal origins. Land and border disputes were legion and mutual suspicion characterised relations. In wars against increasingly expansive French settlers pushing down from the north from what would become Canada, and against the native Indians, the lack of willingness of those colonies further away from the action to provide manpower and money to aid those under attack became a running sore. Indeed, their rivalry was so obvious a feature of life that Benjamin Franklin, American but determinedly Loyalist right up until the break, was writing to his British government contacts as late as 1760 pointing out that the inter-colony jealousy was so intense that there was no danger 'of their uniting against their own nation'.[14]

He based his opinion on practical experience. He had been part of a British effort in 1754 to draw the colonies together in a better arrangement for defending against the French and Indian threat. When the authorities summoned representatives of the thirteen colonies to Albany, in the north of New York colony, only seven colonies bothered to send delegates. Franklin tried to propose a 'plan of union', a forerunner of the future federal government. Not one colony could be found that approved of the concept.[15]

When the first Continental Congress that managed to attract all thirteen colonies met in Philadelphia in 1775 to agree collective action following the opening skirmishes between colonists and British troops in Lexington and Concord, there was still no overriding sentiment towards independence, rather a determination to keep up the fighting in order to persuade King George III and his government to address their grievances, and as late as January 1776 – five months before independence was declared – the King's health was being toasted by the officers of George Washington's mess at Boston.[16]

The 'War of Independence' itself was far from the unified, anti-British uprising so cherished in American folklore. It might be more accurately cast as America's first civil war, as between a fifth and a third of the population remained loyal to the Crown.[17] About another third stayed neutral or apathetic.[18] Historians point out that the American Revolution was no different to most others: it was a minority movement.[19] The rebels prevailed because they had the force of numbers – to convert, or repress. As soon as British troops had moved on from a community, 'patriot' militias appeared ready to politically educate the people, and coerce them if necessary.

They proved remarkably effective. But it is a tale of concerted effort to overcome apathy or resistance, hardly the stirring image of a nation-in-arms that is the popular perception. As George Washington, the rebels' commander, moved his army through New Jersey he said he felt as if he was fighting in 'the enemy country', so strong was the Loyalist sentiment there. At one of the most crucial moments early in the war, when matters hung in the balance, Washington famously camped his troops over the freezing winter of 1777–78 at Valley Forge in Pennsylvania, another strongly Loyalist colony. They were destitute, frost-bitten and starving. At the same time, though, farmers nearby still preferred to sell their produce to the British instead.[20]

Few Americans recall with ease that they never actually managed to inflict the killer blow on the Redcoats. Rather, it was the British who decided to give up the increasingly futile six-year struggle which had turned into an expensive stalemate.

One theory advanced to explain how the British had allowed it to come to this was that they were, in overall strategy, too humane. Seeing the colonists as kith and kin, they were hesitant to use the harsher tactics that they had all too willingly used, with great success, against 'foreign' enemies in continental Europe in the first half of the 18th century, when British military prowess ruled triumphant (think of Marlborough's classic victories at Blenheim, Ramillies, Oudenarde and Malplaquet all between 1704 and 1709 which shaped European politics for a century). It was this lack of decisiveness and ruthlessness that was the ultimate fatal flaw in the British war effort.[21]

Add to this the moment that really tipped the issue: it was not an American final assault, but the arrival of French naval reinforcements during the siege of General Cornwallis's forces at Yorktown on the Virginia coast. This heralded, in British eyes, inevitable eventual defeat and prompted Cornwallis to seek terms – another fact that tends to get buried in stateside accounts.

A new beginning – but what?
And even when the war was won, it was far from obvious that the now free colonies would contentedly wrap themselves together into a union of the like-minded. For many amongst those rebelling, the war was fought not for unification with fellow colonies, but simply for turfing out the British Governor. In the re-telling of history in the centuries since, these two aspirations have become inextricably conflated into the assumption that the search for freedom from Britain was the same as the wish for a union in a new nation.

It is significant that the committee to draw up Articles of Confederation for a new unified state that was established only nine days after the Declaration of Independence took five years – to March 1781, only six months before the British surrender at Yorktown – to get them ratified by all the colonies in order for them to come into effect. Clearly, there was no sense of an urge to unite.

And what was agreed fell far short of a set-up for viable national government. The Articles created a Congress where representatives of the colonies met, but, beyond that, the colonies adamantly refused to relinquish powers they had up to now enjoyed. They dismissed any idea of creating an overriding chief executive or President with its own powers over them and they granted no power for Congress to raise its own taxes to pay for the tasks assigned to the new 'central' government: responsibility for foreign affairs, the power to declare war, the establishment and running of a postal service, standardising weights and measures, and establishing army and naval commands. Colonies also refused the centre any authority to regulate their trade or shipping.

So, after the War of Independence was won, the victorious states embarked on a highly uncertain path. It was no rush toward a new order. Nothing changed dramatically. For six years, the loose arrangements established by the Articles of Confederation carried on. There was certainly little appetite amongst the colonies for shackling themselves with another overbearing authority having just rid themselves of the King's. Colonies resumed their self-serving practices, and the fissures began to develop.

Commerce was a crucial driver of disharmony. As international traders, cities such as New York and Boston earned a lucrative income from charging customs duties on goods arriving in their ports destined for onward carriage to other colonies. Those nearby such as Connecticut and New Jersey suffered especially. They objected to an arrangement that saw them endure higher prices that went to pay for the upkeep of their neighbour's government.

It was these types of pressures, along with intensifying land disputes and the new problem of the debt caused by the war which someone had to pay off, that impelled the calling of the Philadelphia Convention in 1787 that would, seventeen weeks later, produce the Constitution and create a new unified nation, a full federal government with real powers and the office of a President. But all this actually exceeded the Convention's original purpose and intent, which had been set expressly and only to *revise* the Articles, not to replace them by agreeing to the creation of a federal administration. Like the Revolution itself, the turning of the Convention – it was never known as the Constitutional Convention until afterwards – into a nation-building enterprise was the work of a small band of nationalists, led by James Madison, George Washington, Alexander Hamilton and a few others.[22]

The project was hardly the manifestation of any overwhelming urge to combine. Of the thirteen colonies, Rhode Island refused to attend at all. Maryland struggled to find people willing to serve as delegates – the first team of five selected all turned down the offer to go to Philadelphia, and representatives were still being sought when the Convention opened. New Hampshire sent just two, but refused to meet their expenses and the dispute delayed their arrival by several weeks. Of the fifty-five delegates selected in all – now esteemed as America's 'Founding Fathers' – only about thirty were there from start to finish. Six never came at all.[23]

Tiptoeing to a new nation

The negotiation of the Constitution was hardly the studious application of intellect and political cleverness with which history now imbues the events in Philadelphia. It was an exercise in disputation, conflict and compromise. The smaller colonies deeply feared the ambitions of the larger ones. They had not gone through a war to get rid of one tyranny just to place themselves under the thrall of another, albeit a home-grown one.

Hence the bitter battles on a range of issues that each colony saw differently depending on its size and the make-up of its economy: representation in the new Congress (and the egalitarian solution in the Senate that saw every state in the new federation having two representatives, regardless of its size); the powers of the President (there was a strong debate whether there should be a single chief executive or a troika with one elected from the northern states, one from the southern and one from the middle states) – it took sixty separate votes in the convention just to settle the President's role;[24] the division of authority between the federal government and the states; a North–South fissure on how populations should be calculated for the purpose of apportioning Congressional seats (leading to the notorious 'three-fifths' clause in the Constitution that counted slaves as only three-fifths of a person in order to rein back the advantage southern states were seen to have over northern ones); a South-North fissure on the South's fears of interference in its overseas trade, leading to the provision for at least two-thirds of the Senate being required to approve international treaties, which at the time were largely commercial in nature.

By the end, having waded through the weeks of contestation, the finished product was a mish-mash of compromise. Even Benjamin Franklin rose and expressed doubts about some of the provisions,[25] but signed it nevertheless. Far from a sense of a job well done, there was the unease of a cobbled together plan that risked coming apart at any point in the near future. Only thirty-nine of the fifty-five delegates were present at the end to sign, and three of those refused to put their names to it – Virginian Edmund Randolph, George Mason, his compatriot, who felt the provisions would produce 'monarchy or a tyrannical aristocracy', and Elbridge Gerry from Massachusetts, who wanted a guarantee that there would be a second convention to revise what they had just settled on.[26]

So in all, nineteen members of the Convention, over a third, never put their names to the Constitution agreed in Philadelphia. One estimate is that at this point when the new Constitution was about to be launched upon the American public for their approval, a majority of the population was probably against it.[27] Knowing there was no chance of unanimity amongst the colonies, the Founding Fathers had decided that nine ratifications or approvals from amongst the thirteen would be sufficient to bring the new Constitution into force. The battle for ratification was hard fought and is further evidence that the coming together of the colonies into the United States was no manifestation of an impelling urge to create a new country which the modern reader might assume.

In only five was approval easy (the Delaware, New Jersey and Georgia assemblies endorsed it unanimously, Connecticut overwhelmingly (128–40) and Pennsylvania comfortably (43–26). Massachusetts came next, but only just (187–168) which encouraged Maryland and South Carolina to bring theirs to the vote, both succeeding comfortably (63–11 and 149–73 respectively). When New Hampshire voted in

favour 57–47 in June 1788, nine months after the Philadelphia
Convention, this was enough for the Constitution formally to
come into force. However, the two most important members
– Virginia, the largest and most populous, and New York,
the centre of commerce – had not approved. Without them,
it was accepted the new nation could not survive. Virginia
squeaked home four days after New Hampshire by 89–79.
There was then an agonising month before New York voted.
It did so by an even narrower margin of just three, 30–27. Two
of the original thirteen, North Carolina and Rhode Island,
actually rejected the constitution and remained outside for
another year and eighteen months respectively.[28]

Nearly throwing it all away

And then, after all that, America's leaders set down to change
it all again. The very first piece of business in front of the
very first Congress was a set of proposals to amend the brand
new Constitution. We remember these first ten amendments today as the Bill of Rights, which famously includes
the First Amendment right to free speech, the Second
Amendment right to bear arms, the Fifth Amendment right
not to incriminate oneself in court ('pleading the Fifth') and
the Eighth Amendment prohibition of 'cruel and unusual
punishments'. They were thought necessary because many
of the ratification debates in the states showed a strong
sentiment that the Constitution that had been painfully put
together at Philadelphia gave too much power to the new
federal government. A balance needed to be restored by
setting out in explicit terms the rights of the people.

We remember the Ten Amendments as a superlative crys-
tallisation of personal rights. They resonate to this day and are
probably better known in American minds than the original
Constitution itself. What tends to be forgotten, however, is
that these were only the tip of an original iceberg. The Bill
of Rights was just the residue of a much larger list placed

in front of the first Congressmen that amounted to the desire to emasculate everything that the Founding Fathers had just constructed. What faced the new legislators was a set of more than two hundred amendments proposed by the ratifying conventions in the states. As one historian of the episode writes:

> [I]f the structural amendments had been adopted, even in part, the result would have been a dismemberment of the government limned in the Constitution. These proposals would have curtailed the number of terms for the President, Senators and Representatives; abolished the Vice Presidency; limited the scope of jurisdiction of the federal courts; forbidden Congress to create any court but a Supreme Court and federal admiralty courts; restricted congressional powers of taxation and regulation of interstate and foreign commerce; barred any exercise of federal power to raise revenue unless and until the states refused to comply with congressional requisitions; and required a two-thirds vote of both houses of Congress for any statute regulating commerce, any tax law, and any treaty. ... [I]t is doubtful whether such an eviscerated form of government would have lasted long.[29]

Future President James Madison led the moderate side to salvage a workable compromise. His first battle was to prevent a second national convention being summoned. Many of the states had argued that the whole exercise needed to be repeated to address the citizens' rights concerns. Within four days of Washington's inauguration as first President in April 1789, Madison outmanoeuvred the second convention advocates by tabling a motion giving notice that he intended to bring the amendments to the floor of Congress. This neatly ensnared legislators in the debate on the substance before enough states could submit their requests for a separate convention.[30]

He pruned the list of proposed changes that lay before Congress into a manageable seventeen amendments, and coined the phrase 'Bill of Rights'. These were further reduced by the Senate to twelve, and it was these which were eventually put to all the states for another prolonged process of ratification.

Twelve? Not ten? While the Bill of Rights that finally passed contained ten amendments, that was not the original proposal. The first two of the set did not secure the required support of the states, so the famous 'First Amendment' on free speech was actually the original Third Amendment, and pleading the Fifth would have been 'pleading the Seventh'. The first amendment that failed was designed to ensure adequate representation of the people by tying the size of the lower House strictly to population: first to one Representative for every 30,000 citizens until the House had reached 100 members, then one for every 40,000 until the House reached 200 members, and then after that an upper limit of no more than 50,000 citizens to a Representative. Paradoxically, had it been approved (it failed by just one state) the House of Representatives today, with the American population at over 300 million, would have had 6,000 members instead of the present 435.

The second amendment that failed, supported by only six states of the eleven required, had an even more curious history. This sought to restrict pay rises to members of Congress by ensuring that no increase could be made in their salaries until after an election had taken place, the idea being that they could not vote themselves a pay rise without facing the electorate for their judgement on it before it came into effect. Although it failed at the time, the formal process of ratification never stopped, and having languished for over 190 years, states in the 1980s, aggrieved at the bloated size of Congressional staffs, began a campaign to resurrect it. Amazingly, the requisite number of states (now, of course, much higher than in 1789) ratified the amendment so that in

May 1992 it became part of the Constitution at last – as the 27th Amendment, 203 years after it was first proposed.

It took two years, until December 1791, for the required two thirds majority of the states (eleven out of fourteen – Vermont had joined the Union during the ratification process) to ratify the ten amendments that they seemed ready for at the time. (The remaining three – Massachusetts, Georgia and Connecticut did not do so until 1939![31])

Although it was not the end of disputation about the shape and form of the new government – new tussles broke out almost immediately about where the new federal capital should be built and whether the federal government should assume the debts of the states incurred in the revolutionary war[32] – the essential construction work of the new nation had finally moved beyond the point of no return.

So in the end the United States had been created. But the image of its foundation as a heady, unstoppable, unanimous journey to an agreed destination lives on only in the minds of the patriotic (and myth-encrusted) American. At any step along the way, the outcome was far from predictable, still less inevitable. And a generation had passed since the first stirrings of revolt in the 1760s. This was no headlong rush to nationhood. By the end of the process, it came to look less like the culmination of the fervent national dream we are today led to believe it was, and more the making of a grudging marriage of convenience.

Building the foundation story
The founding of the United States was thus a confused and confounding story. Little wonder that history has smoothed out the uncertainties in its telling down the years. A simple, consistent and one-directional narrative is essential, especially for a nation that was built from such fissiparous parts. The familiar story that Americans 'know' lays a blanket of unity over the actual disharmonies that bedevilled the Founding

Fathers and which made the birth of the United States such a prolonged and problematic affair. With a complex reality, and the ever present threat of renewed dissatisfactions with the experiment, from any of the component states, the need for a clear foundation narrative was paramount – even if it meant mangling the facts. This is why so many of the episodes Americans cherish are travesties of the truth.

For example, at the core of the story, deeply-held and firmly believed by Americans ever since independence, is the claim of exploitation that the colonies had to endure at the hands of the British. But the unwelcome truth is different. Colonists in pre-revolutionary America in fact enjoyed a rather enviable economic position.

Although unjust taxation is the defining refrain of the Revolution, this simple narrative is mired in mythology. Levels of taxation in the colonies were actually extraordinarily low. The most controversial measure of the era to raise revenue – the Stamp Act of 1765 which imposed levies on a range of business transactions – would have doubled taxes to just 2 shillings per person per year.[33] This compared enviously with the 26 shillings per person per year that Britons paid at home. No other people in the colonial empire or the rest of Europe (except the Poles) paid less in taxes than the Americans.[34]

Nor did they have to pay taxes for their own defence against Indian and other European intrusions (such as the French). They had Britain to thank for that. Protection of the colonies was estimated to cost the British a staggering £350,000 a year by 1765[35] – in the order of £400 million in modern values – and a more than four-fold increase since 1748, just seventeen years earlier. Meanwhile, the colonists could continue to accumulate their own wealth behind the barrier provided for them.

They were helped here too. The closed British trading system, which required American exporters only to trade with Britain, and which became one of the ostensible grievances of the revolutionary era, in fact accorded the colonists large benefits without undue restriction. The laws governing trading with foreign countries were 'laxly enforced' in the words of one (American) account.[36] Colonial shipbuilders benefited hugely from subsidies the British authorities paid for ships' parts and stores which their English competitors did not receive and about which they complained heavily.[37] The colonists were also guaranteed a monopoly of the British market in tobacco as cultivation was banned in England and Ireland itself. Fortunes were made by widespread smuggling which the British did little to control. The revolutionary leader John Hancock, famed for being the first to put his name to the Declaration of Independence, was at the same time as he signed the document that complained at the heinous illegalities of King George III, making a fortune as one of Boston's biggest smugglers. The same American assessment concluded:

> The average American was probably better off economically than the average English person at home. If the colonies existed for the benefit of England, it was hardly less true that England existed for the benefit of the colonies.[38]

Politically, too, Britain gave more freedom to its colonies than did any other imperial power. The elder Mirabeau, the renowned French economist of the period, described the English as 'the most enlightened of the people of Europe in their conduct in the New World'.[39] Ironically, some historians argue that the laxity of the British enforcement of their own trade laws, coupled with the comparatively free political society, contributed to an atmosphere that encouraged the colonists to rebel. As a respected account suggests:

> The very liberality of the institutions to which the mother country had accustomed them prepared them to rebel ... Naturally, too, the wholesale evasion of commercial laws which

ran counter to the feeling and interests of the country, had
accustomed the people to the defiance of British authority.[40]

The apparent unfairness of Britain's policies is at the heart of the
American foundation story. One of core watershed moments,
the **Boston Tea Party** in 1773 when colonial 'patriots' invaded
British merchant ships in Boston Harbour and threw chests
of English tea overboard, has come down to us as one of the
iconic protests against the home government's unjust taxes. The
episode is a classic example of how an event has become misremembered because it serves a better purpose in being wrongly
told to fit a larger historical account. In fact, the Tea Act against
which the protests were being made, *lowered* taxes on tea. It
was because it did so that the protest was held. It made English
tea far more affordable for Americans and undermined the vast
black market in tea that prevailed locally (an estimated 75 per
cent of tea was smuggled). It was the prospect of cheap, legally
imported tea that was the concern of Bostonians, not higher
taxes. But as the legends of the Revolution bedded down, the
Tea Party became useful to tell a different story.[41]

Contrary to the account that generations of Americans
have been imbued with, no one spoke the rousing words
'No Taxation Without Representation' during these momentous years. Attributed to James Otis, a member of the
Massachusetts House of Representatives, the citation first
appeared in a biography of him published in 1823, sixty-one
years after the date of his agitation, and forty years after his
death. There is no contemporary record of the phrase being
exclaimed during the Revolution, and it never was the rally-
ing cry that modern memories like to think.[42]

Paul Revere's ride, one of the seminal moments of the
outbreak of war, when he supposedly rode from Boston to
Concord to warn of the arrival of British troops, is enshrined
in the folklore of the Revolution. Although he did exist, he
was in fact one of three riders that night, but never made the

journey to Concord, having been arrested rather ignominiously for posterity before he reached the town. His perpetual fame was secured only when Longfellow wrote his famous poem about the ride in 1863, nearly ninety years after the event in which he had the rider successfully reach his destination. Prior to that time, Revere was a nonentity. He was not even mentioned in the register of national fame, the *Dictionary of American Biography*. Overnight, he was parachuted into the pantheon of historical heroes.[43]

Visitors to Independence Hall in Philadelphia, where the Declaration of Independence was pronounced in 1776, see the **Liberty Bell**, which supposedly rang out the news of independence. Its adornment with a quotation from the Bible urging '*Proclaim LIBERTY throughout all the land unto all the inhabitants thereof*' fits neatly with its apparent connection with the foundation story. But history has a twisting tale to tell here too. The bell, while certainly installed in the steeple of Independence Hall at the time, has not been the continuously revered symbol providing a direct connection with 1776. To start with, there was no public announcement of the Declaration of Independence on 4 July 1776, so the bell was not the herald that popular mythology has it. When independence was proclaimed four days later, and bells across the city pealed, it may have been one of them ringing, but it certainly did not perform the pivotal role commonly believed. In fact, its cherished connection with the events of 1776 was only forged in the American consciousness much, much later. That link was simply made up by a local author, George Lippard, who in 1847 – seventy years after the event – published his *Legends of the American Revolution*. It was this that not only gave the bell its central role in America's birth, but saved it from oblivion. The city of Philadelphia had tried to sell it for scrap in 1828. It was, after all, just an old bell. It came to acquire its hallowed fame by a curious and circuitous accident. In 1839, anti-slavery activists used the bell's quotation to promote their abolitionist cause. It was they who invented the moniker of the 'Liberty Bell', and the 'liberty' they marked had absolutely nothing to do with 1776. This labelling along with Lippard's folkloring created the ingredients from which the modern myth emerges. Since Lippard, the 'Liberty Bell' has been inextricably lodged in the American mindset as a fundamental icon of the Revolution, and few have any desire to unscramble the tangled story.[44]

☞

Washington – hero to zero

George Washington's election in 1789 as first President is cast in legend as the inescapable and inevitable outcome of a nation's gratitude to the military leader who had won them their independence. It was not quite so serene. So intense were the divisions in New York – then the capital of the new country – that the state could not decide who to elect to the electoral college that would finally select the new President. Washington thus became President without any votes from New York, in whose city he took the first oath of office in April 1789. New York also failed to agree who to send to the Senate, so for the first session of the first Congress, the state was unrepresented.[45]

While there was no doubt amongst the political leadership that Washington was the obvious choice as the country's first chief executive, this does not mean he was as universally liked or admired as President as later generations seem to assume. As he took on the airs and graces of office, he riled some of his erstwhile friends. When he received official visitors he had all chairs removed from the room so that no guest could sit in his presence, and he adopted the regal style of greeting by insisting on bowing and refusing to shake hands.[46]

His handling of major political issues as President took the shine off his revolutionary credentials, so by the end he was regarded with far less of the 'father of the nation' sentiment than he had started out with. A particular cause of contention was the onset of the French Revolution in 1789, just months after he had taken office. As military conflict seemed inevitable again between France and England, America was caught in the middle. The 'perpetual' US-French treaty signed in 1778, which had been instrumental, as we have seen, in winning the War of Independence, committed the US to helping France defend its islands in the West Indies. But Washington, conscious of the fragile state of the new nation, wanted to avoid war at all costs. So in 1793, he announced America's neutrality, outraging his former revolutionary allies, like author of the Declaration of Independence, Thomas Jefferson.

In spite of the proclamation, British fleets in the Caribbean still went after American merchant vessels – some three hundred were seized and their American sailors pressed into the British navy. This only increased the outrage in America at Washington's tactics. When he solved the problem by concluding a desperate peace treaty with Britain which came into force in 1796 and which amounted to a surrender to the old foe – Britain refused to rule out future seizures of US vessels, and forced a commitment to pay outstanding pre-Revolution debts to British merchants – Washington's political stock fell to its all-time low. He never recovered and when his term of office expired later that year, he happily retired.

These misfortunes had caused many old friends to turn against him, some in deeply vitriolic fashion. Old campaigner Tom Paine, wrote an open letter to Washington castigating his behaviour in office:

> You commenced your Presidential career by encouraging and swallowing the grossest adulation, and you travelled America from one end to the other, to put yourself in the way of receiving it. ... The character which Mr Washington

has attempted to act in this world is a sort of non-describable chameleon-coloured thing, called prudence. It is, in many cases, a substitute for principle, and is so nearly allied to hypocrisy that it easily slips into it. ... [T]he world will be puzzled to decide whether you are an apostate or an imposter, whether you have abandoned good principles, or whether you ever had any.[47]

One summary of his two terms of office, by the Philadelphia *Aurora* newspaper in 1796, leaves us with a very different feeling from the one with which we are usually asked to remember Washington:

If ever a nation was debauched by a man, the American nation has been debauched by Washington. If ever a nation was deceived by a man, the American nation has been deceived by Washington. Let his conduct, then, be an example to future ages; let it serve to be a warning that no man may be an idol.[48]

The *Aurora* was run by Benjamin Bache, grandson of one of America's founding fathers, Benjamin Franklin. How times had changed. 'If ever there was a period for rejoicing, it is this moment,' wrote Bache, on 6 March 1797 when Washington stepped down from office. He continued:

Every heart, in unison with the freedom and happiness of the people, ought to beat high in exultation, that the name of Washington ceases from this day to give a currency to political iniquity and to legalise corruption.[49]

Yet within a generation or two, Washington was being revered as the father of the nation. He could do no wrong. It has remained that way ever since. That he should so rapidly move back again from political anti-hero to national icon says more about the new nation's need to invent a body of history to solidify the country's foundations. Soon it did not matter what the reality of Washington was. He was to play a far more important role for America dead than he had perhaps ever played for it while alive.

☞

French revolutions with history

The motto most famously thought of as *the* slogan of the French Revolution, *Liberté, Égalité, Fraternité,* was not in fact formally adopted by the revolutionary movement until four years *after* the storming of the Bastille in 1789. It became the official mantra only in June 1793,[50] and also originally had the words 'ou la mort' ('or death') as part of it. These were dropped in 1795. By the time the motto had been sanctified as the equivalent of the modern day 'official sound-bite of the French Revolution', most of the revolutionary action had taken place: the storming of the Bastille, (July 1789) the Declaration of the Rights of Man (August 1789), the new revolutionary constitution (July 1790), the attempted escape from Paris of King Louis XVI (June 1791), the storming of the royal palace at the Tuileries by the mob (August 1792), the abolition of the monarchy (September 1792) the King's execution (January 1793), the outbreak of the royalist revolt in the Vendée region (March 1793) and the creation in Paris of the infamous Committee of Public Safety (April 1793) which would turn the Revolution into a dictatorship. There was not much left to go of the Revolution by the time the Club de Cordeliers, one of the influential revolutionary associations, decided on 30 June 1793 to declare the phrase the formal statement of the Revolution. And even then, it was only part of a longer tag: officially, they agreed the motto would be: *Unité, indivisibilité de la République, Liberté, Égalité, Fraternité ou la mort.*[51]

This was consistent with the far more febrile war of words

that went on in the French Revolution than we are given to believe by our history books. As we have just seen with the American revolutionaries and their 'No Taxation Without Representation', the idea that the French masses ran around exclaiming *Liberté, Égalité, Fraternité* as the totemic all-encompassing call of the Revolution is a historical fiction. In fact, the French Revolution worked itself out under a veritable rainstorm of competing slogans. This one was just one of many, and was never the supreme one until after the turmoil had largely settled down. It reflected, rather than drove, the result.

The slogans usually combined three concepts, but embraced the vast permutations of ideals that revolutionaries sought. So there was *Union, Force, Vertu* ('Union, Strength, Virtue'), *Force, Égalité, Justice* ('Strength, Equality, Justice'), *Liberté, Sûreté, Propriété* ('Liberty, Security, Property'), *Liberté, Unité, Égalité* ('Liberty, Unity, Equality'), *Liberté, Raison, Égalité* ('Liberty, Reason, Equality').[52]

When the Declaration of the Rights of Man, the defining manifesto of the Revolution, was issued shortly after the fall of the Bastille, it mentioned only liberty and equality, leaving out any reference to fraternity. According to French cultural historian Mona Ozouf, this was not unusual. While liberty and equality were frequently regarded as a connected pair, fraternity was not an automatic part of the triptych. Other sentiments, such as *Amité* (Friendship) or *Charité* (Charity) just as often featured.[53] And Robespierre, when he drafted a possible extension of the Declaration in 1793, envisaged formulating the definitive message of the Revolution as *Égalité, Liberté, Sûreté, Propriété*.

All of these multiple themes swirled around the Paris of the revolutionary years. None outclassed any other in the way we are led to assume *Liberté, Égalité, Fraternité* did, and historians debate how significant the Club de Cordeliers action in 1793 actually was given that when Napoleon assumed power as First Consul in 1799, he dropped the motto entirely, choosing to go with something completely different: *Liberté, Ordre public* ('Liberty, Public Order').[54]

It was only in 1838 that French historian Pierre Leroux began the trend that associates the phrase as the primary product of revolutionary sentiment.[55] It was picked up again when France went through another bout of revolutionary upheaval in 1848, and promptly abolished four years later when Napoleon's nephew, Charles Louis Napoleon Bonaparte, then first President of France, eradicated it from all official documents. (*Ordre et Progrés* – 'Order and Progress' – became the official mantra.)

The popular memorialisation of France's revolutionary heritage that we currently recognise, and which we are led to believe has been ingrained in national consciousness from the beginning, really only came together during the French Third Republic after 1870. This regime re-adopted *Liberté, Égalité, Fraternité* as the national motto. Surprisingly, too, to modern minds who might reasonably assume that the central event of the Revolution, the storming of the Bastille, had been celebrated annually ever since, it instituted 'Bastille Day' as the French national holiday: only in 1880, ninety-one years after the event.[56]

☞

Full Marx to Karl?

The Russian Revolution of 1917 that ushered in the world's first Communist regime was portrayed at the time, and continues sometimes still to be seen, as the unerring unfolding in reality of the theories of Karl Marx. The intellectual founder of Communism, through his dense and almost impenetrable *Das Kapital*, laid out for those who grasped it a compelling theory of the future evolution of society, an inevitable next stage in civilization that would follow from capitalism.

Communism, a classless society of equality and harmony – 'from each according to his abilities, to each according to his needs' – would replace the exploitative system of capitalism where the workers toiled and the financial benefits they created flowed to profit-seeking business owners. The systematic and near-scientific nature of Marx's account, that this was an inevitable working out of the internal contradictions of capitalism, lent both credence to his ideas and a sense that it was unavoidable. Adherents would maintain throughout the Communist era of the 20th century that the processes involved in the transition to Communism were beyond the control of mere mortals. When the conditions were ripe, Communism had to follow just as night followed day.

And Communism did follow, in a number of places around the world, starting in Russia, and spreading to China, Vietnam, Korea, Eastern Europe, Africa and Central and Latin America over the decades. But despite the apparent cogency of the theory, and the professed attribution by all Communist regimes to their Marxist roots, not a single one of the last century's Marxist experiments ever actually followed the path predicted by the originator of the cause. In one of the great conundrums – and deceptions – of history, the putting into practice of Marx's ideas everywhere failed to conform to how Marx said it should, and would, happen.

The essence of Marx's idea was that the tensions created by capitalism, with its exploited working class labouring under increasingly unendurable conditions, had to lead eventually to a crisis in society, and the emergence of a new structure that would resolve the conflict between the competing interests. He pronounced three laws of economics which flowed from the fact that capitalism produced profits ('surplus capital') for some: *the law of capitalist accumulation*, by which owners, in striving for bigger and bigger profits, would accumulate more and more labour-saving machines to produce more and more goods; *the law of the concentration of capital*, by which the number of business owners would tend to shrink into larger and larger conglomerates, because they were more efficient, with the eventual emergence of monopolies; and *the law of increasing misery*, by which, through replacement by machines and increasing pressure on wages to keep profits high, the workers would be the ones who continually suffered.[57]

To fulfil the Marxist vision, capitalism had to reach its culminating point of furthest development before the forces of change would automatically be triggered. But it never happened that way. In one of history's biggest deviations between theory and practice, Communism took off in a country least close to Marx's prescription for a society ripe for the change.

Russia in the early decades of the 20th century was a peasant-based, not an industrialised, society. Of all of Europe's societies, it was the most unlikely territory for the Marxist vision to come to fruition. Throughout the previous century Russia had been a by-word for backwardness and underdevelopment. The bulk of the population still lived on the land, most in a state not much above serfdom. As late as the 1880s, a quarter of peasants did not even own a horse.[58] Rare amongst the European experience of the nineteenth century, the mortality rate of Russians actually increased during the century, from 27 per thousand at the start to 35 per thousand in 1880.[59] By 1904, only 27 per cent of school aged children actually attended school. Only 21 per cent of the Russian population could read and write.[60] For the most part, Russians simply did not share in the rise in living standards that swept the rest of the industrialising continent. They were going backwards – hardly the scenario Marx anticipated.

What industrial development there was was highly concentrated: only St Petersburg and Moscow could be called significant industrial cities. It was to be this factor, rather than the overall state of economic development, that would make for successful revolution. Nearly half the entire industrial workforce worked in factories of over 1,000 employees. Such concentration made the politicisation of the workers so much the easier.

Such development that had taken place had largely been financed from foreign loans and expertise – even screws and bolts had to be imported from abroad[61] – so the number of actual 'capitalists' in Russia was miniscule.[62] Industrialisation was just beginning in Russia, not reaching its culminating crisis. This was not the fertile ground for change the Marxist template envisaged.

Politically, it was deeply unstable, to be sure. Revolutionary sentiment against the Tsarist regime had festered throughout the 19th century, and had come to a head in 1905 when Russia suffered a humiliating military defeat in the Far East at the hands of the then tiny and insignificant Japan that sent shock waves around the royal courts of Europe. It sparked demonstrations for social and political reform in St Petersburg, but all accounts of the revolt agree that the outburst was spontaneous and unorganised. The forerunner of the Russian Communists, the Social Democratic Labour Party, had been formed outside Russia – in Brussels – just two years earlier, and while it played no role in the ferment inside the country, Lenin always maintained that without the 'dress rehearsal' of 1905, the 1917 revolution would have been impossible.[63]

Between 1905 and the outbreak of revolution in 1917, the intellectual leaders of the movement – Lenin and Trotsky in particular – plotted and planned and theorised. Lenin eventually recognised that the conditions in Russia did not match those laid down by Marx. He pressed on for a full-blown proletarian revolution, leading to the Bolshevik-Menshevik ('majority-minority') split as the Mensheviks wanted to follow the orthodox prescription of an interim stage whereby, as Marx stipulated, an elite-led government should take over first. Lenin was prepared to dump Marxist theory, arguing that what Marx intended most was the overthrow of the existing system rather than being over-concerned about the form it followed.

In the event, it was naked power politics, not the unfolding of an elaborate political theory, that took hold in Russia in 1917. Lenin would face twists and turns in the years that followed to keep the revolutionary ship afloat, often leading to compete reversals of policy (he overturned strict Communist principles in 1921, barely three years after seizing power, by his 'new economic policy' that essentially re-introduced small-scale capitalism). His success in taking power, and keeping it, lay less with his adherence to the Marxist dogma that supposedly would see things through, and more because, in the words of one historian, his party 'was just one degree less inefficient than any other force against which it had to contend'.[64]

And, in fact, every other Communist takeover that followed saw the same pattern. Communism came not through the culmination of capitalism, but the supplanting of largely peasant and underdeveloped societies by hard-edged and zealous revolutionaries. In *Das Kapital*, Marx had prophesied the process as the inner workings of the economic system, thus: 'There grows the revolt of the working class, a class always increasing in numbers, and disciplined, united and organised by the very mechanism of the process of capitalism itself.' In the end, Mao's dictum rang as a truer guide to the Communist means of advancement: 'Political power grows out of the barrel of a gun.'

☞

Organised chaos – the Nazi machine

If asked to visualise the Nazi behemoth, one of the images that will most likely come to mind will be the massed ranks of the German armed might standing in their thousands at one of the infamous Nuremburg rallies, column after column after column, in perfectly choreographed order. We have an ingrained view of Hitler's regime as one of the most ruthlessly efficient political orders ever created. It may not have lasted for long, but while it did, it represented the height of totalitarian discipline.

Not true. In fact, historians point out that the key to Hitler's success in mastering the German political establishment was precisely the opposite. When he came to power in 1933, Hitler launched upon a chaotic, intentionally conflictual system of government, designed to ensure that no potential rivals were able to build a power base to challenge him. He deliberately created government departments with overlapping authorities, so their leaders would expend much of their energy in constant fights with competitors in the system. The approach is summed up admirably thus:

> Seen from either a stylistic or logical point of view, [the Nazi government] was never a uniform or a logical structure. In it, traditional and revolutionary elements comingled uneasily and lent an air of incoherence to the whole. The functions performed in some of its parts seemed to serve no purpose except to offset what went on in others ... It was always difficult for those in one part of the building to know what was going on in others, and lateral communication was often quite impossible. The only clear channels of communication were those that ran to and from the apartments of the architect, and this had been the guiding principle of his creation, consciously intended to make all parts of the whole dependent upon his commands.[65]

While the outside world saw a solid edifice, inside bureaucratic life was one long muddle, with functions duplicated and mutual suspicions among administrators constantly fuelled. Hitler deliberately abandoned the previously used cabinet system so that his ministers would have no ready means of sharing information, or discussing policy. Almost all key political decisions were taken by Hitler in one-to-one encounters with his subordinates, and usually spontaneously rather than as the result of a lengthy consideration of the issues.[66] The Minister of Finance, Schwerin von Krosigk, complained that he only heard about events that had a major impact on the country's finances, such as the 1935 repudiation of the limitation on arms under the Treaty of Versailles which signalled the start of Germany's remilitarisation effort, in the newspapers.[67]

Hitler was also prone to setting up special commissions or separate agencies which further confused the powers of the main departments. When he launched his Four Year Plan in 1936, and charged Hermann Goering to lead it, he created an entirely separate organisation that then competed with the Ministry of Economics. The Ministry of Labour, which had been given the responsibility for manpower was rivalled by the establishment of the German Labour Front organisation set up just two months after Hitler's accession to power. In 1942, at the height of the war, there were fifty-eight Supreme Reich boards, as well as dozens of bureaus and agencies which contested the most mundane of matters.[68] One official complained of receiving contradictory instructions when he was simply trying to arrange a celebration of the solstice.[69]

Hitler himself maintained three separate support offices – a Reich Chancellery office, a Presidential Chancellery office and a Party Chancellery office, reflecting his simultaneous roles as head of government, head of state and head of the party. He did not define their functions clearly or the division of labour between them.[70]Although it might seem self-defeating, there was method in the apparent madness:

> Hitler had learned the old lesson of divide and rule and had become adroit in devising checks and balances that protected his own position by making the contenders dependent upon

his arbitrament of their disputes. Offsetting every grant of authority with a counter-grant to someone else became the hallmark of his administrative practice.[71]

Hitler biographer Joachim Fest has captured the atmosphere succinctly:

> Cabinet ministers, commissioners, special emissaries, officials of party affiliates, administrators, governors, many of them with assignments kept deliberately vague, formed an inextricable knot of interlocking authorities, which Hitler alone, with virtually a Hapsburgian grasp of puppet mastery, could supervise, balance and dominate [72]

If it was incoherent at the top, it was even more so at the local level. The Nazi Party organisation was divided into forty-two *gaus* or regions, each headed by a locally powerful leader (*gauleiter*). *Gauleiters* were responsible directly to Hitler, and in the Nazi way of things their influence stretched across both party and governmental matters. Conflicts with the governors of the fifteen *lands* or states, the main formal unit of regional government, were inevitable. But even within the party, Hitler created tension. The way the party was structured, more actual power lay with the next level down, in the *kreis* or district.[73] So the *Kreisleiters* were yet another source of power dilution. If Hitler seemed positively to encourage friction, it was with a purpose: in-fighting kept energetic people busy.

Such an approach to leadership has led some historians to view Hitler's Germany as not so much a totalitarian state as a modern version of a feudal empire.[74] Appealing to personal loyalty had been a trademark of Hitler's style since the earliest days of his party leadership. What he did after 1933 was to raise his personal survival technique into a form of government.

☞

The Cuban missile crisis
– diplomatic triumph or self-inflicted wound?

By common agreement, the thirteen-day stand-off between the United States and the Soviet Union in October 1962 was the pinnacle of the Cold War. After the discovery of Soviet nuclear missiles on America's doorstep in Cuba, the world held its breath for nearly two weeks as frenetic diplomatic exchanges sought to defuse the crisis. The planet teetered on the brink of nuclear war.

That it came out alright in the end is commonly put down to the calm and cool-headed attitude of the young President Kennedy – in office for less than two years, and now tested to the extreme – who, as the conventional narrative tells it, navigated wisely around the shoals of potential disaster, adroitly handled by the unpredictable and wayward Khrushchev, and brought the world safely through. Dean Acheson, the former Secretary of State, wrote at the time that Kennedy's policy had been 'wisely conceived and vigorously executed'.[75]

Reality, in fact, has a few edges to it that put a different gloss on the affair. The picture of American innocence struggling to respond reasonably and on the moral high ground to an unreasonable Russian challenge usually gives us a comforting glow of a diplomatic triumph. All was not so clear-cut. Did the whole crisis have to happen at all? And furthermore, had the Americans in fact actually brought it upon themselves?

The origin of the idea for cocking a snook at the US is reported to have come when Khrushchev was visiting his satellite, Bulgaria, in May 1962. As he relaxed by walking on the beach at Varna, he gazed out over the Black Sea. He was aware that on the opposite shore, 250 miles distant, lay Turkey, a member of the Western NATO alliance, where the Americans had two months earlier installed fifteen

Jupiter nuclear weapons as part of the hemming in of the Soviet southern borderlands. They could hit Moscow in just eight minutes. From a Soviet perspective, with short range warheads also deployed in Italy and Britain, they had reason to feel surrounded.

Pondering the apparent unfairness of the strategic balance, Khrushchev, on his walk, is said to have mused, 'Why not throw a hedgehog at Uncle Sam's pants?'[76] Cuban leader Fidel Castro in fact took a little persuading – he was more worried it would revive hostility from his near neighbour (he had already suffered an American attempt to overthrow him in the infamous Bay of Pigs fiasco the year before). But when he finally came round, sixty-five Soviet ships were soon en route for the Caribbean.

When spy-planes first discovered the missile installations, Kennedy's reaction told a lot about American perspectives. He is recorded as being horrified, telling McGeorge Bundy, his national security adviser that it was 'just as if we suddenly began to put a major number [of missiles] in Turkey'. Bundy had to remind him, 'Well, we just did, Mr President'.[77]

An oft-unasked question about the crisis, then, is why the Americans ought to feel unduly threatened by the presence of nuclear weapons a hundred or so miles off their coast if they expected the Soviets to put up with the same scenario off theirs. An option that presented itself to Kennedy on day one of the crisis, therefore, was to do nothing. There would then have been no edge-of-the-cliff drama, no bringing humanity to the brink of catastrophe and the world would have gone on, just as it was going on across the Black Sea.

Kennedy was, in domestic politics, caught by his own history. He had, before becoming President, pressed the previous Republican administration to 'do something about Cuba'. Although the subsequent Bay of Pigs disaster had been planned before he took office, he had sanctioned it when he arrived and it had happened on his watch. He could not afford another humiliation. These domestic pressures, not the inter-national strategic dimension, made a non-response impossible and drove the President on to make a crisis out of the episode.

Nor was the diplomacy as carefully managed as we have been led to believe. According to newly-released records, from both sides' archives in the late 1990s, the legendary level-headed Kennedy was exactly that – a legend. Having found himself boxed in to having to do something, tape recordings of meetings with his advisers show Kennedy to have started by wanting an all-out invasion of Cuba.[78] He relented when the generals pointed out it would probably have led to the eastern seaboard of the United States being wiped out. He then wanted massive air strikes on the island; the generals said that probably would not work either. The eventual naval quarantine put around Cuba to block further deliveries of missiles, far from being the conventional picture of an astute and balanced diplomatic response, was the outcome of the President being dissuaded from aggressive military action and having no other response to make.[79]

According to the archives, Robert Kennedy, the President's younger brother and serving as Attorney-General, wanted to provoke a showdown by blowing up a US ship to provide an excuse for initiating hostilities, in a repeat of the sabotage of the battleship the *Maine* which was blown up in Havana Harbor in 1898 to give the pretext for the Spanish-American War. On the other side, unbeknownst to the Americans, the Soviet commander on Cuba had been authorised to fire his nuclear weapons if the US invaded without waiting for further confirmation from Moscow.[80] Truly, the world was lurching into uncharted waters.

In the event, an old-fashioned political deal prevailed. When Moscow proposed that their missiles would be with-drawn if the US removed theirs from Turkey (and publicly promised not to invade Cuba), a basis for a settlement formed. A non-public commitment on the Turkish withdrawal alongside the publicly presented agreement appeared to the world an equitable *quid pro quo*: the Soviets announced that they had been given the guarantee they needed for the security of their Cuban ally: there was no longer any need for the (clearly defensive) missiles to remain.

Within months the Turkish missiles were quietly withdrawn, much to the chagrin of the Turks who had not been told of the secret deal. While the legend tells of the Cuban Missile Crisis being a triumph for careful Western diplomacy – recall Dean Rusk's famous quip that has defined the fortnight that 'we're eyeball to eyeball, and I think the other fellow just blinked' – and the flowering of Kennedy as a statesman, the truth is that it was Khrushchev who emerged as the short-term victor. He secured the withdrawal of the missiles from his doorstep and a guarantee that the communist regime in Cuba would be allowed to continue without the threat of invasion.

And if you believe the conspiracy theorists, this second let-down of Cuba by the Americans was to trigger subterranean moves amongst the Cuban and mob underworld that would eventually come together in Kennedy's assassination in Dallas just over a year later.

☞

References

1 S. E. Finer, *The History of Government, Vol 1*, Oxford University Press, 1997
2 M. I. Finley, *Politics in the Ancient World*, Cambridge University Press, 1983
3 Finer, *op. cit.*
4 *Ibid.*
5 C. L. Wayper, *Political Thought*, The English Universities Press, 1965
6 *Ibid.*
7 *Ibid.*

8   *Ibid.*

9   *Ibid.*

10   *Ibid.*

11   *Ibid.*

12   H. Brogan, *History of the United States*, Longman, 1985

13   A. Cooke, *America*, Weidenfeld and Nicolson, 1973

14   Quoted in T. Draper, *A Struggle for Power*, Little, Brown & Co, 1996

15   Draper, *op. cit.*

16   T. A. Bailey & David M. Kennedy, *The American Pageant*, D C Heath, 1994

17   R. Raphael, *The American Revolution: A People's History*, Profile, 2001

18   *Common Errors in History*, Historical Association, 1951

19   Bailey & Kennedy, *op. cit.*

20   Bailey & Kennedy, *op. cit.*

21   J. Black, *War for America*, Alan Sutton, 1991

22   C. Collier & J. L. Collier, *Decision in Philadelphia*, Ballantine, 1986

23   B. Bryson, *Made in America*, Secker & Warburg, 1994

24   D. Wallechinsky & I. Wallace, *The People's Almanac*, Doubleday, 1975

25   *Ibid.*

26   Collier & Collier, *op. cit.*

27   *Ibid.*

28   M. A. Jones, *The Limits of Liberty*, Oxford University Press, 1995

29   R. B. Bernstein & J. Agel, *Amending America*, Random House, 1993

30   *Ibid.*

31   *Ibid.*

32   *Ibid.*

33   J. P. McKay, B. D. Hill & J. Buckler, *A History of Western Society*, 4th ed., Houghton Mifflin, 1991

34   *Ibid.*

35   Draper, *op. cit.*

36   Bailey & Kennedy, *op. cit.*

37   *Ibid.*

38   *Ibid.*

39 Quoted in J. Holland Rose, A. P. Newton & E. A. Benians (eds), *The Cambridge History of the British Empire (Vol 1)*, Cambridge University Press, 1929

40 *Ibid.*

41 R. Shenkman, *I Love Paul Revere, Whether He Rode or Not*, HarperCollins, 1992

42 Draper, *op. cit.*

43 R. Shenkman, *Legends, Lies and Cherished Myths of American History*, HarperCollins, 1988

44 Shenkman, *ibid.*

45 Shenkman, *ibid.*

46 W. Garrison, *A Treasury of White House Tales*, Rutledge Hill Press, 1996

47 W. A. Degregorio, *The Complete Book of US Presidents*, Barricade Books, 1993

48 *Ibid.*

49 D. J. Boorstin, *The Americans: The National Experience*, Random House, 1965

50 *Oxford Dictionary of Quotations*, 3rd ed, Oxford University Press, 1979

51 *Ibid.*

52 *Liberté, Égalité, Fraternité* at www.worldlingo.com

53 In *Realms of Memory*, Columbia University Press, 1998, cited in *ibid.*

54 *Ibid.*

55 *Ibid.*

56 F. Furet, *Revolutionary France 1770–1880*, Blackwell, 1993

57 R. N. Carew Hunt, *The Theory and Practice of Communism*, Penguin, 1963

58 L. Kochan, *The Making of Modern Russia*, Jonathan Cape, 1962

59 *Ibid.*

60 K. Perry, *Modern European History*, W. H. Allen, 1976

61 Kochan, *op. cit.*

62 D. McLellan, *Karl Marx: The Legacy*, BBC Books, 1983

63 Carew Hunt, *op. cit.*

64 *Ibid.*

65 G. A. Craig, *Germany 1866–1945*, Oxford University Press, 1978

66 I. Kershaw, *The Nazi Dictatorship*, Edward Arnold, 1985
67 Craig, *op. cit.*
68 J. Fest, *Hitler*, Weidenfeld & Nicolson, 1974
69 *Ibid.*
70 Craig, *op. cit.*
71 Craig, *op. cit.*
72 Fest, *op. cit.*
73 R. Grunberger, *A Social History of the Third Reich*, Penguin, 1974
74 R. Koehl, quoted in Kershaw, *op. cit*
75 Quoted by H. Thomas, *The Times*, London, 16 October 1987
76 J. Isaacs & T. Downing, *Cold War*, Bantam Books, 1998
77 *Ibid.*
78 A. Fursenko & T. Naftali, *One Hell of a Gamble*, J. Murray, 1997
79 *Ibid.*
80 *Ibid.*

4

Battling for Truth

The most common metaphor for history's attempts to portray the almost perpetual conflicts that man inflicts upon his fellow man is 'the fog of war'. It is a very apt phrase, for of all humanity's undertakings, war is the most encumbered with falsehoods, lies and deceptions. Not only is war, by its very nature, chaotic, meaning that any clear picture is a challenge to historians, but the sacrifices it calls for tend to demand clear justifications for actions, and the losses that follow. Where the picture is not clear, mythologising, deliberate or accidental, tries to make it so.

Crusading zeal?

A snippet to start with to set the tone. We may feel we remember the Crusades for their fearsome religious purity, but war then was pretty much as it has always been. When Richard I ('the Lionheart') got to Marseilles en route to the Third Crusade in 1190, he discovered that his advanced guard of 'trusty' knights had spent the entire campaign funds on prostitutes.[1]

☞

The English Civil War – a most confusing conflict

The English Civil War now seems to be remembered for little beyond a handful of fleeting images – King Charles storming into Parliament to try to arrest five members (the 'birds' who had 'flown'), Cromwell, the upstart farmer, later occupying the Speaker's Chair in the Commons shouting, in reference to the Mace, the symbol of Royal authority, to 'throw away those baubles', the beheading of a King and a vague collection of battles between proletarian Roundheads and flouncy Cavaliers. It is a largely unremembered conflict today. If you think that is unfair, who can name more than two Civil War battles? (And extra points if they don't include Edgehill, Marston Moor or Naseby.)

It deserves more. This seminal moment in the course of British history remains the bloodiest the nation has ever witnessed. The nine years of war between 1642 and 1651 involved more military activity on English soil than the rest of the millennium (from the Norman invasion to now) put together. From 1066 to 1640, there had been twenty battles where more than 5,000 men were engaged. Since the Civil War, there has been just one engagement over 1,000. In those nine years in between, there were twenty-two battles involving more than 5,000 troops, including eight of the ten greatest battles in our history. It is a sobering fact that a larger proportion of the population died in the Civil War than in the First World War.[2] The war cost 600,000 lives from battle and disease, out of a population of just five and a half million[3] – 11 per cent of the entire nation, the equivalent of a holocaust of over six million Britons today.

When it is remembered, the Civil War is invariably misconstrued. It is most often characterised as a battle for political liberties between an illiberal monarchy and liberalising Parliament, representing the common people. Yet the rule that followed was clearly even more repressive than the authority it overthrew. Under Cromwell, the military were authorised to enter private houses to ensure that the Sabbath and fasts ordered by the Puritan Parliament were being observed, theatres and other forms of public entertainment were shut down, alehouses were sharply reduced. Christmas was famously abolished, and the playing of football and cards outlawed. In 1647, Parliament enacted a law decreeing that anyone who had acted in any playhouse in London was to be punished as rogues (a year later, anyone who had watched them could now be fined).[4]

Recent research has tended to explode long-held interpretations about the causes of the war (without necessarily leaving any clearer picture behind on what did lead to conflict). It seems clear now that it is wrong to see the Royalist and Parliamentary sides as representing the culmination of long-standing social or economic divisions that seeded an inevitable outbreak of war. Positions were far more fluid than is often portrayed. Many who opposed the King's attempts to levy taxes without Parliamentary support – one of the supposed key dividing lines – actually supported the King when it came to religious issues or relations with Scotland.[5] Nor was it a case of Parliament, which Charles had ruled without for eleven years, wanting to assert its primacy over the King, another traditional explanation. As one historian of the period has summarised:

> No one had intended to increase the powers of the two Houses, but only to insist that Parliament be allowed to meet regularly to discharge its ancient duties: to make law, to grant supply, to draw the King's attention to the grievances of the subjects and to seek redress.[6]

The truth appears to lie more in the direction of personal mismanagement of politics by the King and religious turmoil, not least the separate feuds breaking out in Scotland and Ireland that destabilised the kingdom at crucial moments and fed disorder (as well as the need for funds). When war broke out between King and Parliament it did so 'to the dismay and bewilderment of almost everyone'.[7] In short, more accident and blunder than the once fashionable theorems that saw the war as the working out of deep forces of historical change.

Cromwell, the leader whose legacy as King-killer defines his commonly accepted place in history, also presents a mercurial picture. He, in fact, came close to accepting the invitation of his pliant Parliament to assume the title of King for himself in 1657, a year before his death. He eventually declined, re-taking the title Lord Protector instead, but not until he had considered the idea for six weeks.[8] He nevertheless lived in the old royal palaces in Whitehall and Hampton Court, dressed in ermine and was addressed as 'Your Highness'.[9]

The first First World War

The term 'First World War' was only coined as a recognised historical label in 1947[10] (the 1914–18 conflict had been known as the Great War at the time, and then more popularly 'World War One' from 1939 as a second one began to loom). The concept of a global war, emerging only in the last century, has tended to diminish our appreciation of earlier periods of warfare. In fact, in terms of geographical spread, the first truly world war took place a century and a half earlier, and surpassed the First World War, both in length and in territorial span.[11]

The Seven Years' War, 1756–1763, was the first to involve all the major powers of Europe – Britain, Prussia (the forerunner of Germany) and Hanover on the one side against Austria, France, Russia, Sweden and Spain on the other. As in 1914, the origins of the war lay in the growing anxieties of the traditional monarchies in Europe with the emerging might of the central powerbase, Prussia. And also like 1914, but to a much greater extent than popularly realised, it ranged across the globe. As well as major battles on the continent of Europe, Britain fought France (and their native Indian allies) in North America in a conflict that saw Canada's future become definitively an Anglophone one; in the Caribbean where Britain would seize island after island from the French; in the Mediterranean where she also secured a number of island outposts that would have lasting significance; and in India where military success destroyed French hopes of developing their settlements and made India a British preserve. The war also saw action as far as the Philippines where Britain captured Manila from the Spanish four months before the peace treaty was signed and ransomed it handsomely for $4 million (about $120 million in modern values).

By the time it ended in February 1763, France had to renounce all its claims to Canada and all territory east of the Mississippi River except New Orleans. Its imperial hopes in North America were extinguished for good. Britain won Florida from Spain in return for restoring the captured Havana in Spanish Cuba, and kept most of the Caribbean islands it had seized – Grenada, St Vincent, Dominica and Tobago. In India, the British East India Company ended up as the supreme power in the sub-continent, a base from which the British Raj would develop in the century to come.[12]

The naval success of Britain in the Seven Years' War laid the foundations for the complete control of the seas that the Royal Navy enjoyed for the next hundred and fifty years. Not until the battleship building programme of the new German Empire in the first decade of the 20th century, which would trigger the next global outbreak, did the British navy ever feel fundamentally challenged.

On the European mainland too, the war saw a shift in the power balance with Prussia, despite some heavy defeats in battles, managing to preserve its growing strength and set the foundation for the emergence of a united Germany a century later. In an uncanny precursor of the 'second' First World War, when the defeated Germany of 1918 revived to challenge the European balance again within a generation, in this 'first' world war the great power that lost most – France – would also re-emerge, within a generation, to unsettle Europe again, first by revolution in 1789 and then outright war against the other powers under Napoleon. There were similarities in the reasons too: the debts incurred by France in the war went a long way to create the social tensions that led to revolution, just as Germany's lingering sense of national grievance after 1918 seeded the Nazi rise to power.

The Seven Years' War – the first truly world war – is not one of the conflicts that readily comes to the modern mind. Unlike other more memorable wars of history, it lacks an eye-catching name, and the multitude of battles are almost forgotten today. It is one of the most neglected, but most significant, series of military engagements in history. It set the course of empires that resonate still today. But these were long term consequences, not immediately discernible. Coming just before more earth-shattering episodes as the American War of Independence, which launched a new nation, and the French Revolution, which unleashed a new political philosophy, the Seven Years' War has all too often been relegated to the shadows. But as a defining moment in the imperial fortunes of Britain and France, it stands as a monumental watershed: no more would France threaten the British settlements in America, Canada or India. The Seven Years' War was a pivotal conflict, a genuine global military undertaking, its magnitude not to be seen again for over a century and a half. Yet ask most knowledgeable people today about it, and the chances are most will know nothing about it.

☞

Culloden – A Scottish national fairy tale

Dear to Scottish nationalists' hearts is the romantic, though ultimately unsuccessful, campaign of Bonnie Prince Charlie to claim the British crown in the Jacobite Rebellion of 1745–6. It culminated in one of Scotland's most iconic episodes, defeat on the moor at Culloden, and the Young Pretender's igno-minious flight 'over the sea to Skye' (and eventual escape to

France). It has come down to us in our schoolbooks as a defeat of Scottish national aspirations by the English, another of the seemingly endless conflicts between the two nations over the centuries. But this presentation is a myth. What is usually missed out from the telling is that there were more Scots in the 'English' royal lines than there were in the rebel highlander army. Some 4,000 rebels faced 9,000 Redcoats under the Duke of Cumberland. Among his battalions were three comprised of Lowland Scots, and two more raised almost entirely from the Clan Campbell.[13] To call the other side enthusiastically nationalist would also be far from the truth too. Many had been dragooned into the rebellion by threats of eviction and roof-burning. Those that did join willingly did so more out of antagonism to the Campbells' siding with the English than any loyalty or interest in the Jacobite cause.[14]

The '45 was no simple anti-English crusade. It was instead a complex, fratricidal civil conflict. By the end, Prince Charles had more clans hostile to him than had ever been for him. Although he would never set foot in Scotland again, his image would constantly evolve and the events be spin-washed until it has become a totem of the struggle of a united Scotland against the hated English.

☞

The charge of the Light Brigade – futility immortalised or tactical success?

It is the most famous lost cause in military history. Immortalised in Tennyson's elegiac poem, the fate of the Light Brigade at the Battle of Balaclava in October 1854 during the Crimean War has resonated down the years as the epitome of fruitless sacrifice:

> 'Forward the Light Brigade!'
> Was there a man dismay'd?

Not tho' the soldier knew
Some one had blunder'd
Their's not to make reply,
Their's not to reason why,
Their's but to do and die:
Into the valley of Death
Rode the six hundred.

Cannon to the right of them
Cannon to the left of them,
Cannon in front of them
Volley'd and thunder'd.
Into the jaws of Death,
Into the mouth of Hell.

The charge of the (actually 673) cavalrymen was against the Russian field batteries at the end of a narrow ravine a little over a mile long. On both sides of the defile were enemy guns too. It looked suicidal. In fact, the manoeuvre was entirely the result of a miscommunication between Lord Raglan, commander of the British forces stationed high on a ridge overlooking the battlefield who sent a messenger with the instruction to the Light Brigade to 'head off the guns' by which he was referring to some escaping Russian cannon that he could see from his position. The ambiguity of the order, and the fact that down in the valley the recipient of the message, General Lucan, could not see the escaping Russians, just the stationary battery at the far end, led Lucan to assume the command was to assault the Russian lines.

Whatever its origin, the received version of the outcome is that catastrophe followed. Long accepted casualty figures put the death toll at nearly half the brigade, with a significant number of the rest wounded. The tallies were based on initial reports from the pioneering war correspondent of *The Times*, William Howard Russell, which reached London three weeks later. Tennyson's poem, which appeared barely four weeks after that, in the first week of December, accentuated the sense of an 'annihilation' (the word used in an editorial in *The Times* to describe the debacle).[15]

However, research published in 2004 by the official archivist of the Queen's Royal Lancers, successor regiment to one of those that took part in the charge, has turned the received wisdom on its head. Having tracked down more than twenty eyewitness accounts and testimonials about the charge, a different conclusion emerged: that losses were actually far fewer than popularly imagined, were not out of the ordinary at all, and that most of the apocalyptic rendering of the event can be laid at the door of Tennyson's mood-magnifying work.

According to the modern account, only 110 cavalrymen died. Others had their horses shot from beneath them but later struggled back to camp on foot. These were not included in the first roll call of survivors, when at the count only 195 men reported in that evening. From that, it was deduced that more than two-thirds of the force had perished, been captured or were missing, presumed lost.[16] No one bothered, or were inclined, to correct the impression later, not least because of the inverted glory that ensued amongst the public for the scale of the sacrifice – *The Times* had commenced its editorial with the stirring sentiment:

> We now know the details of the attack on Balaklava [sic] on the 25th, and with them much that is glorious and much that is reassuring.[17]

'In the popular misunderstanding of the charge, the Light Brigade was virtually wiped out with most of the men killed or wounded,' said the archivist, Terry Brighton. 'This is totally untrue. ... An incredible 395, or 60 per cent, rode the one and a quarter miles under fire from the Russian guns, attacked and pursued the Russian cavalry behind the guns, and returned up the valley with the enemy at their backs, unscathed except for minor wounds.'

Other military historians backed up the new findings. The Marquess of Anglesey, a noted cavalry historian, told the press, 'It was a foolish thing to do and it was all to do with a muddle, but the actual losses were not that great or exceptional in any way.'

It was Tennyson's quick-off-the-draw popularisation that 'caught the feeling of the hour'[18] and cemented the episode in the national story as an unmitigated and unparalleled disaster. When the truth came to dribble out in the weeks and months that followed, no one had the slightest interest in upsetting an imagery that had begun to emerge from the War, and which the Charge of the Light Brigade concisely typified: that of a bungling and incompetent military leadership that was not fit to command the brave troops of the ranks.

☞

A war to end slavery?

The American Civil War which lasted four years between 1861 and 1865, tore a nation in two, cost over 650,000 lives – one in every three soldiers who participated became a casualty from either battle or disease – and scarred the American consciousness forever. Scarred and also moulded it. For all is not as clear cut as history often seems to make out when it comes to understanding the reasons why the war was fought. Slavery may have brought the country to the point of conflict, but the common assumption that the Civil War was a war to end slavery is far from the truth. The war was about preventing the break-up of the Union, not the freeing of slaves. That it is seen today as synonymous with the struggle to end slavery is the work of decades of finessing the memory, doubtlessly spurred on by a national urge to find a moral justification for the appalling cost.

Slavery was, for sure, the issue that divided the nation. The southern states, reliant on mass labour for producing cotton, needed the 'peculiar institution' to continue unfettered. The North had an economy that was built on trade in manufactured goods, and was suffering from an economic depression that had barely touched the South since worldwide demand for cotton was booming. The two halves had reached an uncertain compromise in the years before the outbreak of war as America expanded westward. As new states joined, it was ensured that there was always a balance: when a slave state joined, it was mirrored by a 'free' state to ensure in Congress that neither mindset would outnumber the other.

The North's biggest fear was the break-up of the Union: the balance of economic activity that the North and South together represented was essential for the continued viability of the United States. Cotton, the product of the South, accounted for 60 per cent of all the country's income from exports at the time of the war. In contrast, the South's nightmare was political: to be out-voted by an accumulation of free states that would bring the basis of their social and economic existence to an end.

Indelibly identified with the War is Abraham Lincoln, elected President in late 1860 as abolitionist sentiment was reaching a noisy crescendo. The spark was a Supreme Court decision in 1857 that ruled that it was not constitutional for Congress to set conditions on a state's entry into the Union. The spectre of the balancing provision of one slave state for each free state disappearing set the South on edge. Lincoln's election, on a platform to oppose any further extension of slavery in new states, was the trigger. It was doubly so as the South's antipathy towards Lincoln and the abolitionist cause was increased by the fact that Lincoln hardly appeared to carry the nation with him: he won the election on a minority of the votes cast, under 40 per cent (as he faced three other opponents).

So even if Lincoln *had* been an out and out anti-slave visionary, his mandate to act was less than overwhelming. But he was not. Lincoln's attitude to slavery has been the subject of vast historical smoothing over the decades. Seen today as the arch abolitionist, he, in fact, was dogmatic in his own mind about the differences between the races. In the famed debates with rival Stephen Douglas when Lincoln challenged him for his Illinois Senate seat in 1858, Lincoln made himself very clear:

> I have no purpose to introduce political and social equality between the white and the black races. ... There is a physical difference between the two, which, in my judgment, will probably forever forbid their living together upon the footing of perfect equality.[19]

In the fourth debate, he stated his opposition to ever giving blacks the vote, allowing them to hold public office or to inter-marry with whites.[20] His position on slavery was also a considered one and consistently held. In all 175 speeches that he made between 1854 and 1860, he insisted that it would be unconstitutional to abolish slavery.[21] When he ran for the presidency in 1860, he was fully signed up to the Republican party platform that opposed the extension of slavery in new territories that would eventually become states. But that platform also explicitly upheld the right of the southern states to continue with it.[22]

It was Lincoln's opposition to the *extension* of slavery into the new areas lining up to become states that really struck fear into the South and set them on course for secession as soon as Lincoln won. They realised that that policy would inexorably lead to the South – and slavery – becoming a minority interest in the Union, and vulnerable to being eventually outvoted on abolition. That was the kind of union they wanted no part of. They could see the writing on the wall and the first declaration of secession, by South Carolina, came on 20 December 1860, just weeks after Lincoln's victory.

But Lincoln made it as clear as he could where he stood. He used his inauguration speech as President the following March to take up the slavery issue as the very first topic after his opening introduction, and he did so in order to commit to not interfering with it:

Apprehension seems to exist among the people of the Southern States that by the accession of a Republican Administration their property and their peace and personal security are to be endangered. There has never been any reasonable cause for such apprehension. Indeed, the most ample evidence to the contrary has all the while existed and been open to their inspection. It is found in nearly all the published speeches of him who now addresses you. I do but quote from one of those speeches when I declare that—

I have no purpose, directly or indirectly, to interfere with the institution of slavery in the States where it exists. I believe I have no lawful right to do so, and I have no inclination to do so.

Those who nominated and elected me did so with full knowledge that I had made this and many similar declarations and had never recanted them; and more than this, they placed in the platform for my acceptance, and as a law to themselves and to me, the clear and emphatic resolution which I now read:

Resolved, That the maintenance inviolate of the rights of the States, and especially the right of each State to order and control its own domestic institutions according to its own judgment exclusively, is essential to that balance of power on which the perfection and endurance of our political fabric depend;[23]

Nothing could have been starker as to where Lincoln's sentiments lay. He was not about to fight the South on the battle-
ground of slavery. Whenever the purposes of the war were
questioned, Lincoln was persistent in his view of where his
priorities lay:

> My paramount object in this struggle is to save the Union,
> and is *not* either to save or destroy Slavery. If I could save the
> Union without freeing *any* slave, I would do it; and if I could
> save it by freeing *all* the slaves I would do it; and if I could
> do it by freeing some and leaving others alone, I would also
> do that. [24] (emphases in original)

Although revered in the pantheon of American heroes as the
President who freed the slaves through his famous and selfless
Emancipation Proclamation, the actual historical record on
Lincoln's later policy on abolition is of a rather different hue.

The origin of the Proclamation, announced in September
1862 and formally signed into law on New Year's Day, 1863,
was driven by political necessity rather than social morality.
Casually assumed by modern folk to have been the great
social stride forward brought about by the war (and why ever
not, given the title?) the Proclamation was, in fact, a deft
exercise in deception.

The motivation behind making a declaration freeing the
slaves lay in the political atmosphere in the north in the early
part of 1862. Lincoln's Republicans were deeply divided about
the conduct of the war. He was losing the support of the
abolitionist wing of the party. Lincoln reasoned he needed
a policy platform to bring them back. But he needed also to
avoid going too far by upsetting the conservative wing of the
party which worried about eroding the rights of states, and
for whom the issue at stake in the war was the preservation of
the Union, not the fate of slaves.

He waited until the Union had won a significant victory

(to have announced the Proclamation on the back of a string of defeats would have given the impression that it was a cry for help – which it was – rather than an elevated statement of principle). The victory at Antietam, in September 1862, gave him the opportunity, and he immediately declared the intention of emancipating slaves as from 1 January next.

But the Proclamation was able to do nothing of the kind. It freed slaves only in the Confederacy, where the President's writ no longer ran, and not in the states over which he actually had legal control. It did not even stretch to the Confederate territories that had been occupied by the Union. These were all expressly excluded. It was not as if no one noticed at the time – only the passing years have conveniently erased the reality. The *New York World* newspaper editorialised with scathing mockery:

> The President had purposely made the proclamation inoperative in all the places where we have gained a military footing which makes the slaves accessible. He has proclaimed emancipation only where he has notoriously no power to execute it.[25]

It was a splendidly 'political' act that propagandists of any age would have been proud. Lincoln lifted his Union government onto the moral high ground and, for the first time, declared the freeing of slaves by law, without either condemning slavery as a practice (it was noted that the Proclamation contained no declaration of principle adverse to slavery)[26] or actually doing anything material to achieve it.

Only some 200,000 out of the estimated three and a half million slaves were freed during the war as a consequence of the Proclamation. Lincoln would enter the annals of history for an act that was meaningless but which pragmatically kept the Union together until military victory was secured. That he would later propose in two State of the Union speeches a scheme to rid the United States of the Negro problem by shipping them all off to another country was entirely consistent with his lifelong beliefs about the impossibility of the two races living together. But it is not a line that modern readers are likely to come across in the mythologising paeans written about the national folk hero.

> I believe it would be better to export them all to some fertile country with a good climate which they could have to themselves.[27]

The irony of history is that Lincoln succeeded in winning the objective he stood for – preserving the Union – but he is remembered, and worshipped, for an objective he never intended, never strived for and never achieved.

☞

In Flanders fields – the First World War

> The rain drives on, the stinking mud becomes more evilly yellow, the shell-holes fill up with green-white water, the roads and tracks are covered with inches of slime, the black dying trees ooze and sweat and the shells never cease. ... It is unspeakable, godless, hopeless.
> *Paul Nash, war artist, letter from the Western Front, November 1917*

The First World War was this, for sure – but it was not all this. Nash's classic image will almost certainly be the one conjured up if offered 'the Western Front' in a word association game. It was, after all, a front that had seen 955,000 French casualties in the opening four months of war in 1914, along with a million German. In all, by 1918 nearly nine million French, Britons, Germans and a host of other nationalities had perished, been wounded or simply disappeared, blown out of existence never to be found. It was truly humanity's first experience of war on an industrial scale. With the War Poets giving the conflict a literary legacy that fixed in posterity a unique and enduring imagery of horror, the 'Great War' quickly gained superlatives that set this one apart from anything previous. Not only did it become 'the war to end wars' but it also came to be seen as one that had, in four short years, erased an entire generation.

The 'lost generation' has become a lingering, iconic image of the sense of loss. It has cast the First World War as a sociological watershed. Modern analysis, however, suggests that the 'lost generation' is, in large part, a myth. Historian Gordon Corrigan pointed out in 2003, after researching the census records of 1911 and 1921, that 86 per cent of men of military age survived the war. As for the war destroying the country's future elite, 80 per cent of those from public school and university returned home.[28]

Other perspectives that were pushed into the background in the immediate post-war construction of memory also call into question the popular imagery we carry with us. One of the most persistent motifs of the Western Front is the environment of ceaseless fire and perpetual stress. This turns out to be far from the truth. For the majority of soldiers, for the majority of the time, the story is one of idleness, inaction and boredom. British troops on average spent just a week every month up at the front, and that was split equally between the 'real' front line, the so-called fire trench directly opposite the enemy's line, and the support trench a hundred yards behind[29]. The French average was similar – eight days a month. The balance then – up to three quarters of their time – was spent at 'rest' far behind the lines, kicking heels, idling, and for those led by more officious commanders, pointlessly parading.

Renowned expert on the war, Lyn Macdonald, after spending more than twenty years recording the memories of veterans, confirmed that the most common recollection of the troops was not the horror of the occasional battle but of the long periods of inactivity, the boredom, the indolence of life in the rear. Thus, Macdonald found, it was common to hear them in fact relish the fighting as a break from the sterility of inaction. 'Every veteran I have ever interviewed I have asked the same question: "Would you do it again?" And not one has said no.'[30]

For many, life in the trench was actually preferred to that of the enforced routine at the rear. Lance Corporal Ramage of the Gordon Highlanders probably spoke for many when he wrote in his diary in June 1915:

> Were it not for the scarcity of food, water and sleep in the trenches, we have a much harder time when we return for rest at billets, a rest crammed full of parades from early morning till eve.[31]

And although the usual imagery of the trenches is one of muddy swamp, rudimentary construction and appallingly primitive living conditions, many units created veritable homes from home. A lieutenant from the Argyll and Sutherland Highlanders described theirs in 1915:

> Our own trench is a magnificent piece of work, exceedingly strong and comfortable. ... Dugouts are numerous and those of the officers luxurious. Captain Henderson has a suite of rooms! He has a sitting-room ... a dressing room with a chest of drawers and full-length mirror, a bedroom with a spring bed and mattress. A pull bell connects the bedroom with the sitting room and orderlies; the bedroom has a stained glass window with muslin curtains and a flower box outside, with pansies![32]

It was far from all horror. Charles Carrington, a young subaltern who wrote his wartime memoirs in 1929, painted a politically incorrect picture of life in the trenches, observing:

It is not honest to deny the existence of happiness which was actually derived from the war. First, the horrors and the discomfort, indescribable as they are, were not continuous. The unluckiest soldiers, whose leave was always stopped, who never had a 'blighty' wound, still spent only a comparatively few days in the face of the enemy, and of these only a few were of the most horrible kind. Their intensity, when they came, sharpened the senses…[33]

And few seem to have experienced the supposedly archetypal fate of seeing streetloads of comrades blown away. According to Corrigan's analysis of the statistics, the average soldier was likely to suffer the loss of no more than half a dozen of his comrades.

Ultimate success in the war too appears more clearly now to have been down to other factors than military endeavour. Despite the depiction of the war as one of merciless attrition, the meat-grinding of opposing forces until one slowly overcame the other by sheer weight of numbers, the dynamic of the war, and particularly the way it ended, was anything but. The consensus amongst historians for some years now has been that victory was due to the collapse of German morale in 1918 that resulted from the realisation that the conflict was unwinnable once American forces arrived on the continent.

This much is clear about the First World War: victory was not due to military success by the original Allies. It has been shown that throughout the war the British army lost more men than it killed in every offensive it launched.[34]

The influence of the War Poets on our understanding of the war is immense. The visions they evoked have often come to define our appreciation of the trench experience. However, it comes as a surprise to realise how perhaps the most famous of them managed to do so from minimal real life exposure. Wilfred Owen, the most iconic of the band, whose output has come to popularise the imagery of the First

World War, drew his poems from just five months of experience on the Western Front in the first half of 1917. He was never wounded, never spent a long stretch in the trenches and saw, in those five months, about 30 days of action (and according to his biographer, just three personally alarming events: a four-day shelling, which prompted *The Sentry;* two nights lying out in the snow, which produced *Exposure;* and two days sheltering in a dugout with the decomposing remains of a colleague). It was this last episode that sparked the mental collapse that saw him sent home for 17 months.[35] Many of his poems were actually written whiling away time during his recovery in England, not during his time in France. He returned to the Front six weeks before the end of the war, and his place in the pantheon of heroic victims was guaranteed when he was shot by a sniper a week before the Armistice.

☞

Armistice – universal rejoicing?
It is a commonplace in the accounts of the end of the war that the Armistice in November 1918 was seized upon by a warweary nation once the Germans had encountered a sudden and unexpected stalling of their 'last push' offensive and sued for a truce.

In fact, Prime Minister Lloyd George was initially against stopping the war, worried that the absence of a clear defeat of the enemy would merely seed opportunities for German warmongers in the future to claim the war had been unjustly lost. He told ministerial colleagues, 'If peace were made now, in twenty years' time the Germans would say ... by better preparation and organisation they would be able to bring about victory next time'. He suggested the war should continue until Germany was seen to be 'really badly beaten'. But the urge for peace prevailed and history, sadly, went on to prove Lloyd George absolutely right. One historian reached the conclusion that the timing of the Armistice was 'the most completely successful of all the manoeuvres carried out by the German generals'.[36]

☞

Our finest hour?

Mythology in war provides a vital support mechanism for a society enduring a threat to its very existence. Grievous setbacks become heroic stands, shining successes turn out to be much closer calls than first thought. Only later does the historical record get properly calibrated.

Britain's experience in the Second World War is no exception, and some of the most cherished parts of the wartime folk narrative have come to be revealed as fictions. The full story has been told elsewhere.[37] In short, some of the things that may come as a surprise:

- far from the self-satisfying image of Britain going to war on behalf of little Poland, it emerged in 1999, on the 60th anniversary of the outbreak of the war, that Britain had made a desperate and secret last-minute effort to negotiate a deal with Nazi Germany which would have got Britain out of its guarantee to Poland, repeating the sell-out of Czechoslovakia the year before. It failed, so the country played its predicament as the magnanimous action that history remembers.[38]

- the role of the little boats in the 'miracle of Dunkirk', when hundreds of them made the perilous journey across the English Channel to rescue a third of a million trapped soldiers, was in fact vastly overplayed. They were only brought in when the operation was more than half complete, and they removed just 18,500 of the 338,000 troops saved. The vast majority were taken home by regular warships or large cross-Channel ferries.[39]

- the stalwart effort of the Royal Air Force in the apparently uneven battle for the skies over Britain that evoked Churchill's glowing tribute to 'the Few', turns out to be far less the uphill struggle that we have come to believe. Post-war analysis has shown that although British intelligence believed the RAF was outnumbered, in fact the British always held a slim numerical advantage, and always managed to outproduce the Luftwaffe in new aircraft. Arguably, the belief that the RAF was outnumbered helped to induce a caution into tactics that preserved the overall strength better than it might otherwise have been. Fighter Command used smaller formations to tackle the incoming fleets, which again tended to accentuate the impression of being out-numbered.[40] And although we are told that it was radar that enabled the Spitfires and Hurricanes to be efficiently targeted, later analysis revealed that on 69 per cent of occasions when fighters were directed to a location where controllers thought the enemy was, nothing was found.[41]

- the Dambusters Raid in 1943 which attacked three dams deep in Germany's industrial heartland and hailed as one of the most successful feats of the war, in fact failed to disrupt Nazi steel and weapons production by even a day. 1,200 civilians died in flooding, and eight of the nineteen Lancasters used in the mission were shot down, losing fifty-six of the 133 airmen involved. Within ten days of the raid, water supply in the areas targeted was back to 96 per cent of the pre-raid level. [42]

- the evacuation programme that sought to remove women and children from British cities was largely ineffective. By the end of 1939, 43 per cent of evacuees had drifted back into the cities. By the time the Blitz started in 1940, ninety per cent had returned. Even when a second effort was made, by the winter of 1940 more children of school age remained in London (520,000) than had been billeted throughout England and Wales.[43]

- at the height of the Blitz, only a minority of central Londoners used the air raid shelters. A census in November 1940 found that only nine per cent of the population slept in them, just four per cent used the Underground stations and 27 per cent used their domestic shelters. The rest – a staggering 60 per cent – simply stayed in their homes.[44]

- the habit of carrying gas masks – a legal requirement under wartime regulations – never took off. In the first weeks, 75 per cent obeyed the instructions to carry a mask at all times when in public. By November 1939, only a minority were doing so; by the following spring, almost nobody bothered.[45]

- it was revealed in 2000 that the famous photograph of St Paul's Cathedral taken at the height of the worst raid in December 1940 that saw almost all of the surrounding buildings destroyed, was touched up to enhance the imagery. Appearing to rise ethereally from a sea of smoke, the image of the dome of St Paul's standing defiant has become an icon for the wartime spirit of resistance. Experts analysing the original, however, said the two-thirds of the picture appeared to have been treated, to define more clearly the outlines of wrecked houses in the foreground and to sharpen up the structure of the dome and clock towers which accentuates the cathedral's 'other worldliness' difference from the surrounding murkiness.[46]

☞

The Blitz – scaring folk out of their wits
The stoic attitude of city dwellers as the bombs rained down is another of the cherished images of the war. The smiling

faces in adversity beaming out from the newsreels, the 'we can take it' signs that appeared in shop windows crafted for later generations a sense of remarkable fortitude in the face of unremitting death and destruction. But part of the reason for this apparently surprising response is likely to have been that what Londoners and others were suffering was not a patch on what they had been led to expect would happen.

For a decade, the public had been brought up on a diet of warnings that promised unfathomable disaster should aerial warfare break out. They were told that they would be virtually defenceless and that civilization would effectively come to an end. In the event, Londoners could take it largely because the reality turned out to be far less frightening than the picture politicians had forecast.

'The bomber will always get through' was the accepted wisdom throughout the pre-war period as military planners grappled with the new form of warfare. The introduction of bombing from the air represented a huge leap forward. Physical frontiers were rendered meaningless, possessing territory – the historical way of securing a nation – became less and less relevant, and the forms of defence – land armies, artillery and navies – became not only useless against airborne raiders, but vulnerable to them as well. It also added a new dimension to war – for the first time, civilians were clearly in the firing line. Air bombardment, however much it might be declared to be targeted on military and industrial locations, eliminated the distinction between combatant and non-combatant. Mass bombing of cities would bring normal people right up to the front line of war.

Few defences could be foreseen to prevent aircraft from enjoying complete freedom of action. Throughout the 1920s and 1930s, fear of the bomber became almost a national psychosis. A former Secretary of State for War and veteran of the First World War airship raids told the House of Commons as early as 1922 that defence against aircraft was impossible:

Nobody ever attempted to bomb a place with more than 50 aeroplanes during the War. The biggest air raid on London was, as a matter of fact, conducted with 36 aeroplanes. It will be quite easy, and no doubt it will be done if ever we go to war again, for an enemy to bombard, not with 30 aeroplanes, but with 300, and those aeroplanes will not carry the little bombs which were carried by the 36 – and they were quite small bombs which were used in that daylight raid upon London – but they will carry bombs at least ten times as weighty. ... It is hopeless to attempt to protect yourself against this raid of 300 aeroplanes. It took 32,000 men to protect London against the raids of the 36 machines. An hon. and gallant Member tells me that they did not succeed, but still they made it rather difficult for them, although they did not prevent them from flying over.

It will be seen at once that to attempt to prevent an enemy from bombarding your town, by preparation in time of peace in the way of land defence, is, frankly, impossible. All that you can say is, 'If you are going to destroy my town, I will destroy yours.' [47]

The starkness of the threat was most notoriously voiced by Stanley Baldwin, the Conservative party leader in the National coalition government, in November 1932:

In the next war you will find that any town within reach of an aerodrome can be bombed within the first five minutes of war to an extent inconceivable in the last war ... I think it is well also for the man in the street to realise that there is no power on earth that can protect him from being bombed. Whatever people may tell him, the bomber will always get through. ....

It is a matter of mathematical calculation that you will have [air defence] sectors of from 10 to hundreds of cubic miles. ... Imagine 100 cubic miles covered with cloud and fog, and you can calculate how many aeroplanes you would have to throw into that to have much chance of catching odd aeroplanes as they fly through. It cannot be done, and there is no expert in Europe who will say that it can. The only defence is in offence, which means that you have got to kill more women and children more quickly than the enemy if you want to save yourselves. I mention that so that people may realise what is waiting for them when the next war comes. [48]

Such authoritative statements of complete vulnerability induced a dread of the future much the same as that of the nuclear age. Churchill himself got caught up in the doom-mongering:

No one can doubt that a week or ten days' intensive bombing attack upon London would be a very serious matter indeed. One could hardly expect less than 30,000 or 40,000 people would be killed or maimed. [49]

This was in fact a rather conservative view. The Air Ministry itself was, in the same year, advising the Cabinet that Germany could drop seventy-five tons of bombs on Britain a day from her home bases (and 150 tons if she occupied airfields in Belgium and Holland). This was calculated to cause fifty casualties per ton. By 1936, the estimate had risen to 600 tons, with casualties in the first week of war of some 150,000. On the brink of war in 1939, the official estimate was 700 tons a day[50] but the estimate of casualties had risen exponentially. Drawing misleading lessons from events in the Spanish Civil War, such as the bombing of the small Spanish town of Guernica (which was unusually packed for market day) and the bombing of Barcelona, experts now estimated that each ton of dropped explosive would cause 72 casualties.[51] The forecast for the first enemy raid was that some 600,000

Britons would be killed and twice that number injured. One Briton in twenty-five would be a casualty.

In practice, when the bombing came, casualties were a fraction of those forecast. In the entire first year of war, only 257 were killed and 441 hospitalised by air raids.[52] In the whole war, just 60,000 British civilians perished from all causes.[53] The average casualty rate from aerial bombing was closer to fifteen to twenty per ton, and major raids across the country saw between 400 and 500 tons of bombs dropped, well below the pre-war estimates.[54]

So the indomitable spirit of the British, so long carved into our collective memory as a distinct feature of the national race, may have had far more to do with a simple sense of reprieve that the long-held predictions of utter disaster failed to come true. When reality hit, people found that life, for most, went on. Compared with what they had been led to expect, it all turned out to be less fearsome and not the apocalypse that was foretold. Seen in this light, 'We can take it' may be as much an expression of surprise and relief than the defiance it is usually taken for.

☞

The greatest deception in history?

In the usual telling of the D-Day landings in Normandy on 6 June 1944, the success of the operation lay in the 'bodyguard of lies' that was created by Allied intelligence around the location of the invasion, deceiving Nazi defenders into believing that the cross-Channel assault would take place further north, in the Calais-Boulogne area where the sea distance from England to France was at its smallest. For decades, the Anglo-American victory on the battlefield was garlanded with the additional cachet of having pulled off one of the most audacious deception tricks in military history. Latterly, however, research in the German archives and the publication of Britain's intelligence record has put a rather different gloss on the claim to have completely outwitted Hitler's forces.

There is no doubting that an intricate and long-running deception campaign was run by the British and Americans. Part of the stratagem was to convince German military eavesdroppers that a huge army was taking shape in Eastern England in the Dover-Cambridge-King's Lynn area (while the real invasion force was assembling to the south-west, between Brighton and Falmouth). This was done by transmitting thousands of fictitious radio messages that appeared to be the day-to-day preparations of a massive army. In the waterways of Eastern England, four hundred fake 'landing craft' could be spotted by German aerial reconnaissance.[55] They consisted of little more than canvas and scaffold constructions floating on oil drums, replete with smoking funnels, laundry hanging from rigging and 'tell-tale' patches of oil in the water. Inland, thousands of fake inflatable tanks, guns, armoured vehicles and campsites were strewn across the countryside, and at night, thousands of lights were shone in an elaborate display intended to give the impression of convoys of supply trucks feverishly loading the fleet. The RAF kept up the pretence of air defence in the area, keeping German aircraft to above 30,000ft, from where it was impossible for their cameras to detect anything amiss.[56]

But despite the impressive effort, as D-Day neared, there was increasing uncertainty among the Allies as to whether Hitler, and more importantly, Rommel, the German commander in the Normandy region, had bought the deception. A week before the landings, intelligence showed that Rommel had inexplicably moved his 91st Airlanding Division, a unit specialising in defending against parachute assaults, to the precise area near Cherbourg where the US paratroop divisions were due to land. Further evidence uncovered in the 1970s suggests that German commanders on the ground were quite certain that an attack would descend on Normandy. The only area of doubt was whether it was the main assault or a diversionary operation.

In the spring of 1944, German intelligence had penetrated the French Resistance and knew that cells had received orders to prepare sabotage plans in support of the invasion. These were to focus on the area between the Normandy coast and Paris.[57] By contrast, there were to be no sabotage operations in the Belgian or Dutch resistance groups, inconceivable if the more northern area was the true landing ground. Another tell-tale clue picked up by the German military machine was the pattern of RAF bombing that had in recent weeks concentrated on the corridor between the Normandy coast and Paris, in an attempt to destroy the approach routes of German tank reinforcements. A map prepared for the German Commander-in-Chief West showing the clear evidence of the RAF's focus was first published by a German historian only in 1975.[58]

According to intelligence author Phillip Knightley, the conclusion that German commanders expected an attack on Normandy is supported by evidence in the German Naval Staff War Diary. On the day before the invasion, an entry cites an intelligence report of a week earlier that recorded Allied bombardment of German supply lines between the Seine estuary and Normandy. It ended: 'This factor may indicate intentions of enemy command against Normandy.'[59] Knightley adds the view of Major Oscar Reile, the German officer in charge of intelligence for one of the army groups stationed in the region: '[We] were surprised neither by the time of the invasion nor by the place or direction of the enemy advance.'

Even British intelligence suspected that all might not be plain sailing. On 22 May, just two weeks before the operation, the Joint Intelligence Committee issued a grim assessment of the state of the enemy's knowledge:

The main assault is expected against the Northern coast of France from Boulogne to Cherbourg inclusive. Although German High command will, until our assault takes place, reckon with the possibility that it will come across the narrow Straits of Dover to the Pas de Calais area, there is some evidence that the Le Havre-Cherbourg areas [the actual landing site] ... (are) regarded as a likely and perhaps even the main, point of assault.[60]

A week later, it reiterated its warning even more clearly:

The recent trend of movement of German land forces towards the Cherbourg area tends to support the view that the Le Havre-Cherbourg areas is regarded as a likely, and perhaps even the main, point of assault.[61]

And five days before the invasion, an intercepted telegram from the Japanese ambassador in Berlin reporting home on an interview with Hitler on 27 May recorded that the Fuhrer was convinced that after diversionary operations in Norway, Denmark, south-west France and on the French Mediterranean coast, they would establish a bridgehead in Normandy or Brittany; and that after seeing how things went, they would embark on establishing a real second front in the Straits.[62]

So, far from the deception plan being the unadulterated success that our nationally favoured version has it, the last days of preparation were wracked with self-doubt as to whether the Germans had fallen for the months of elaborate hoaxing. In the end, all Allied intelligence could conclude – in its final assessment of the German mind on the eve of D-Day – was that the enemy 'appears to expect several landings between the Pas de Calais and Cherbourg'.

In fact, it was an even closer run affair than the Allies suspected. Little did the Allies know that the only factor stopping German defences being ready for the arrival of the invaders was a self-defeating disbelief in Allied tactics. The German success in penetrating the Resistance mentioned earlier had revealed not only sabotage plans but the meaning of the coded radio broadcasts that the British would transmit to signal the date of the invasion. A verse from a poem by French poet Paul Verlaine ('The long sobs of the violin') was to be broadcast in two parts, the first on the 1st or 15th of the month in which the invasion was to take place, and the remainder 48 hours before the actual date of the attack.[63]

On the evening of 1 June, a German radio reconnaissance post picked up the first part of the poem and forces in part of the northern command were put on alert. When the same post then picked up the second part of the message days later, the warning was sent straight to the highest command in the region. But bizarrely, Field Marshal von Rundstedt dismissed the whole thing as a hoax. No enemy, he is recorded as saying, would broadcast its intent to invade over the radio.[64] So the army facing the oncoming invasion fleet were left in an ignorance that was actually self-inflicted.

It would seem, then, that the proper historical verdict on the D-Day deception scheme is equivocal at best. Outlandish in conception and execution for sure, we *want* to believe that it worked, and the Allies' eventual success in the battle for Normandy reinforces our conviction that it did. But examined dispassionately, the evidence is far from clear that it convincingly persuaded the German defenders on the northwest coast in the way we like to think it did. And in the end, it was German unwillingness to take notice of evidence it had in its possession that contributed to its state of unreadiness on the morning of 6 June.

The enigma of Enigma

The other great perception of the Second World War that governs particularly Britons' perspective on the outcome is that at the heart of victory lay the breaking of the German military code system. Nicknamed Enigma from the devilishly complex ciphering machine invented by German engineer Arthur Scherbius just after the First World War, the system produced codes which were impenetrable to traditional methods of code breaking. Without the triumph in breaching Enigma, the thought stream goes, the Allies would not have won. Bletchley Park, the home of the British code breakers, has secured for itself a hallowed place in the war effort, and it is hard to escape a narrative now that fails to place it at the core of the success. One even suggested that the breaking of the Enigma ciphers was:

> [T]he greatest single British scientific achievement of the Second World War. Its influence upon victory was more important than that of asdic [submarine sonar], the proximity fuse, the bouncing bomb, probably even of radar.[65]

That it remained a secret for nearly 30 years after the war – its existence was only revealed in 1974 – doubtlessly added to the mystique and importance of the operation to the war effort.

The reality, however, is far more complicated, and a detached look at the evidence suggests that its value, while important, has been overstated. Once the euphoria of the discovery died down, more sober analyses beginning in the late 1980s painted a less conclusive picture.

Since the Allies had to take exceptional care not to reveal to the other side that its messages were being read, an immediate difficulty arose of how to convey to operational commanders the information that was being obtained – which was codenamed 'Ultra' – without the ability to reveal the extent of authenticity known to be behind it. One expert assessment has estimated that after a time, as little as 5–10 per cent of Enigma output sent to the field was actually used operationally.[66]

Commanders were simply not able to be told how 'reliable' the intelligence really was. An example is cited of the caution exercised by General John Lucas commanding the Allied landings at Anzio in Italy. Pinned down on the beachhead, he was urged to break out by his seniors who had access to Enigma traffic and knew for a fact how weak the German forces were at that particular moment. Success was assured – but they could not tell Lucas the basis for their confidence. Lucas, on the ground, had made his own assessment which was far less optimistic, so he stayed put. The Germans were given time to reinforce, re-establish their defensive positions and the landings became a byword for a bogged-down failure. Lucas ended up losing his command for his apparent timidity, later writing with understandable bitterness in his diary, 'apparently everyone was in on the secret of German intentions except me'.[67]

As one account has put it, knowing the secrets could actually inhibit a commander's position:

> ... because he knew that his political bosses had received the same secrets and would, rightly or wrongly, consider themselves in a position not only to advise him but to remove him if he failed to act as they would have. Churchill sacked two fine generals, Wavell and Auchinleck, early in the North African campaign because he felt that he knew from Ultra as much about the Germans and Italians as his generals did, and he disapproved of their performance in that light. Yet in this case, Ultra was wrong.[68]

The last point illustrates another of the problems with handling the eavesdroppings of the other side. The intelligence was only as good as what the Germans were saying to each other. And that was not always the whole truth. After the war, it became clear that, just as with any human organisation, German military units often lied and misled their seniors about their conditions. Many exaggerated their deficiencies in equipment or strength in manpower to squeeze more out of their High Command. Intercepting such messages led to numerous confusions.

> When Rommel wrote reports [from the desert] he developed a tactic of exaggerating [shortages] in order to make sure of receiving at least part of the material he needed. This meant that Churchill, who was fascinated by Ultra reports, forced the British commanders to mount attacks they did not intend and which then failed. This led to the removal of Wavell and Auchinleck.[69]

The same account shows how the intercepts could mislead disastrously if commanders said one thing and changed their mind, as arch tacticians like Rommel were wont to do.

> [If] the opportunity beckoned, [Rommel] would change his plans, often without bothering to say so. One of the reasons for the disaster at the Battle of Kasserine Pass in February 1943 was that Ultra indicated an attack in one direction, but Rommel disobeyed the order coming from Italy and attacked in another. The Americans, who had relied on Ultra, lost almost half an armoured division.[70]

The sheer number of messages to be transcribed, decoded, translated and then assessed – running at 3,000 a day by mid-1942[71] – often overwhelmed the interceptors at Bletchley Park. And even this was only a small portion of the overall traffic. One German historian estimates that only a quarter to a third of Nazi forces communications went by radio.[72] The rest went by landline teleprinter or telephone, which was not capable of interception. And often the outgoing part of a message was sent by radio, and intercepted, but the reply (or the original question if it was the reply that had been intercepted) had gone by landline or telegraph, so all the time the Allies were dealing with partial messages, and, even if they had got intelligible exchanges, then the problem was trying to work out which were significant war-wise and which were mundane day-to-day organisational dross.

There is also evidence that over-reliance on Enigma interceptions had the effect of reducing the level of alertness normally expected on the ground for keeping an eye on the enemy's movements. One case in point is said to be the German counter offensive in the Ardennes in the winter of 1944, which significantly held up the Allies' post-D-Day advance. The Germans achieved complete tactical surprise over the Allies when Hitler imposed strict radio silence. Since no warning of the offensive had come through Enigma, the Allies were caught unawares. They had dropped their guard on all the other means by which knowledge about the enemy was usually gained locally on the ground.[73]

A further problem surfaced. Where the evidence emerging from Enigma conflicted with prevailing prejudices at home, it was simply ignored. It was known early on from intercepts that the RAF's strategic bombing of the German homeland had not damaged civilian morale as it had been assumed, and that larger Allied losses in raids compared with the damage being done were turning the continued bombing raids into serial Allied defeats in men and materiel. The higher echelons of the British and US war effort were made aware of the realities, but the bombing continued because the facts revealed by Enigma went against the ingrained convictions of Bomber Command.[74]

In all, the more recent assessments conclude that Enigma was far from the unalloyed blessing it is so frequently portrayed to have been in the narratives that immediately followed the revelation of the intelligence coup. While doubtless it was a healthy morale boosting asset for the hard-pressed Allied military command to know that it had an ear to the Nazi military mind, the practical usefulness of this advantage was much less clear cut. It seems evident now for large swathes of the war effort, Enigma had little or no impact, and in some instances positively hampered the conduct of operations. In only a very few cases was Enigma actually critical to success.[75]

☞

Desperate remedies – snaring a traitor (1)

The tale of William Joyce, Lord Haw-Haw, who was executed in London's Wandsworth prison in January 1946 for treason on account of his wartime Nazi propaganda broadcasts on German radio, is often recounted as a simple and cast iron case of a British traitor meeting his just desserts. But such a version masks the remarkable sequence of events that was the denouement of the most famous turncoat in modern British history. It involved labyrinthine manoeuvring by the British legal authorities to get its prosecution to stick. For few now recall that Joyce was not actually a British citizen, but American by birth (and a naturalised German at his death) and that almost all the period he spent broadcasting for Hitler came after his British passport – the only legal document that connected him to Britain – had expired.

He had been born in New York, son of an Irish emigrant father and English emigrant mother. Michael, his father, had become a naturalised American citizen in 1894, six years after arriving in America and twelve years before William was born. At the time, the procedure involved signing a declaration renouncing 'for ever all allegiance and fidelity to any and every foreign Prince, Potentate, State and Sovereignty whatever, and particularly to the Queen of the United Kingdom of Great Britain and Ireland, whose subject he has heretofore been'.[76] The family, travelling on a US passport, returned to Ireland when William was three years old. He was to grow up there, and later moved to England in December 1921, a few months before his sixteenth birthday.

The controversy about his allegiance – formal and political – began in the 1930s as he became attracted to the far right politics of Oswald Mosley's British Union of Fascists. Hoping to accompany Mosley on a visit to Germany to meet Hitler, Joyce applied for a British passport in July 1933, falsely declaring himself to be British. (At the time a birth certificate was not required; applicants were merely warned of the consequences of making false statements.) He renewed the passport, curiously for a single year, when it expired in 1938, and again for a year in the summer of 1939 as he prepared to flee to Germany as war loomed and as he increasingly foresaw his future life being on the other side. His British document was valid until 1 July 1940.[77]

He left England for Germany in late August 1939, a week before war broke out. All accounts agree he intended it to be a permanent break from England (hence the reason for the short period of renewal of his passport). He initially got work in Berlin as a translator of Hitler's speeches, but as the radio propaganda war hotted up, he secured a newsreading position on the Nazi English service in late September 1939. He would make his first overtly propaganda commentary the following month. He would only be firmly identified by British intelligence as the voice behind the broadcast in August 1940. By then, Joyce had applied for German naturalisation – his British passport had expired – and this was granted on 26 September 1940.[78] For the rest of his life, Joyce, the American, was officially German.

When he was captured by British troops in May 1945, the problem of whether he could legally have committed treason arose. The authorities took no chances. They rushed through Parliament a procedural Treason Act to ensure that the notorious ambiguities that surrounded the 1351 Act that Joyce was charged under did not complicate matters. Only one debate took place on the changes in each House: the House of Lords took thirty-one minutes; the Commons despatched it in just nineteen.[79] Amongst other simplifications, the Act quietly repealed the requirement for a witness to corroborate a traitor's actions. Legal authorities argue that had this not been done, a successful prosecution of Joyce on the evidence available would have been unlikely. The authorities could only produce one 'witness', a detective inspector, who claimed to be able to recognise Joyce's voice as the broadcaster during the period when his passport was valid.[80]

Despite this, when the trial opened in September 1945, it took until just the second day for the judge to accept as 'overwhelming' the evidence that Joyce was, in fact, an alien. His fate then hinged on the question of whether he owed any allegiance to the Crown as a consequence of owning the passport, even though he had lied about his nationality to obtain it. On the third day, the judge ruled that he did, and jury took just twenty-three minutes to convict him.

The single piece of 'evidence' from the single witness who claimed to identify Joyce as broadcasting between August 1939 when he got his passport, and 2 July 1940 was sufficient for a conviction of treason against Britain. Joyce was hanged in Wandsworth on 3 January 1946.

During the war, the British public treated Joyce's broadcasts with a mixture of odium and ridicule. Not long after they began, they had become more an amusing diversion from the rigours of the day than a threat to national morale. When he fell into their hands at the end of hostilities, the British had a most unwelcome dilemma. They hardly wanted to make life difficult for their American allies by palming him off to the rightful legal jurisdiction (and after all, Joyce had broadcast largely against Britain, not America, so it was doubtful the Americans would eagerly embrace the hassle of a prosecution as they prepared for the far more onerous task of the Nuremburg trials of the top Nazi leaders). So Britain's best legal brains were applied to securing the conviction and execution of a man who had spent less than half his life in Britain, had never taken British citizenship and was, for most of his broadcasting career, a German national.

☞

Desperate remedies – snaring a traitor (2)
Another notorious wartime legal episode that easily gets mis-remembered is the case of the First World War femme fatale, Mata Hari, executed in 1917 by a French firing squad for spying for the Germans. The account that history commonly tells is only part of a sordid story that did not fully emerge until 2003.

Far from the eastern exotic that her stage name suggested, at the time of her death the Dutch-born Margaretha Gertrude Zelle was hardly an alluring spring chicken. She was forty-one years old, and had been a celebrated risqué dancer in the bohemian music halls of Paris since 1905. When in 1914 war, and arguably the passage of time, put paid to her stage career, she accepted 20,000 francs from a German spymaster to sleep with French officials and pass back secrets. So far, this is the common account. But according to French historian Philippe Collas, the great-grandson of the magistrate who sent Zelle to the firing squad, here the story becomes murky.

In 2003, he published for the first time records of the case that painted a different version of events.[81] These showed that Zelle was brutally manipulated by the French secret services, and then sacrificed to protect an already endangered reputation.

The French security services had not had a good war: they had failed to procure meaningful intelligence on Germany throughout the war, and were aware that they had been penetrated by German spies. When they were tipped off, by the British, about Zelle's exploits, according to Collas, they turned her as a double agent and persuaded her to act on behalf of the French. Unknown to them, the Germans had already written her off as ineffective. She had signally failed to produce any secrets of value to them.

Working now for France, she immediately seduced a German army major and secured valuable military intelligence. She was not a reliable asset to either side. It was not long before the Germans suspected her treachery. When the French services became aware that her cover had been blown, they salvaged the situation in a callous deception operation to preserve their own reputation.

They arrested her themselves, brought her before a pliant magistrate and, in a closed court, presented the evidence of her treason against France. Fatally for Zelle, Captain Georges Ladoux, a senior member of the French counter-intelligence branch, withheld the vital information that Zelle had agreed to change sides and was providing information to the French authorities.

Although her defence lawyers made the assertion to the court, the magistrate, according to Collas, was predisposed against Zelle because of her scandalous stage profession. Collas discovered that his great-grandfather had, at the time the case was referred to him, become aware that his own wife had started an affair. His private notes were full of seething disgust for Zelle and her wily manipulations of men. According to the new interpretation, this hostility towards women that his own personal tragedy had stoked in him swayed his judgement against the notorious flighty female. He overlooked the suspect official account, and condemned her to death.

Zelle went to her death not the arch spy traitor that history commonly brands her but more a weak and manipulated victim of the machinations of desperate officials coupled with the vindictiveness of a trial judge unhinged by his own very personal anguish.

☞

Falkland mythology

In one of the celebrated actions of the Falklands War in 1982, a British Vulcan bomber flew 4,000 miles from Ascension Island to bomb the airstrip at Port Stanley in an attempt to prevent Argentines from using it to resupply their invasion force. The mission involved *seven* mid-air refuellings. Bad weather prevented air reconnaissance from establishing for certain whether the airfield had been put out of action. Two days after the attack, a photograph was obtained showing a crater in the middle of the runway and three others running off in a line. To this day, the commonly received belief is that the raid effectively closed the airport to the enemy's attack jets and stalled the invaders' grand plan.

In fact, after the recapture of the islands it was discovered that the Argentines had already concluded before the attack that the runway was too short for their Super-Etendard fighters.[82] To confound the British, following the bombing, Argentine sappers built fake craters on and near the runway using earth and rocks which the spy planes photographed, and from which Britain's war leaders deduced the runway to be out of action. No more raids were deemed necessary. The false craters were then removed each night to allow transport planes to land and continue the resupplying of the troops. In all, over thirty flights by Argentine Hercules transporters were made to the islands between May 1, the date of the Vulcan raid, and the eventual surrender on June 14.[83]

☞

Planning for the unthinkable – nuclear war

We have had until late a (comparatively) cosy image of the Cold War built on the tacit assumption that our leaders, all too conscious of the issues at stake, had pulled out all the stops to ensure planning for the unthinkable was the best it could be. Horrendous though the contemplation of all-out nuclear conflict was, we rested less uneasy in our beds with the thought that everything possible was being done to ensure our national safety. If only we (or the enemy) had known.

British preparations for dealing with an all-out nuclear attack from the Soviet Union included a war game run in 1956 by the RAF to assess how the country might cope after 200 nuclear bombs had fallen. One of its conclusions was that British Rail would have half the normal train services running again within four weeks.[84]

Confidence in the level of civil defence that would be possible in the wake of a nuclear attack was not confined to this study. An earlier one in 1952 forecast that after four direct strikes on London – at Trafalgar Square, and the railway junctions at Clapham, Lewisham and Dalston – London Transport would need to deploy 500 of its buses to run 'a shuttle bus service between the London centre and the undamaged part of the railway line south of Clapham Junction'. Although this would cause 'severe delay' in getting bus-using workers home, it was thought not more 'than Londoners would readily accept when they hear of the disaster and the task for which the buses are withdrawn'.[85]

Documents released by the Public Record Office only in 1998 also revealed that despite spending an estimated £100 million developing its nuclear arsenal, the government lacked a reliable radio communications network to keep in touch with the Prime Minister should a 'bolt from the blue' attack occur while the PM was away from Downing Street. The Cabinet Secretary proposed to the Chief of the Defence Staff in 1961 that arrangements were needed to ensure that the PM was always instantaneously reachable wherever he was. In these pre-mobile phone days, this meant a radio set, along with an operator. As that proved too costly, a typically British compromise was envisaged. A radio set would be installed in the PM's car which would enable messages to be relayed to him using the AA's breakdown service network.[86]

Documents released in 2005 confirmed how naive government thinking actually was. The Home Office was exercised in 1952 with making sure there would be arrangements allowing coroners to go through their formal procedures for identifying the dead and recording the cause of their demise. Given the likelihood that lots of bodies would not be recoverable, the government concluded that a year would have to pass before death could be presumed. This was not thought likely to cause financial hardship for the family concerned since, as one official wrote, 'the banks would no doubt permit overdrafts in view of the circumstances'.[87]

References

1   D. Wallechinsky & I. Wallace, *The People's Almanac 2*, Bantam Books, 1978

2   J. Morrill, 350th anniversary essay, *The Times*, London, 4 April 1992

3   C. Hibbert, *The English: A Social History*, Grafton, 1987

4   *Ibid.*

5   C. Russell, *The Causes of the English Civil War*, The Clarendon Press, 1990

6   J. Morrill, *Stuart Britain – A Very Short Introduction*, Oxford University Press, 2000

7   *Ibid.*

8   R. Howell, *Cromwell*, Hutchinson, 1977

9   P. Gaunt, *Oliver Cromwell*, Blackwell, 1996

10 J. Ayto, *Twentieth Century Words*, Oxford University Press, 1999. Lt-Col Charles Court Repington, a military correspondent of *The Times*, entitled his memoirs published in 1920 *The First World War*, but the term was not widely adopted at the time.

11 F. D. Margiotta (ed.), *Brassey's Encyclopaedia of Military History and Biography*, Brassey's, 1994

12 R. E. Dupuy & T. N. Dupuy, *Encyclopaedia of Military History*, HarperCollins, 1993

13 J. Prebble, *The Lion in the North*, Penguin, 1981

14 *Ibid.*

15 *The Times*, 13 November 1854

16 T. Brighton, *Hell Riders: The Truth about the Charge of the Light Brigade*, Viking, 2004

17 *The Times*, 13 November 1854

18 Brighton, *op. cit.*

19 W. Degregorio, *The Complete Book of US Presidents*, Barricade Books, 1993

20 *Ibid.*

21 J. Morris, *Lincoln: A Foreigner's Quest*, Viking, 1999

22 Degregorio, *op cit.*

23 www.presidency.ucsb.edu/inaugurals.php

24 Letter to the editor of the *New York Times*, 22 August 1862, quoted in S. Foote, *The Civil War,* The Bodley Head, 1991

25 Foote, *op. cit.*

26 Foote, *op. cit.*

27 L. Bennett Jr, *Forced Into Glory: Abraham Lincoln's White Dream*, Johnson Publishing, 2000

28 G. Corrigan, *Mud, Blood and Poppycock*, Cassell, 2003

29 J. M. Winter, *The Experience of World War I,* Grange, 1994

30 Quoted *Sunday Times*, 8 November 1998

31 Quoted in *Facing Armageddon*, Leo Cooper Books, 1996

32 *Ibid.*

33 *Ibid.*

34 N. Ferguson, *Pity of War*, Allen Lane, 1998

35 D. Hibberd, *Wilfred Owen: A New Biography*, Weidenfeld, 2002

36 J. Grigg, *A Peace Too Soon, The Times*, London, 6 November 1998

37 P. Mason, *What Needled Cleopatra ... and other little secrets airbrushed from history*, JR Books, 2009

38 Report, *Sunday Telegraph*, 8 August 1999

39 N. Harman, *Dunkirk: The Necessary Myth*, Hodder & Stoughton, 1980

40 R. Overy, *The Battle*, Penguin, 2000

41 J. F. Dunnigan & A. A. Nofi, *Dirty Little Secrets of World War II*,
    William Morrow, 1994

42 R. Boyes, *The Times* London, 17 May 1993

43 A. Calder, *The People's War*, Jonathan Cape, 1969

44 *Ibid.*

45 *Ibid.*

46 Report, *Daily Telegraph*, 29 December 2000

47 Maj-Gen John Seely, House of Commons, 21 March 1922

48 House of Commons, 10 November 1932

49 House of Commons, 28 November 1934

50 R. Lamb, *The Drift to War*, Bloomsbury, 1989

51 A. Calder, The People's War: Britain 1939–45, Jonathan Cape, 1969

52 F. D. Margiotta (ed.), *Brassey's Encyclopaedia of Military History
    and Biography*, Brassey's, 1994

53 A. Reid, *A Concise Encyclopaedia of the Second World War*,
    Osprey, 1974

54 Lamb, *op. cit.*

55 A. Cave Brown, *Bodyguard of Lies*, W. H. Allen & Co, 1976

56 *Ibid.*

57 P. Knightley, *The Second Oldest Profession*, Andre Deutsch, 1986

58 Gert Buchheit, cited in Knightley, *op. cit.*

59 Knightley, *op. cit.*

60 F. H. Hinsley, *British Intelligence in the Second World War*,
    HMSO, 1993

61 *Ibid.*

62 *Ibid.*

63 R. Overy, *Why the Allies Won*, Jonathan Cape, 1995

64 *Ibid.*

65 M. Hastings, foreword to R Lewin, *Ultra Goes To War*,
    Hutchinson, 1978

66 R. J. Spiller, *Assessing Ultra*, Military Review, August 1979, cited in
    Knightley, *op. cit.*

67 Knightley, *op. cit.*

68 *Ibid.*

69 *Ibid.*

70 *Ibid.*

71 D. Stafford, *Churchill and Secret Service*, The Overlook Press, 1998

72 J. Rohwer, cited in Knightley, *op. cit.*

73 Knightley, *op. cit.*

74 *Ibid.*

75 *Ibid.*

76 J. A. Cole, *Lord Haw-Haw*, Faber and Faber, 1964

77 *Ibid.*

78 *Ibid.*

79 House of Lords Hansard, 30 May 1945, cols 265-276; House of Commons Hansard, 11 June, cols 1393-1398

80 *Ibid.*

81 Report, The Times, London, 10 November 2003

82 L. Freedman & V. Gamba-Stonehouse, *Signals of War: The Falklands Conflict of 1982*, Faber and Faber, 1990

83 *Ibid.*

84 Public Record Office releases, report, *Daily Telegraph*, 7 August 1998

85 Report, *Daily Telegraph*, 20 April 2001

86 Public Record Office releases, report, *Daily Telegraph*, 13 October 1998

87 Report, *Daily Telegraph*, 12 August 2005

5

Creative Shocks

This chapter is about human ingenuity. Our sense of history is often most strikingly brought home to us through our perceptions and recollections of human invention and creativity. The 'advance of science' is a veritable cliché, but one which reveals that an abiding theme of the way we tend to think about historical progress is the assumption that technical advance runs in the same direction as the advance of history. In other words, the more modern we are, the more advanced we are. But, surprisingly, that is not how history has often happened. Large parts of the dramatic advance in technological knowledge in the Western Enlightenment of the 17th to 19th centuries were actually a re-discovery of what past civilisations already seem to have been familiar with. In this chapter, we also take a look at the vagaries of historical reputations in science and creativity. How we remember who deserves the honours can be a hit and miss affair.

Cultural milestone or mere figment of the imagination?

The Renaissance – the flowering of the arts in Europe between the 14th and 16th centuries – traditionally occupies a pivotal point in the historical narrative of our social and cultural development. In the common telling, it marks the sudden and energetic departure, most noticeably in Italy, from the dreary, uncivilised barbarism of the Dark Ages to the elevated artistic and scientific achievements of masters such as Michelangelo and Leonardo da Vinci. It comes down to us from our history books as one of the most radical shifts in human progress ever recorded, a self-engineered

explosion of enlightened thinking and a breathless urge
to learning.

There are two things wrong with this common stereotype
that we are presented with. First, any assumption that those
living through it knew it was happening to them, that it was
a conscious experience, in the same way that society experienced, for example, 'the Swinging Sixties'. The Renaissance
was, in fact, much more a retrospective construct. And second,
that it is portrayed as this sudden, almost inexplicable burst
of energy, 'coming from nowhere', which has had the effect
of accentuating its character as a distinctively home-grown,
Eurocentric affair.

The first surprise about the Renaissance is that it was
not so-called at the time, or even widely appreciated to be
happening (we are, after all, talking of a period of three
centuries or so). Apart from a single use of the phrase by the
Italian art historian Giorgio Vasari in his *Lives of the Painters*
in 1550, the term 'Renaissance' did not originate contempo-
raneously with events. Remarkably, it did not appear as a
historical description of the phenomenon until 1855 when
French historian, Jules Michelet, used the word to entitle
one of the nineteen volumes of his monumental *Histoire de
France*. It acquired more popular recognition from its use
five years later by Swiss historian Jacob Burckhardt who first
conceptualised Italy as the core of the 'movement' in his *The
Civilization of the Renaissance in Italy*.[1] Before then, the term,
and the perception of a Renaissance, simply was not a part
of history's characterisation of its past. It is a creation of the
mid-19th century, and thus barely 150 years old.

The second artifice that gets promoted is the sense of the
period being a stark departure from the recent past, an emergence out of the wasteland left by the Dark Ages, Europe
rediscovering for itself new heights of culture. This is far
from an accurate depiction of reality. While it may pander
to Europeans' sense of a fresh start, and, importantly, under

their own steam, the carving out of the Renaissance as a mysterious blossoming of local talent, hides a long-running continuum of artistic, architectural and scientific advance that had, in fact, been seeping into Europe over the previous three centuries – care of Arab Spain.

It is a fact rarely acknowledged by Europeanists that almost our entire understanding of the classical Greek masters – Aristotle, Euclid, Plato, Pythagoras, Socrates and a host of others – derives from the translation into Latin of Arab translations of the original works after the creeping Christian 'reconquest' of Spain from Arab settlers between the 11th and 13th centuries. Arab libraries across the Spanish peninsula held vast treasures of both Arab learning and their translations of the original works of ancient Greece. Cordoba, the Arab capital, boasted 700 mosques, 300 public baths, seventy libraries and paved and lit streets. The library in the Royal Palace had 400,000 books; its catalogue alone comprised forty-four volumes.[2]

It was these immense repositories that were plundered by European scholars as military victories fell in favour of the Christians and the Arabs retreated. Europe discovered unheard of treasures of knowledge – science, mathematics, astronomy, biology, medicine, optics, geometry, mechanics, hydrostatics, navigation, and a wealth more, including the political and social philosophies of Socrates and Aristotle.

Fundamental changes followed. Europe absorbed the Arabic counting system – which we still use today – seeing how much better it was for practical use than the clumsy Roman numerals. Europe's knowledge of medicine and pharmacy was transformed by acquiring the Arab translations of Greek masters such as Hippocrates and Galen.

The dripfeeding of these new ideas into Europe from an army of translators who stationed themselves in Spain had turned into a flood by the start of the 13th century. At the time of the supposed Renaissance, Europe was already driving fast forward on a learning curve towards vast new horizons. That is why the image of the Renaissance as a sudden upwelling of culture, seemingly out of the blue, in the mid-14th century, set against the supposed backdrop of mass ignorance and stunted lives, and supposedly a process self-generated by Europe, is far from the truth. As a leading author of world history has concluded:

> [The Renaissance] formed in the culture which the great changes in Christian civilization from the twelfth century onwards had made possible. ... [I]t is to falsify history if we take it to imply a transformation of culture masking a radical break with medieval Christian civilization. The Renaissance is and was a myth ... There is no clear line in European history which separates it ... from the [preceding] Middle Ages.[3]

Yet that is pretty much how our common view of history still tends to see it.

☞

Borrowing from the past

We tend to assume that scientific advance is an entirely modern phenomenon, and see the post-Renaissance period from the 16th century as a time of 'great discoveries' that transformed our world – of the unpacking of the physical world into its chemical elements, of unravelling the laws of physics, of the unleashing of unparalleled power through steam and then the hidden wonders of electricity. We picture our most recent centuries as the breakthrough from an ignorant past. But as we have already seen in Chapter 1, we have often forgotten that our long lost ancestors knew quite a lot more than we often realise, or prefer to remember. The Ancient Greeks had already worked out through calculation that the Earth was round along with a decent go at its size too, and as we will see shortly, knew about the potential for steam as a source of power. It may surprise us to know what else they had become familiar with. The story of modern Western invention is far more a tale of re-acquaintance with ancient knowledge than we often realise.

Democritus, who lived around 460 bc to 370 bc, first proposed the concept of matter being made up of individual **atoms**. He formed the essential framework that we know today of physical objects being built from masses of discrete particles, these particles having different forms and properties depending on their combinations. It was he who coined the term 'atoms' (from the Greek *a-tomein* meaning 'indivisible') for these building blocks of nature.[4] It would not be until Dalton in the first decade of the 19th century that the idea was picked up again with scientific rigour.

The **underwater diving suit**, not patented in modern times until 1715, was in use as early as the 4th century BC. Aristotle (384 BC–322 BC) describes equipment that appears to be remarkably similar to that of the modern era's usage. He describes metal containers with glass plates that seem to be helmets, and tube mechanisms that supplied fresh air.[5]

Shorthand, often assumed to be a 19th century invention, was first practised by Greek historian Xenophon (430 BC–354 BC) who used the technique to record his conversations with philosopher Socrates.[6] And the first form of **telegraph** – semaphore style signs visible from a distance that became the standard practice for European communication from the 17th and 18th centuries until the arrival of electric telegraphy – was described by Greek historian Polybius in the 3rd century BC. Unlike simple fire beacons which could only warn of, but not specify, a danger, the Greeks invented the system of having symbols for each letter of the alphabet. Combinations of signs could convey a specific message over long distances. And until the electric transmission by wire came along, there was no better system.[7]

The gunpowder-based **cannon**, which made its appearance on European battlefields only in the 14th century to revolutionise land warfare, had its forerunner in a design by Archimedes in the 2nd century BC for a steam-powered weapon. We only know of the device through Leonardo da Vinci who sketched it out attributing the idea to a description by Archimedes.[8] The contraption consisted of a tube, possibly made of copper, the end third of which was heated. Water was introduced, creating steam and thus pressure, which was used to force the projectile out of the tube. No accounts have come down from Greek sources of its actual use on the battlefield, and it may have been simply a conceptual exercise. (Archimedes, from Syracuse in Sicily, and the pre-eminent scientist of his day, was roped in to help his city repel a Roman siege in 213 BC. He appears to have designed some fiendish defensive machines which prolonged the city's defence for a year before the Romans succeeded. Archimedes was killed in the final assault in 212.)

Greek engineer Ctesibius appears to have invented the first **hand gun** in 245 BC, over 1,800 years before gunpowder-powered muskets appeared in Europe around 1570. His was powered by compressed air. It consisted of a metal tube with a piston that could be retracted, increasing air pressure behind it, and held by a catch. The catch was released by means of the equivalent of a modern-day trigger to fire the projectile.[9]

Ctesibius, almost unheard of today, was a prolific inventor. He is recorded by several contemporary historians to have built a **hydraulic organ** which, from the description, appears to foreshadow the same approach of forcing air by bellows through reed pipes as is the foundation for modern organs.[10] It also represented the first development of a keyboard, necessary to open and shut valves to the individual pipes. He also invented the **thermometer**, which did not reappear in Europe until Galileo in 1592.[11]

The basic principles of mechanics and transmission

of energy for work, all appeared far earlier than we like to think they did. Philo of Byzantium (about 280 BC–220 BC) is recorded as first describing the use of **cogwheels and chains** to perform work. And Hero of Alexandria in the 1st century BC first conceived of the **crank shaft and connecting rod** system by which energy generated can be transferred from one direction to another, essential for all machines from steam engines to motor cars.[12] Hero also is credited with inventing **gear systems** familiar to us today but demanding precision engineering on a scale often not assumed to exist in ancient Greece. The use of different sized interlocking cogged-wheels to transfer energy and magnify power and motion was chiefly put to use for lifting devices, including the earliest **cranes**.[13] He used them also to invent the first distance measuring devices – odometers – for land vehicles and ships. Germinus, a mechanic from Rhodes, in around 87 BC even invented a mechanism that made allowances for the **differential,** the ability to drive an axle that provides different speeds of rotation of the two ends, for example for wheels going round a corner where wheels need to move at different rates. Essential for many practical machines including clocks and other devices involving complex movement, the differential only came back to practical use in the 19th century as road vehicles developed. It seems the Greeks used it for astronomical devices for calculating the movements of the planets.[14] The concept of **soldering** for joining metals was described by Hero[15] as well as a tripod-mounted device which measured angles for building and ensuring straight lines – what we would know today as the theodolite.[16]

In understanding the human body, the Greeks also made discoveries which were then destined to disappear for nearly two millennia. Although we would assume that **electrical cardiac stimulation** is a modern medical technique, the earliest form was in fact practised by the Greeks. Texts from the 5th century BC record torpedo fish, a type of electric ray common in the Mediterranean, being applied to the chest to stimulate vital reflexes.[17] The Romans also picked up the method, it being well described by 1st century physician Scribonius Largus, whose handbook of drug recipes survives.[18] Erasistratus (c304 BC–c250 BC), often known as the founder of physiology, worked out many of the bodily systems including the basics of **blood circulation** (except he got the role of veins and arteries wrong)[19] and the principle of **oxygen exchange** as the explanation for how humans breathed. He also conceived, against the norms of the time, the novel idea of the **brain** as the centre of human senses – contempories held the heart to be the controlling organ of the body.

As we have seen, the Greeks knew far more about the Earth than we often give them credit for. It was the Greeks too – through Hipparchus (190 BC–120BC) – who first divided the world into 360° of **longitude**, the basis we still use today.[20] He also mapped out the **longitude and latitude** grid we use today, proposing that each place in the known world be located by references to their unique co-ordinates.[21] He calculated the **length of the day** to within six minutes of its actual length, and that of the **month** to thirty seconds.[22] Hicetas (400 BC–335 BC) and Heraklides (388 BC–315 BC) had both already maintained that the **Earth spun on its own axis**, pre-empting Renaissance astronomers by 1,800 years.[23] Aristarchus, who lived around 320 BC–250 BC, even proposed that the **Earth revolved around the Sun**, and was not the centre of the solar system, an idea that was not to find final favour until Copernicus in 1543. He also conjectured, like Heraklides, that the movement of the stars in the sky was the effect of the Earth rotating on its axis, a concept for which he was ridiculed by the prevailing theorist of the day, Ptolemy, who rejected the idea of a spinning Earth because he claimed it would create catastrophic winds.[24]

☞

A forgotten pioneer

Think of pneumatic tyres and, if asked who invented them, the almost certain answer would be Mr Dunlop. Everyone knows that. Expect that what John Boyd Dunlop invented in 1888 was the pneumatic *bicycle* tyre. Almost entirely forgotten in motoring history is that the pneumatic vehicle tyre had actually been invented over forty years earlier – and it used an identical approach to Dunlop's. The only difference was the inconvenient assembly method that made the tyres extremely difficult to change if punctured.

It was London civil engineer Robert Thompson who first patented the concept of a pneumatic tyre built around and encasing an inflated inner tube in December 1845.[25] He fitted them to his carriage and demonstrated them publicly the following summer. The patent described the inner tube being made of india rubber, and enclosed inside a canvas cover. A 'strong outer casing' was then constructed 'by riveting a series of circular segments of leather and bolting them to the tyre'.[26]

A contemporary magazine reporting the public display painted a quaint picture of the 'silent wheels'. They were 'so silent as to suggest a practical inconsistency of a most startling character between the name and quality of the thing'. It reported that the tyres had by then apparently been tested for a hundred miles and that 'the outer leather casing is (contrary to what might have been expected) as sound and entire as at first'.[27] Another account reports that Thompson's 'air wheels' eventually broke the endurance record of over 2,000 kilometres.[28]

It was, however, the elaborate leather casing that proved the undoing of the invention as the long term solution. Demand was limited for the tyres as it took over seventy bolts to fix the leather straps in place to contain the rubber inner tube. They were consequently extremely difficult to replace, expensive, and, until mechanised locomotion came along, not an economic proposition for most contemporary users. It would be Dunlop, a generation later, who would re-engineer the idea (after a false start – his original scheme envisaged inflating the tyres with water) and secured for himself the place in history that he enjoys. Thompson, the originator of the inner tube, lies largely lost to the modern memory.

☞

More undeserved honours

Dunlop's lasting fame is an example of how we can often be guilty of ignoring the true pioneers. Our historical road map of scientific invention has in fact more false trails than we might assume. Taking a closer look at the fixtures on our usual story reveals a surprising litany of now forgotten heroes.

The concept behind the **Diesel engine** was not, in fact, invented by Diesel. True, his name has been irrevocably attached to the device conceived in 1893 and first made in 1897 which was an alternative way of making internal combustion engines work – by heat of compression to create ignition of the fuel in contrast to the petrol engine which used a spark. However, Diesel was pre-empted by the now entirely unknown English inventor, Herbert Akroyd Stuart. Halifax-born Stuart was just twenty-six years old when he took out two patents in 1890 for a heat compression ignition engine, pre-dating Diesel's same idea. He had even built a number of machines using the method by 1890, three years before Diesel's patent, and seven years before Diesel had ever made his first working engine.[29] By 1896, the year before Diesel would capture history for himself, Stuart had built both tractors and a locomotive using the principle. Quite how he came to be sidelined is one of the many little personal tragedies of historical fate and memory.

Edward Jenner is usually cited as the 'inventor' of vaccination through his work against smallpox in 1796. Yet Dorset farmer Benjamin Jesty was vaccinating his family in exactly the way that Jenner would achieve fame for as early as 1774.[30] Jesty's village of Yetminster was suffering an epidemic of smallpox and, mirroring the oft-told story of Jenner's supposed inspiration, Jesty had noticed how his milking servants had looked after smallpox affected neighbours without catching the disease themselves. He followed the same thought pattern that Jenner would be credited with, obtained pox from a cow in a nearby village and, using a needle, injected it into his wife and sons – a generation before Jenner. Years later, after the House of Commons had generously awarded Jenner £10,000 (some £750,000 in today's values) for his 'invention' in 1802, supporters pressed the cause of Jesty to be recognised – and rewarded – for his pioneering role. He gave evidence to the Vaccine Pock Institute in 1805 which then led public opinion on the issue. All he got was a long testimonial commending him and a pair of gold mounted injection needles.[31] Even he is not likely to have been the first to practise the technique. Letters from Lady Mary Wortley, the wife of the British ambassador to the Ottoman Empire, published in 1763, but dating from the second decade of the century, describe vaccination by needles as being commonplace in the near east at the time, nearly a century before Jenner. She had her own five-year-old son treated in 1717 when an epidemic of smallpox broke out in Constantinople.[32]

William Harvey is usually credited as the discoverer of the circulation of the blood, in 1628. However, the concept of the blood flow system of the human body had already been identified by 13th century Arab physician Ibn al-Nafis al-Quarashi. Unnoticed by western scholars until 1552, it came back into the light through the works of a Spanish doctor and theologian, Miguel Serveto. Unfortunately for him – and history – he wrote about it in a controversial religious work and was burned at the stake for his ideas.[33]

James Watt certainly did not invent the steam engine. Although popularly assumed to be the creator of the modern steam-powered revolution of the 18ᵗʰ century, his contribution to science built on the originality of others. He was an arch adapter rather than an originator. While he made milestone advances in the application of steam power in making engines that could power other machinery and mobile locomotion, the concept of the generation of power though steam was actually a fairly dated invention by the time Watt came on the scene in the early 1760s. The true inventor of the first practical working steam engine was Devon engineer Thomas Newcomen who produced the world's first working steam engine in 1712, half a century before Watt, and twenty four years before he was even born.[34] It was used for the straightforward purpose of pumping water out of mineshafts. Watt's genius was to see how Newcomen's machine could be made more efficient, and he genuinely turned a rather limited device into one that had multiple potential uses. That is probably why it is his name, instead of the true inventor, that gets remembered.

There is an astonishing postscript to the story of the steam engine: that the concept of steam power was actually known to the ancient Greeks, eighteen hundred years earlier. The mathematician and mechanical genius Hero of Alexandria is now known to have constructed a steam powered device in the 1ˢᵗ century BC. The 'aeolipile' was a simple machine consisting of a hollow sphere pivoted on an axle with two hollow spouts protruding from opposite sides. When water in the sphere was heated, steam was produced from the spouts which turned the sphere. It seems that while Hero had worked out the concept and power of steam energy, he could not think of any practical uses to which it might be applied.[35]

We revere **Johannes Gutenburg** for inventing the process of movable type that ushered in the modern world of printing. But as with many things, China beat the West to the mark. Although Gutenburg pioneered the combination of movable type and a printing press that could use it time after time, the claim for invention of the concept of changeable type pieces belongs to a Chinese alchemist, Pi Sheng, who created the process three hundred years earlier around 1045.[36] He did not advance so far as to create a machine for continuous printing, but he was the first to perfect the method for creating and then fixing together individual letters. He did this with a mixture of clay and glue to form the letter pieces which were then baked to hardness. They were stuck on an iron baseplate which had been coated with resin to keep the combination of letters in place. Once the page had been printed, the letters were released by heating the printing block which melted the resin and loosened the pieces ready for re-use.[37]

It was 1313 before printer Wang Chen developed machinery capable of printing on a repetitive scale. He is recorded as having a catalogue of 60,000 characters in use.[38] Clay had given way to hardwood as the base for the letters. This was still more than a hundred years before Europe's hero Gutenburg first managed the same, in around 1439.

Rather more scurrilous are the antics of **Samuel Morse** whose name is synonymous with the electric telegraph and the code that bore his name. He invented neither the telegraph system nor the code. Both were the work of other collaborators whom Morse mercilessly pushed out of history's fame frame. A fellow American inventor Joseph Henry had actually pioneered much of the development of the electromagnet which lay at the foundation of the system. He built his in 1831, a decade before Morse. As Henry did not patent his device, Morse drew on it slavishly and when, on the point of getting the contract with the American government, he slapped his own patent on the work in 1840 and secured the profits and fame that followed. When it came to the code for which he achieved immortality, he would have had a much more complicated method than the dots and dashes. He based his on the flag-based semaphore system, with words being made up of individual four digit codes. It needed a massive directory to de-code. Alfred Vail had come up with the simpler idea of giving each letter its unique dot-dash combination. Morse simply patented it as his own.[39]

☞

Not what it would seem

Other creations are not all we assume them to be.

The most famous index finger in the history of art – that of Adam's outstretched towards God's finger in the central scene of **Michelangelo's** 16th century ceiling of the Sistine Chapel in Rome – is not by Michelangelo. At some time in the past, the original plaster fractured. What we see today is a restoration, by an unknown hand.[40]

For all their symbolism of longevity, we actually have an entirely false impression of the collective significance of the **Seven Wonders of the World**: they only existed all at the same time for about 30 years – between the completion of the Pharos lighthouse at Alexandria around 260 BC and the destruction by earthquake of the Colossus of Rhodes in 226 BC.

The Pyramids of Giza were built around 2550 BC and are still, of course, around, the only one of the seven to survive to the modern era. The Hanging Gardens of Babylon were first constructed around 604 BC, but were in ruins by 150 BC. The Temple of Artemis at Ephesus was begun about 560 BC, rebuilt twice after a fire (in 356 BC) and sacking by Goths (AD 263) and finally destroyed in AD 401. The statue of Zeus at Olympia was started in 438 BC and lasted 800 years until destroyed by fire in AD 475. The Tomb of Mausolus, at Helicarnassus, the original mausoleum, was started around 350 BC and survived in parts until 1522. The Colossus of Rhodes was completed in 282 BC. The Pharos lighthouse was started in 297 BC, completed in 260 BC and lasted until its destruction in an earthquake in 1303.

☞

Our national bard – unclear Shakespeare?

One of the abiding myths about Shakespeare is that we know so very little about him. It has become a common lament in popular accounts that the record is thin, very thin indeed. It fuels compelling and endless controversies, how this product of a rural Warwickshire backwater emerged almost overnight to stand at the pinnacle of his trade, how he was able to switch with such ease across the wide variety of subjects he covered and, of course, whether he actually wrote the plays that are credited to him (over fifty other candidates have been proposed in the last 150 years).[41]

Recent scholars have begun to argue that we probably know more about Shakespeare than any other Elizabethan who was not of royal or noble birth.[42] A collection put together in 2002 of copies and transcripts of documents connected with Shakespeare runs to over 300 pages, including records of his family, the theatre companies with which he was involved and all significant contemporary references to him up to 1612, the year before he ceased writing.[43]

It is true that no personal correspondence to or from him survives. Biographers contrast this with other contemporaries like Jonson and Donne who have left copious amounts to posterity, so Shakespeare's invisibility begins to look a touch deliberate.[44] It seems to have been a rather persistent trait. He made no effort to publish or preserve his plays – the first collection of his works was only put together by actor colleagues seven years after his death. Unlike the image we have fostered of the energetic, artistic genius, labouring away for the passion of theatrical production to the exclusion of all other considerations, it looks increasingly likely that Shakespeare may simply have not been bothered about reputation or fame, but was interested only in accumulating money.[45] He appears to have kept his head down. He was the only playwright of his generation never to be imprisoned or censured by the authorities for his writings.[46]

This was, after all, the same man who managed to dodge the legal requirement of registering with his local Southwark borough throughout the twenty-five years he spent in London, thus avoiding local parish taxes.[47]

But it is also true that the injection of controversy into Shakespeare's life is a distinctly modern phenomenon, elevating the 'mystery' of the man far beyond anything he encountered during his life or for a prolonged period after it. In the 250 years following Shakespeare's death (in 1616), no one expressed the slightest doubt about his credentials.[48] Brought up on the ceaseless controversy about his authorship, most modern readers would find it difficult to appreciate the *uncontroversial* and settled consensus that prevailed for so long about Shakespeare and his accomplishments, that nothing struck anyone as mysteriously out of the ordinary. Indeed, the author of the acknowledged standard work on Shakespeare's historical reputation notes that his death occasioned no great outpouring of homage, in marked contrast to his arch rival Ben Jonson when he died twenty years later.[49]

It was only in the mid-19th century, when an obsessive American, Delia Bacon, became convinced that her namesake (but no relation), Francis, had authored the plays, that a hare was set running. She came to England in 1852 on a mission to prove it, produced a dense 675-page treatise in 1857 and ended up dead in a lunatic asylum in 1859. But she started a craze that has shown no sign of letting up.

There remains one aspect of Shakespeare's life that has been manufactured, and no one is keen for it to questioned – the uplifting coincidence that our national bard was born on 23 April, St George's Day and England's national day. The long-held assertion is based on a single unsubstantiated reference from an 18th century antiquarian, William Oldys, who around 1750 seems to have misread the inscription on

Shakespeare's memorial in Stratford church to mean that he had died on the same day as he was born. As his death in 1616 was documented on 23 April, the claim as to his birth entered history, to be picked up and popularised by one of Shakespeare's earliest aficionados, George Steevens. His assumed authority ensured it stuck. That there is not one reference to this striking coincidence from any contemporary during Shakespeare's life – surely it would have been an attribute worthy of remarking upon? – or in the hundred and fifty years after his death until Oldys, should have been a clue to its doubtfulness. But in the tradition of not allowing facts to get in the way of a good story, the myth became enshrined in the record.[50] (The only verified record for Shakespeare's birth is for his baptism, on 26 April 1564. Recent research points to the wedding date of Elizabeth, Shakespeare's granddaughter, on 22 April 1626 as being held on that date to honour her grandfather's birthday. It is the strongest evidence we are likely to get as to the real birthday of the Bard.)[51]

References

1   R. Stemp, *The Secret Language of the Renaissance*, Duncan Baird, 2006

2   J. Burke, *The Day the Universe Changed*, BBC, 1985

3   J. M. Roberts, *History of the World*, Pelican, 1980

4   R. Tarnas, *The Passion of the Western Mind*, Ballantine Books, 1991

5   G. Messadié, *Dictionary of Inventions*, Wordsworth, 1995

6   Messadié, *op. cit.*

7   Messadié, *op. cit.*

8   Messadié, *op. cit.*

9   Messadié, *op. cit.*

10 Messadié, *op. cit.*

11 Messadié, *op. cit.*

12 Messadié, *op. cit.*

13 Messadié, *op. cit.*

14 Messadié, *op. cit.*

15 Messadié, *op. cit.*

16   Messadié, *op. cit.*

17   Messadié, *op. cit.*

18   R. Porter, *The Greatest Benefit To Mankind*, HarperCollins, 1997

19   *Hutchinson Dictionary of Scientists,* Helicon 1996

20   Messadié, *op. cit.*

21   D. J. Boorstin, *The Discoverers*, J. M. Dent, 1984

22   H. C. Corben, *The Struggle to Understand*, Prometheus Books, 1991

23   Hutchinson, *op. cit.*

24   Hutchinson, *op. cit.*

25   P. Robertson, *Shell Book of Firsts,* Ebury Press, 1974

26   *Ibid.*

27   *Ibid.*

28   Messadié, *op. cit.*

29   *Dictionary of National Biography*, online edition at www.oxforddnb.com

30   *Ibid.*

31   *Ibid.*

32   A. S. E. Ackermann, *Popular Fallacies Explained and Corrected*, The Old Westminster Press, 1923

33   V. A. Giscard d'Estaing (ed), *The Book of Inventions and Discoveries*, Queen Anne Press, 1991

34   Hutchinson, *op. cit.*

35   Messadié, *op. cit.*

36   Boorstin, *op. cit.*

37   *Ibid.*

38   Messadié, *op. cit.*

39   P. Mason, *What Needled Cleopatra ... and Other Little Secrets Airbrushed from History*, JR Books, 2009

40   R. King, *Michelangelo and the Pope's Ceiling*, Chatto, 2003

41   S. Wells, *Shakespeare: A Dramatic Life*, Sinclair-Stevenson, 1994

42   M. Wood, *In Search of Shakespeare*, BBC, 2003

43   C. Loomis, *William Shakespeare, The Life Records*, Gale, 2002

44   S. Greenblatt, *Will In The World: How Shakespeare Became Shakespeare*, Cape, 2004

45   *Ibid.*

46 J. Bate, *Soul of the Age*, Viking, 2008

47 K. Duncan-Jones, *Ungentle Shakespeare*, Arden, 2001

48 J. Bate, *The Genius of Shakespeare*, Picador, 1997

49 S. Schoenbaum, *Shakespeare's Lives*, Oxford University Press, 1991

50 P. Honan, *Shakespeare: A Life*, Oxford University Press, 1998

51 *Ibid.*

6

We Remember It Well (?)

Here we take a look at some of history's most momentous social changes, and see them in a completely new light. Our understanding of many of these events shapes the way we think about ourselves today – yet on closer inspection, it is clear that our interpretations are based on a wild, perhaps wilful, misreading of the past.

The Roman Empire – sudden fall or a longer trip?

The classic view we popularly have of the end of the Roman Empire comes from Edward Gibbon's monumental six volume, million and a half word epic, *The History of the Decline and Fall of the Roman Empire*. Twenty-four years in the making, from conception in 1764 to the publication of the final volume in 1788, its title has shaped our mental framework for this pivotal point in human history. The concept of the 'fall' of the Empire has created a mindset that bases itself on the image of a sudden, cataclysmic collapse, and the villains of the piece are easily located. The traditional story in our history books is simple: the (comparatively) civilised Roman Empire was overrun by invading (and uncouth) barbarians. The Sack of Rome in AD 410 by Alaric the Goth is seen as the crucial tipping point. The Vandals followed in a second Sack of the city in 455, after which it was all over.

The real story was anything but. And lurking beneath the commonly accepted simplicity is a tale far more complex that reveals surprising new insights into the much-maligned tribes whose names – Goths and Vandals – have stayed with us as archetypes of wanton destruction.

The various tribes that have been convicted by history of destroying Rome are painted as being classic invaders from outside the borders of the Empire. One popular history typifies the metaphor that we commonly conjure up: 'the steppe barbarians, forever battering at the gates.'[1] And the esteemed *Encyclopaedia Britannica* tells its readers that the Sack of Rome in 410 was 'an event that symbolised the fall of the Western Roman Empire'.[2] In fact, these are not really true reflections of the realities at all.

For a century before they reached Rome as the Empire's opponents, the Goths, originally a Germanic people from the modern Balkans, had arrived on the edge of the Empire seeking peaceful co-existence with Rome. They themselves were suffering oppression from the encroachments of the nomadic Huns moving in from the vast steppes of what is now Russia. The Goths sought the predictabilities of life by converting to Christianity and, in 376, obtained permission to cross the Danube – the Imperial border – and set up home within the Empire. For its part, Rome needed the cheap labour, particularly for the stretched army, so accounts suggest it was happy to accommodate them. The Emperor, Valens, is recorded by the Roman historian Ammianus as welcoming the prospect:

> The affair caused more joy than fear and educated flatterers immoderately praised the good fortune of the [Emperor] which unexpectedly brought him so many young recruits from the ends of the earth, that by the union of his own and foreign forces he would have an invincible army.[3]

It is a rarely remembered fact that Alaric, the Goth who would lead the assault of Rome, was a career Roman soldier.[4]

So the first 'barbarian invasion' was actually a process of asylum seeking, not the military confrontation that we tend to have figured in our minds. True, it got off to a bad start, within two years the Goths, unhappy at their initial treatment, revolted and defeated a Roman army led by Valens himself, leaving the Emperor dead. Relations were never harmonious after that, and a vicious war ensued for three years before a peace deal was agreed. Goths were to be a constant trouble to Rome, but not more so than any of the troublesome tribes of the borderlands. They were certainly not the conspicuous single force about to derail the entire Empire: that was not to come for another thirty-two years. As one modern historian writes:

> We are still a long way from imperial collapse. The war on the Danube had affected only the Empire's Balkan provinces, a relatively poor and isolated frontier zone. ...At the end of the war, moreover, both eastern and [the new] Western emperors remained in secure occupation of their thrones, with their great revenue-producing centres such as Asia Minor, Syria, Egypt and North Africa entirely untouched. And most parts of the Empire hadn't even seen a Goth.[5]

The Vandals, from what is now southern Poland, were one of a number of migrations which followed in the next decades, again from the pressure exerted by the Huns from the east. These developments are quite different to the usual picture we have created of rapacious peoples possessing in advance an intent to attack and subvert what is presented as a weakening Roman Empire. They came across the borders between 405 and 408 in a major crisis which saw four separate incursions by large swathes of populations fleeing the Huns.

But it was to be the Goths, under Alaric, whom history would record as committing the shattering assault on the capital of the Empire. Here, too, the story is not so clear cut as we think. He had been in revolt to re-write the peace agreement of thirty years before. He did not set out to overturn the Empire.[6] In 408, he set up a siege around Rome to get the Emperor to negotiate. He would spend two years patiently trying to cut a deal. In fact, he had no intention of sacking the city – he wanted booty. By the end of the year, the Roman Senate had agreed to his demands for 5,000 pounds of gold and 30,000 of silver, along with a supply of silks, skins and spices.[7]

Having secured this, he pressed for a longer lasting settlement. He retreated to Ravenna, 175 miles north of Rome, and began a protracted bout of diplomatic negotiation. He demanded an annual amount of gold and corn, the right to live in two areas of the Empire, and that he should be appointed a general in the Roman army. He was offering a future that would see his people live in peace (and no little comfort) and the perpetuation of the status quo as far as the Roman Empire was concerned.[8] The Emperor was prepared to concede the first two demands, but not the generalship. Amazingly, in light of the reputation he has been saddled with, Alaric changed his offer. He would no longer ask for the gold or the generalship, but simply the right to live peacefully in the outback provinces he had identified and be satisfied with as much corn annually as the Emperor thought fit to provide.

This was hardly the rampant assailant that history has handed down to us. Historians muse that Alaric's vision was based on an assumption that Rome, far from dying, would recover its strength. All he wanted was to secure a modest extraction while he held the temporary upper hand.[9] Incredibly, the Emperor still held out from agreeing a settlement. At the end of 409, fifteen months after first setting siege to Rome, Alaric and his force returned to besiege the city once more. His patience seemed unending. He sat it out for a further seven months trying to win his demands peacefully. Only in July 410 when, while waiting at Ravenna for the Emperor for another of the seemingly interminable parleys, a group of rogue Romans attacked Alaric and his deputation, did Alaric's tack change. He returned to Rome again, and proceeded with the 'sack' of the city.

The Sack of Rome in 410 has been described as 'one of the most civilised sacks of a city ever witnessed'.[10] The two main basilicas – St Peter's and St Paul's – were spared depredations as holy places. Witnesses even described their incredulity as the Goths escorted many nuns to the sanctuaries for their personal safety. Over three days, the Goths removed all other valuables from the city, but the historical picture of mayhem, death and destruction is wildly misplaced:

> All in all, even after three days of Gothic attentions, the vast majority of the city's monuments and buildings remained intact, even if stripped of their moveable valuables.[11]

A very different explanation to the normal one seems to be the more accurate interpretation of these events. Far from seeking the destruction of Rome as history tends to recount it, Alaric was desperate to find a political solution with the Emperor. He could, after all, have taken the city by force at any time in the nearly two years he had spent outside its walls in fruitless diplomacy. That the Emperor felt that Rome was dispensable also suggests that the commonly held sense of an end-of-days fatalism is also misplaced. It was certainly a milestone on a very long road to oblivion for Rome, but 410 was not at the time, and does not appear in retrospect, to be anything like the fatal blow it is popularly assumed to be. The end game therefore seems to turn the commonly held view of these events on its head:

> Alaric's letting his troops loose there for three days was an admission that his whole policy, since entering Italy in the autumn of 408, had been misconceived. It had not delivered the kind of deal with the Roman state that he was looking

for. The sack of Rome was not so much a symbolic blow to the Roman Empire as an admission of Gothic failure.[12]

It was to be another forty-five years before Rome was sacked for the second time, by the rather more fiery Vandals. If Rome was falling, it was a long, long stuttering affair. The 455 sacking came about not, as we often perceive, as the culmination of a classic invasion campaign but of an opportunistic assault by a maritime Vandal force coming over from North Africa for, in the words of one historian, 'fun and profit'.[13] Far from occupying Rome as one might expect from the standard presumptions of the 'fall of Rome', the Vandals took their loot back to North Africa. This was no takeover of the Empire, more the usual predatory raid exploiting a period of instability.

Emperors continued to rule in Rome for another generation, albeit in increasing turmoil, the last one being dethroned in 476 by Odovacar, son of one of Attila the Hun's chief warriors, who then ruled as a king in Italy. He nevertheless continued to acknowledge the authority of the eastern part of the Roman Empire that had set itself up in Constantinople 140 years before, and he even sent the Western Emperors' imperial insignia and robes back to Constantinople.[14]

So at the end, the 'fall' of Rome was hardly the sudden cataclysm, bathed in blood and violence, that our history makes us prone to assume by its overstating of the importance of the two sackings of Rome. It was more a low political coup, accompanied by deft sartorial diplomacy. Rome did not so much fall as slowly, and hardly perceptibly, evaporate. The imagery of a step change in history is misleading. One account suggests a more subtle evolutionary perspective:

> There is no real reason even to accept Gibbon's concept of a 'fall' or 'decline' of the Roman Empire. ... Rather the concept of change and development, instead of decline, has much to recommend it, particularly since so many aspects of the

Roman world survived. Both barbarians and popes eagerly embraced Roman political forms and ideas, and a great many aspects of the Roman world survived to influence the medieval and eventually the modern world.

Roman law left its traces on the legal and political systems of most European countries. Roman roads, aqueducts, bridges, and buildings remained in use, not as museum pieces but rather as constant practical reminders of the Roman past that became a part of the growing present. The Latin language lay at the root of many of the modern languages of Western Europe. ... For almost two thousand years, Latin language and literature remained at the core of Western education.[15]

☞

Persecuting Jews – a British contribution

Think of the persecution of the Jews and the forced wearing of a humiliating yellow star as a mark of one's race, and you think of 20th century Nazi Germany. But it may be a surprise to learn that the origin in Europe of such a heinous practice lies not there but ... in Britain.

In the late 13th century, there were 16–20,000 Jews living in Britain in a population of two and a half million. Most had come from France since the Norman Conquest a hundred and twenty-five years earlier. By the end of the century, there were sizeable Jewish communities in all of England's main cities. They had been subjected to regular bouts of persecution, the most notorious massacre coming at York in 1190 where the whole Jewish community was slaughtered during a single night.

On his return from crusading, Edward I followed the edict of Pope Gregory X to outlaw money-lending for interest, and the Jews were the natural target. The Statute of Jewry in 1275 banned usury, required all debts to be repaid by the following

Easter, and restricted Jews from living outside certain towns and cities. In a foretaste of future persecutions, this English law also required that every Jew over seven years old had to wear a yellow badge on their outer garment measuring at least six inches by three to identify them as Jews.[16]

A decisive 'final' solution was soon pressed. On 18 July 1290, Edward promulgated an edict requiring every professing Jew to leave the realm by 1 November. Any who remained were liable to be executed. They were permitted to take as much of their moveable possessions as they could carry. The non-moveable property of every Jew was to be forfeited.

Their flight was marked with episodes of great cruelty. Many parties fled through the southern counties to the coast, the quickest route to the continent, presenting opportunities for highway robbery as they were laden down with their worldly goods. Those who put themselves at the mercy of ships' captains often fared little better. The most infamous incident of all involved a ship sailing from London which had arrived off Queenborough, on the Isle of Sheppey, where the captain anchored at the ebb tide near an exposed sandbank. He invited the passengers to disembark to stretch their legs, and then abandoned them on the sandbank. All drowned as the tide came in.[17]

☞

The Industrial Revolution – manufacturing myths

According to the standard narrative we learn in our school-days, the eighty or so years between around 1750 and 1830 utterly transformed Britain from the agricultural society it had been since time immemorial to an energetic, industrialising economy built upon making, rather than growing, things – manufacturing. A seismic population shift ensued from countryside to new and burgeoning cities. Factories supplanted farms as the most lucrative places of employment for the labouring classes. Cotton mills, iron foundries, mines, canals and steam engines took over as symbols of national life: this was the Industrial Revolution, and it changed the face of Britain. It is also held to have ushered in an era of exploitation of the masses, changing their lives for the worse and making a few better off at the expense of the poor.

None of this is entirely wrong, but neither is this version the complete truth either. The Industrial Revolution is enveloped by a swirl of myths, false histories and often forgotten perspectives.

For the modern mind, the era is indelibly defined by a distinct set of images which comes from the particular lens through which we usually regard the period. What are those icons that regularly come to mind? William Blake's evocative 'dark Satanic mills'; teeming tenement slums in wildly expanding cities housing armies of new factory slaves; the destitution of exploited labour; the grime of newly industrial Britain. Charles Dickens perhaps captured the spirit of the age in 1854 in *Hard Times* with his description of 'Coketown'. It was based on the experience of a visit to Preston in Lancashire:

> It was a town of red brick, or of brick that would have been red if the smoke and ashes had allowed it; but as matters stood it was a town of unnatural red and black like the painted face of a savage. It was a town of machinery and tall chimneys, out of which interminable serpents of smoke trailed themselves for ever and ever, and never got uncoiled. It had a black canal in it, and a river that ran purple with ill-smelling dye, and vast piles of buildings full of windows where there was a rattling and a trembling all day long, and where the piston of the steam-engine worked monotonously up and down, like the head of an elephant in a state of melancholy madness.

This excerpt appears in an anthology of eyewitness accounts of the period detailing 'the Coming of the Machine'. Tellingly, its title is *Pandæmonium*.[18] The urgent, headlong charge towards industrialism, and unremitting misery, are the motifs of this standard narrative of modernising Britain.

Yet taking a wider view, the changes induced by the Industrial Revolution appear rather less precipitous. Eighty years, after all, is around three generations, so use of the term 'revolution' suggests a pace of change that was far quicker than actual reality. (Think of the computer and digital 'revolution' that has transformed the modern world in less than a single generation.)

We should remember that for all the industrial explosion, it would take these eighty years for Britain to become a predominantly industrial economy. A generation into the 'revolution', in the 1780s, Britain was still overwhelmingly an agricultural society with the largest number of people being employed on the land.[19] It was not until 1830 that manufacturing would make a greater contribution to the national income than agriculture,[20] and while individual towns clearly experienced dramatic growth, as far as the overall profile of the country is concerned, the rise of urban living was less a rush to the city than a gradual migration. In 1801, two-thirds of the way through the 'revolution', still only 30 per cent of the population in England and Wales lived in cities. It did not reach 50 per cent until 1851.[21] And as we shall see, the image of this change as being a physical trek of people from village to city is far from the truth. The growth of British cities derived largely from a massive increase in the country's population, not by a depopulation of the countryside.

And contrary too to popular perceptions, innovation and invention progressed rather more gradually than we tend to think. The cotton industry, renowned for being one of the most advanced of the textile trades, was not in fact predominantly mechanised until far into the 19th century. As late as 1830, hand looms were reckoned to outnumber power looms by four to one.[22] The Darbys of famous Coalbrookdale, who pioneered the coke-fired furnace, took forty years to bring the invention to a state where it could be widely replicated. As one economic historian comments, 'hardly rapid progress'.[23]

Other textile industries were even more resistant to mechanisation. Most of the 120,000 workforce in the hosiery trade, centred in the Midlands, was, as late as 1862, still working in their own homes under the 'putting out' system – where weaving and spinning was done by workers in their homes and paid by the amount they produced rather than the time they worked, and working by hand.[24] Long after the invention of the sewing machine, clothes makers more often preferred to keep production by hand.[25]

And far from the stereotypical image of grasping businessmen seizing every opportunity to advance their profits, the evidence is rather to the contrary. Outside the cotton industry, overall growth rates in output per person at the supposed height of the 'revolution' in the last decades of the 18th century were low, much lower than for most of the 19th or 20th centuries.[26] This suggests a much steadier pace to the beginnings of industrial development than the tag 'revolution', and our image of overnight riches, implies.

The abiding theme that structures our received view of the early years of industrialisation is the long sequence of Factory Acts designed to improve hours of working and the restriction of employment of women and children in the new centres of production. This is often the core of the story. Yet seeing the period through this lens creates the sense that the issue of working hours and ages was the only social impact arising from the growth of factories. As one eminent historian has pointed out, the main difference that worried workers between the earlier forms of labour – the 'putting out' system – and factory work was not the one we usually assume:

It was not the long hours or poor pay or physical conditions which made the factory detested. In the domestic system working families worked long hours in hovels for pittances. What was detested in a factory was a feeling of servitude and discipline. In a man's own home he could work twenty hours and be drunk for four: in the factory he worked to a time-table and was not his own master even to sweat himself.[27]

It was often cottage workers' reluctance to work in factories that led early factory owners to turn to abandoned and pauper children for much-needed labour.[28]

Friedrich Engels, who bankrolled Karl Marx in his lifelong endeavour to analyse the social implications of the new industrial environment that ended with the theory of Communism, undertook one of the most thorough assessments of the evolving new order. His *The Condition of the Working Class in England* of 1845 exposed the horrors of the lives of workers in Manchester and the north-west of England, and concluded with a vitriolic summary that epitomises our commonly held view of the period:

Masses of refuse, offal and sickening filth lie among standing pools in all directions; the atmosphere is poisoned by the effluvia from these and laden and darkened by the smoke of a dozen tall factory chimneys. ... The race that lives in these ruinous cottages ... in measureless filth and stench, in this atmosphere penned in as if with a purpose, this race must really have reached the lowest stage of humanity. This is the impression and the line of thought which the exterior of this district forces upon the beholder. But what must one think when he hears that in each of these pens, containing at most two rooms, a garret and perhaps a cellar, on the average twenty humans beings live? ... At the bar of world opinion, I charge the English middle classes with

mass murder, wholesale robbery, and all the other crimes in
the calendar.

Conditions were indeed appalling by modern standards, but
perhaps hardly less so than what had been endured by weav-
ers and spinners quietly and privately at home. What the
factory system did was not so much *create* the social ills it is
often accused of doing – female and child labour, for example,
existed long before the factory, and long hours and job inse-
curity were just as prevalent before factories came along – but
it enabled the evils of the manufacturing system to be more
readily visible.

By focusing on the outpouring of harrowing tales of misery,
our history of the period becomes excessively negative, and
tends to lose sight of the longer term repercussions that were
less tangible and less obvious. It is no accident that the eminent
historian Asa Briggs entitled his seminal survey of the period
(in contrast to 'Pandæmonium') *The Age of Improvement*. For
despite the imagery of hardship and squalor that dominates
our conventional view of the Industrial Revolution, the era
was in fact one of unprecedented *human* progress.

The health of the population improved markedly. Britain's
population tripled in a century, from six million in 1750 to
nearly 18 million at the 1851 census. However, the birth rate is
now known to have peaked around 1780–90,[29] meaning that
the biggest cause of this massive growth in population was
not more births but a falling death rate. Many, many more
who were born managed to survive. The death rate plunged
by a third between 1780 and 1820.[30]

This leads to a compelling theme. There is a tendency in
conceptualising the period of the Industrial Revolution to
imagine that Britain moved from a tranquil, rural idyll to
the Stygian smokes of hellish new cities. But this is a false
perspective. The agricultural way of life was by no means the
placid, healthy state it started to be seen as, in retrospect, by

critics of urban capitalism. The fragility of growing up in agricultural Britain was in fact staggering. In 1740, an astonishing 75 per cent of children died before they reached six years of age.[31] By the start of the 19th century, fifty years into industrialisation, it had fallen to 41 per cent, and would continue to fall consistently throughout the century.[32] Improvements in the understanding of contagious diseases (for example the invention of vaccination in the 1790s, and the realisation of the importance to health of clean water and sanitation) and the fact that public health issues started to force themselves on local authorities through the very visible congestion of new urban living conditions, lifted the health status of the nation by a degree unparalleled in our history.

This general improvement in people's wellbeing – of astonishing proportions – almost warrants a label of a 'health revolution' itself. The change in health status looks to have happened at a faster pace than industrialisation appears to have done, yet its intangibility has made it fade from our historical outlook. We are left with a more parlous view of the period, the one more obvious to the eye.

The celebrated Austrian economist Friedrich von Hayek wrote in 1954 that our historical view of the Industrial Revolution leads us to draw the wrong conclusions on its impact. Far from our common assumptions deduced from the standard telling of the tale – that the Industrial Revolution brought about new heights of social evil and a tragic departure from the halcyon days of a peaceful rural existence – the real story of this changing profile of Britain was that the Industrial Revolution fostered 'an increasing awareness of facts which before passed unnoticed ... Economic suffering became both more conspicuous and seemed less justified.'[33] The concentration of economic activity in factories enabled social observers to see economic relationships far more starkly than before, and the physical concentration of workers in establishments created new prospects for organising labour.

Historians still debate the inter-relationships between industrialisation and the improvement in health. The former did not wholly or directly cause the latter, but there were connections. For a start, the growing numbers of people were more easily absorbed into the new industrialising economy than they would have been into a fully agricultural setting. So the image we carry of a national workforce that was 'degraded' from agriculture to industrial slavery is a rather misguided one. Industrialisation provided the means by which a population that could not have existed under the old static agricultural economy was able to survive. It also added resilience to the economy. The intense extremes of distress and famine that occurred when agriculture went wrong were smoothed out as, with greater importing of food as trade boomed as a result of industrialisation, nutrition became more varied and more reliable.

The Industrial Revolution produced more than hardship and exploitation. It produced new ways of thinking about social relations, only possible because of the very visible impact that new ways of working had. The era was one of constant change, but perhaps not so fast-paced as the traditional label would suggest, and not remittingly in the negative direction we tend to think. Overall, it was hugely for the good. As one historian sums it up, even in the middle throes of the Industrial Revolution,

… it was better to be born in 1800 than in 1760.[34]

And it would be even better in any year after that.

☞

Imperial lore
Of all the periods of our history, few have as many false trails as the British Empire. Always controversial – both at the time and even more so in hindsight – Britain's imperial past comes

down to the modern mind in some well-cast forms, many of which turn out to be untrue. The four most persistent views of Empire are all not as clear cut as we tend to believe.

The chief popular characterisation of the British Empire is that at its high point in the middle and late nineteenth century, the imperial 'mission' was a greed-driven, graspingly aggressive, deliberate and state-orchestrated programme to amass as much overseas territory as possible. Not so. In fact, most of the accumulation of the later Empire was not the pre-planned enterprise of common folklore, and some colonial possessions were acquired more with reluctance than relish. 'Trade follows the flag', was the catchphrase of the time. In practice, the opposite turned out more often than not to be true: British governmental control tended to follow on from what private traders had started, rather than the other way around.

The next two familiar assertions rest on explaining the motivation of Empire, and point to economics as the callous driving force. According to the classic Marxist analysis, Britain acquired its colonies because it needed markets for the surplus production that was churning out of the home country. Colonialism was the inevitable consequence of growing industrialisation at home. In fact, the Empire never provided a major source for British exports. On the other side of the economic coin lay the third critique of imperialism: that colonies were seized so they could be exploited for their tropical resources. In this view, the British imperial monster ransacked its well-endowed possessions, gaining vast riches from their natural wealth. In fact, the Empire was never a major source of imported goods either.

The final sentiment is so taken for granted that it is almost a definition of imperialism. This is that, taken in the round, Empire was gigantically and self-evidently a lucrative undertaking for the British; that the profit and loss account was overwhelmingly in favour of gain over cost. The evidence on this, too, is actually far less clear cut than most people assume.

Together, these four 'facts' of Empire – its deliberateness, its unquestioned financial value, and its two economic drivers – are almost certainly to be the received wisdom that any modern Briton has about their imperial past. Each 'fact', though, fares badly when it comes to the raw facts.

A grand scheme?

To begin with, the view that the Empire was a calculated, methodically implemented 'grand plan'. As long ago as 1883, the Cambridge University historian John Robert Seeley coined a famous phrase when he wrote in his history of the *Expansion of England*, 'We seem as it were, to have conquered and peopled half the world in a fit of absence of mind.' The idea that the Empire was a pre-planned operation of conquest, driven from the centre and maintained with methodical control is attractive to critics of empire who hold up its exploitative evils, but is largely misconceived. The growth of the empire was rarely systematic, rarely done purely for hopes of economic gain, and in many cases not state-drive at all, but following from the demands of private traders who sought protection. The flag more often followed, not created, trade.

The components of the early Empire that would eventually become the Dominions all showed such features. None was taken primarily or solely for reasons of economic gain: **Canada** was taken in 1759 in a tussle with rival France. Its acquisition was primarily to protect the northern flank of the American colonies – hugely ironic for Britain since the American rebellion would begin in less than a generation. Canada would become a sought after home for hundreds of thousands of 'loyalists' fleeing from the American Revolution. **Australia** was, as is well known, secured for a prison colony, as a substitute for the American colonies which had been used for that purpose while they were under British control. **New Zealand**, although Cook made first landfall in 1769, was not regarded with the slightest interest by the British government for seventy years. British settlement started as a result of a private initiative by an enthusiastic emigration society in the late 1830s. Apparent interest in colonisation by the French prompted government intervention in 1840 to claim the land for Britain to protect the settlers that had arrived – one of the first examples of a somewhat reluctant acquisition under pressure from private interests. **South Africa** was always a military undertaking. Securing the Cape was vital for control of the route out to India. **India** itself originated in private interests, this time trade, too. The East India Company 'ran' India – albeit towards the end under heavy government influence – from its foundation in the 17th century. The British government only took over the running of the place after the disastrous Indian Mutiny in 1857. The following year, the Company was abolished and responsibility for governing India became an explicit responsibility of the government.

So even at the start, Empire was a far from organised enterprise. And even as these settlements matured, they would not necessarily show any move to systematisation of development. As James Morris has written:

> It was all bits and pieces. There was no system. ... In fact the very essence of this Empire was its formless improvisation, its stagger. Four million people of British stock lived in the six self-governing colonies of Australia. British settlers had been there for rather more than two hundred years, and the organisation of affairs was entirely theirs. They had started from scratch. The six colonies had six different sets of tariffs, mainly directly against each other. They had six separate postal and telegraph services, and six uncoordinated defence forces. The judicial processes of one colony could not be enforced in another. The railways were built to different

gauges. If an inventor took out a patent in Queensland, it did not protect him in Victoria.[35]

This was true even more for the growth of the later Empire during the heyday of expansion in the Victorian era. In a period when Britain acquired in just ten years in the late 1880s and 1890s territory fifty times the size of the British Isles,[36] the achievement masked a considerable degree of chaos and uncertainty in the increasingly widespread obligations Britain was taking on.

The growth in African possessions was more often than not an unplanned and incremental affair, a mixture of responding to pressure from religious missionaries who had ventured into the hinterland and then demanded protection, backed by the vocal Christian societies at home pushing the popular Victorian civilising 'mission' of Empire; business interests that wanted the extra security of the gunboat or the British Resident to press their case against foreign competitors; and the strategic response to the ever-fluctuating actions of political rivals.

All this came together, for example, in the settlement and eventual absorption of Uganda in the 1890s. Within just four years of the foundation of a private company to explore economic opportunities in the region, the government came under pressure from the Imperial British East African Company to take over the area as a colony. Formed in 1888 by a Glaswegian shipping magnate, the Company had, within two years, sent a representative to Uganda 'to forestall their German rivals'.[37] The local ruler, the Kabaka of Buganda, was victimising missionaries and atrocity stories appeared widely in the European press.[38] The threat of Germans arriving to occupy the headwaters of the Nile, with all that that implied for the security of Egypt, was added into the toxic mix. In the summer of 1892, the Company appealed to the government to come to its rescue.

Far from the common assumption that governments enthusiastically extended their domains whenever the opportunity offered itself, government ministers baulked at the prospect. The Chancellor of the Exchequer bemoaned the preposterousness of the case for holding on to Uganda (the Company was due to evacuate the country at the end of the year):

> Is it *trade*? There is no traffic. Is it religion? The Catholics and Protestants ... are occupied in nothing but cutting each other's throats. ... I see nothing but endless expense, trouble and disaster in prospect if we allow ourselves to drift into any sort of responsibility for this business.[39]

The War Minister accused the Company's representative in Uganda of being a 'second General Gordon' and this ate into Prime Minister Gladstone's nerves. He had been at the helm when the 'heroic' Gordon had died at the hands of the locals in Khartoum in 1885, and had stood accused of failing to do enough to rescue him. It had scarred the nation. A huge public campaign to 'Save Uganda', with 174 petitions flooding into the Foreign Office in the space of a few weeks, coloured the decision too.[40] Eventually, the external pressure prevailed, and by June 1894 a protectorate had been declared. The Company could now look to a resident British government presence in Uganda to guard its interests.

While other examples are not as extreme, the general picture is one of far more hesitancy about the benefits of Empire than is believed by modern readers. The possessions grew by stealth and consequence (of previous decisions) rather than by deliberate desire to expand. The Uganda commitment, for example, led to the necessity of the 500 mile railway that had to be built from Mombasa on the coast to Lake Victoria. That, in turn, led to the settlement of Kenya which lay in between. Hong Kong, Burma and Fiji all became British possessions after private traders complained to the government over oppression by local authorities. (In Fiji, Britain resisted for fifteen years before accepting the inevitable.[41]) Possessions in Malaya and Borneo were taken largely because of the disorganisation of the local Malay States which led to piracy that disrupted the business of the existing small trading stations in Singapore, Malacca and the Straits Settlements. Bechuanaland (now Botswana) was taken in 1885 as a consequence of the German arrival in South West Africa (modern Namibia) the year before with the prospect that any eastwards drift would cut off the Cape from the British territories to the north. Annexation preserved the road to the north.[42]

Morris again:

> Accounted for in these diverse ways, one acquisition seemed to lead logically to the next. Trade led to the defence of trade, exploration to settlement, missionaries needed protection ... It was like a monumental snowball.[43]

The Empire had been, according also to Morris, 'haphazardly acquired'.[44] There was no great plan. If it was not quite 'absence of mind' it was more detour than design.

A mission to exploit?

The most trenchant criticism of Empire is, however, reserved for the accusation that it fuelled rampant exploitation of colonial populations. The commodities of the tropical paradises were, it is commonly held, plundered for the benefit of the home country, which then heaped further disfavour on them by dumping manufactured goods in the colonies as a solution for providing outlets for the new over-productive, profit-gorging monsters of British capitalism. In the most extreme version of the argument, Marxist thought holds that the British economy was only able to survive because of the availability of the colonial possessions that enabled it both to obtain the raw materials essential to keeping the new businesses producing and to offload the resulting output.

But surprisingly, this often unquestioned view of the Empire turns out to be far from true. To get to the truth, we'll have to wade through some numbers. It's worth bearing with it. Throughout the high point of Empire, between the 1850s and the First World War, when the supposed machinations of exploitation were at their worst, the Empire's contribution to imports into Britain of primary goods, that is, the foodstuffs and raw materials that critics maintained were what was being plundered from the new territories, never rose above a quarter, and sometimes fell to just one fifth.[45] In 1854, colonial possessions accounted for just 22.4 per cent of these imports. After more than half a century of alleged exploitation, by 1913, that figure had barely changed.[46] And unhappily for those who casually assert that it was the new African colonies that were bearing the brunt of this extraction, and that Britain was getting rich on the backs of the poor, exploited natives, Africa accounted for just 3.4 per cent of Britain's imports in the 1909–1913 period.[47] And this was dropping, not rising – it had been nearer 6 per cent in 1854.[48] The Empire was therefore not, in fact, the overwhelming supplier of Britain's late 19th century economic success.

Looking at the other side of the coin, matters are little better. Against the assertion that the Empire was the essential and convenient release valve that enabled surplus production to be sold, the truth is that throughout the Victorian era, exports to the Empire never accounted for more than 35 per cent of Britain's output, a figure it reached just before the First World War.[49] For the vast majority of the 19th century, it was under a third. And the biggest recipients were the 'old' Empire – the long settled dominions of Australia, Canada and New Zealand. When exports to India and to British possessions in Europe are taken out of the equation too, it leaves the paltry figure of 18 per cent as the proportion of exports that went to the newly acquired colonies in Asia and Africa that had supposedly been captured to be the principal sources for Britain's excess produce.[50] By 1913, this had risen slightly, to just under 27 per cent. However, taking out from this the phenomenal increase in exports to South Africa that were the result of the spectacular, but fortuitous, gold boom, the remaining 'new' colonies accounted for less than 15 per cent of Britain's total export trade.[51] The contention that these colonies were vital for boosting trade is, therefore, also fantasy. As James Morris has written:

> Trade scarcely flourished in the enormous new African territories: in 1897 [*the year of Queen Victoria's Diamond Jubilee, often acknowledged as the apogee of the Empire*], the whole of tropical Africa took only 1.2 per cent of British exports.[52]

So much then for the new colonies grabbed in the era of the 'Scramble for Africa' being essential to keeping the capitalist economy alive. Morris concludes:

> [T]he assumption that the Empire made Britain rich, that the more imperially she behaved the wealthier she would be, was a misconception. It was partly an honest delusion, based upon insufficient evidence, and partly a kind of fraud, devised by men who stood to gain from aggressive national policies.
>
> The colonial trade, which looked so heart-warmingly portrayed in thick black arrows on diagrammatical maps, was not so important as it seemed. ... In 1896 Britain had imported 64 million hundredweight of wheat – 30.7 million from the United States, 17.2 million from Russia, and only 3.6 million from Canada. Only in potatoes, cheese, apples and fresh mutton was the Empire Britain's chief food supplier: other foodstuffs came overwhelmingly from foreign countries, the Empire generally providing less than 10 per cent.[53]

In practice, economic relations with non-Empire parts of the world – the United States, South America and Europe – were much more important for Britain's wellbeing.[54]

A financial success?

Schoolchildren since the demise of the Empire in the 1960s have had drummed into them the exploitative nature of Britain's colonial past, how riches were drawn from the poor and uncivilised, how Empire was one great profit-making machine. A more sober assessment, however, strikes a rather different note on the costs, as well as gains, of Empire. The balance of account in the end looks rather different from the one we have been commonly brought up to believe.

While an accurate balance sheet will never be possible, there are sufficient pointers to suggest that our usual assumptions that the Empire was an entirely one directional route to untrammelled wealth is a long way off the mark. For a start, it is less often remembered that the Empire offered an alternative place for British investors to put their money instead of in Britain itself. Some economic historians argue that the diversion of investment money from domestic use to investing in the new overseas colonies had the effect of retarding growth in Britain in key infrastructure development:

> The loss to Britain went beyond the funding itself. Investment embodies new knowledge and stimulates change ... Investment at home would have raised the rate of growth and the level of consumption. Conversely, diversion of investment to safe and undemanding projects overseas undermined the urban fabric, and deprived Britain of the technological and institutional dynamism which would have delivered greater economic growth. ... The development of the telephone system in Britain, and of urban electric public transport, lagged far behind the United States. Britain also lagged considerably in the production and application of

electricity and motor transport. Some estimates suggest that the rise of [domestic] investment ... could have delivered dramatically higher standards of living in Britain.[55]

Then there was the issue of the cost of patrolling and defending the new and increasingly widespread possessions. To begin with, this was not excessive. Britain spent about 3 per cent of national income on defence around the time of the high point of empire, between 1870 and the First World War.[56] This was less than her continental rivals, Germany and France, who had to maintain large standing armies (Britain relied on the extensive capacity of the Royal Navy to ferry troops around to colonial trouble spots, so could afford to keep an army only half the size in peacetime.) The problem for Britain started in the last decade of the 19th century and the early years of the 20th leading up to the First World War when the basis of naval superiority changed from cheap gunboats to expensive, armoured battleships. Britain's prevailing advantage rapidly evaporated. Within a decade, the costs of defending the sea lanes began to become excessively expensive for Britain and rival navies matched or outclassed British sea power. What had been a set of possessions cheaply defended (something of a recompense given that they were not generating the overwhelming 'profit' popularly supposed) ended up being a larger and larger millstone around Britain's economy.[57]

Economic historians today tell of a far more modest place for Empire in the development story of Britain:

In comparison with a world that had not been colonised by Britain, other things being equal, the benefits of Imperial trade alone contributed at most 5–6 per cent to British national income [by 1914], and perhaps even less. ... In total, then, the direct contribution of Empire to Britain was not entirely negligible, but in its absence British average incomes would still have been ahead of such contemporary first-rank economies as France and Germany, Sweden and Switzerland.[58]

The British Empire undoubtedly had huge impacts on global settlement patterns – the spread of English-speaking communities to the far-flung reaches of the Earth created new, young, prosperous nations. But many of the benefits of Empire accrued there, not back in Britain. The value of the Empire to the homeland is much more equivocal. Empire certainly changed the world, but the customary view that it was a pre-conceived and systematic enterprise undertaken for mercenary acquisition that produced unqualified gains, is a fiction of nostalgia and retrospective guilt. Empire was a muddled process of accumulation, of limited, if not questionable, financial value to the homeland, and did not come free of cost, some of which went an awfully long way to outweighing the benefits.

The myth of the Victorians

It is now fairly fashionable to deride the popular myths that grew up in the 20th century about the Victorians. Almost everything we have come to believe about their social mores is a mask. One recent author has compellingly assailed our misguided attitude towards them:

> We think of the Victorians as racists, yet they had no anti-immigration laws and elected Britain's first Asian Members of Parliament. We think of them as religious, yet church attendance figures fell just as dramatically in the nineteenth century as in the twentieth. We think of their society as violent, yet their crime figures were lower than ours ... we think of them as royalist, when the period was the zenith of British republicanism. We think of them as puritanical, and

when mountains of evidence are produced to the contrary,
we insist that they were forced to conduct clandestine sex
lives and used it to amplify their reputation for hypocrisy.[59]

Although usually looked back on as a period quintessentially
defined by its attention to public and private morals, the
Victorian era was not, in fact, the paragon of straitlaced recti-
tude. The defining motif of the covered piano leg was never a
practice in English Victorian society. It has now been traced to
a diary entry by author Captain Frederick Marryat (he of the
naval novels of the 1830s and 40s). Marryat observed the covering of piano 'limbs' in America in 1839 and wrote of it in his *A
Diary in America*, poking fun at our American cousins' excessive
prudery.[60] Somewhere along the way, it transferred to the British
instead, and latter generations of Britons were brought up to
chuckle mercilessly at their predecessors' hypersensitivities.

Life was, in fact, lived on the edge. The idea of a sexually
repressed society could not be further from the truth. According
to research published in 1994, throughout the 19th century
between a third and a half of British brides were pregnant on
their wedding day.[61] The sudden craze for roller-skates which
raged in the 1870s was partly fuelled by youthful lovers who
found that they made it difficult for chaperones to keep up. [62]
This was hardly a circumscribed society. *The Lancet* reported
in 1857 that there were 6,000 brothels in London, and 80,000
prostitutes.[63] The age of consent was just twelve until 1875 (when
it was edged up to thirteen).[64] The minimum age for marriage
for a girl was also twelve (that would not change until 1929).[65]

Even Queen Victoria herself notoriously suffered in the
image handed down to posterity. It is only in recent decades
that it has been unpicked. Far from the dowdy killjoy often
painted, contemporaries all point to her keen sense of
humour[66] and she was, by recent revelations, an avid fan of
nude portraits and statues. She and Prince Albert bought
each other quite remarkable numbers of them.[67]

Piety of a different sort – religious – also shapes our common view of the era. Contrary to the standard impression of an upright and diligently spiritual society, church-going was, as in later periods, actually diminishing. The Religious Census of 1851 revealed that in the order of half the people who would be expected to go to church in 1851 did not do so.[68] A later pair of surveys of church-going across the London metropolis in 1886 and 1902, the latter just after Victoria's death, showed clearly the trend of religious commitment at the moment of the supposed apogee of Victorian values. Although the population of the city had increased by half a million in the period between the two surveys, actual attendances had dropped, from 1,167,312 to 1,003,361. For Anglican services alone, the rate of decline was even more pronounced, from just under 536,000 to 396,000.[69] The 1902 survey identified how many people attended more than one service on the day. Taking this into account, it showed that just 830,000 people in the capital attended a religious service – that from a population of some 4.5 million, or around 18 per cent.

And then the crime. Our stereotyped view might summon up fog-bound alleyways, murderous cutthroats and perpetrators being sentenced to hang for next to nothing, but most historians now agree that crime in Victorian times was lower than in previous centuries, and was decreasing.[70] Murder declined by over 50 per cent between the early 1870s and the First World War. Robbery fell by a factor of seven from 1857 to the end of the century.[71] It became particularly rare after 1890, resulting in only 150 arrests in London annually. At the serious end, too, crime was far less prevalent than we have become accustomed to imagine. After 1890, London, with its population some four million, had only around twenty murders a year, and forty cases of manslaughter.[72] Life may not have been pretty or comfortable in the growing jungle of urban existence, but so far as a Victorian's vulnerability to losing it through violent attack goes, it seems to have been comparatively secure.

So why all this mischievous misleading? Author Matthew Sweet offers a tantalising theory: jealousy. We cannot get over the fact that they progressed so far in so many directions, invented so much of the modern world that we inherited and benefited from (the railways, the motor car and steam-ship; public provision of education, health and sanitation; electric lighting, the telegraph and the penny post; soccer, rugby and tennis; public libraries and the popular press, Darwin's evolution and fish and chips ... the list goes on) that we have reacted by casting our forebears in as many falsely disparaging lights as possible:

> The Victorians are the people against whom we have defined ourselves. We are who we are because we are not the Victorians. And if we concede that they moulded our culture, defined our sensibilities, built a world for us to live in – rather than being the figures against whom we rebelled in order to create those things for ourselves – then we undermine one of the founding myths of modernity.[73]

True or not, we have had a problem with the Victorians throughout the 20th century. We are only just getting over it.

☞

Boom and bust?

The history of the 1920s and 1930s are popularly characterised as years of boom – the Roaring Twenties – and then bust – the Great Depression. Iconic images of these periods are cast in our collective memories as symbols of the times: dancing 'flappers' of the champagne-fuelled, Charleston-obsessed jazz age; rain swept hunger marchers and dour queues for the soup kitchen of a dispossessed and out-of-work generation. Yet behind these motifs is hidden an astonishing reality, one barely known to the broad sweep of history's labelling.

The boom of the 1920s, most exuberantly on show in the America of Fitzgerald's *The Great Gatsby* and the extravagance of the emerging Hollywood, has left an historical image of unrestrained excess. Yet later research in the 1950s by the respected Brookings Institute[74] cast doubt on this picture of widespread and generalised prosperity in America. There was certainly an increase in economic activity – American industrial production almost doubled in the 1920s[75] – but the benefits were far from broadly spread. The Brookings research found that in 1929, at the height of the supposed boom and just before the Wall Street Crash of that year, only 8 per cent of American families had an income over $5,000 (equivalent to $63,000 in modern values or around £40,000). The vast majority of families – over 70 per cent – existed on $2,500 or less. Of that, 60 per cent had under $2,000, the level assessed as below the income level sufficient to meet basic necessities. So at a time commonly perceived to be an era of surfeit, more than half the population lived below the recognised poverty line of the time.

Compare this with modern America, and in conditions far from a boom. At the depth of the 2008–10 economic crisis, according to the most recent US Census report, 50 per cent of families in 2009 had an income of $50,000 or more (equivalent to $4,000 in 1929).[76] Indeed, in the past 40 years, the figure for the income of half the nation's families has never been lower than $40,000, the 1929 equivalent of $3,175.[77] In 2009, in the order of 41 per cent of American families earned the $63,000 or more that was achieved by just 8 per cent in the 1929 'boom'.[78] Success and abandon there may have been in the Roaring Twenties, but it seems it was far less widely spread throughout the populace than our common belief holds. A popular song of the period perhaps caught the contrasting mood:

Not much money, oh but honey
Ain't we got fun?

It tellingly went on:

> There's nothing surer,
> The rich get richer and the poor get poorer[79]

Likewise, the 'bust' of the Great Depression is normally portrayed as the cataclysmic collapse that condemned an entire generation to destitution. Imagery of the drabness of the Thirties shapes and conditions everything we think we know about that decade. Yet the usual simplistic depiction of this period also masks a rather more complicated story.

In Thirties Britain, contrary to what would be assumed from the classic narrative, the living standards of the majority of people actually got better – far better – rather than worse, as a result of the economic conditions. At its height, unemployment reached three million, which represented 16 per cent of the workforce. (This itself was not as catastrophically out of line with the recent past as we might commonly think: unemployment had averaged around 12 per cent throughout the supposed boom decade of the 1920s, and had been far higher in the immediate aftermath of the First World War when it had been 23 per cent in June 1921.[80]) It meant that 84 per cent of the working population retained and enjoyed a job and an income. And for them, the vast majority, the effect of the depression was hugely beneficial.

A general fall in prices and lower interest rates, along with stable wage levels, meant that those who did have work experienced rising real incomes and became markedly better off. This showed in higher consumer spending, which most economists agree was one of the main factors getting Britain back on the road to recovery. Expenditure on household durable goods – supposedly the inessentials that are sacrificed in hard times – increased by 40 per cent between 1931 and 1936.[81]

The lower interest rates meant lower mortgage rates and

these fuelled a housing boom in 1930s Britain. Between 1932 and 1934, construction spurted upwards from 200,000 houses a year to 350,000, an increase of 75 per cent in a mere two years.[82] For those who had work, Britain was actually a booming place to live. The leafy and salubrious suburbs of Britain's cities were all created in the Thirties. Car ownership doubled in the decade.[83] Chain stores like Woolworths and Marks & Spencer vigorously expanded the number of their outlets.[84]

The working conditions of the employed improved too. Holidays with pay were becoming a more common part of working lives. In 1937, some four million workers enjoyed at least one week off with pay annually. By 1939, this number was eleven million[85] – 56 per cent of the nation's workforce.[86]

So while those who suffered suffered deeply – unemployment was concentred in the industrial heartlands of northern England, and in Scotland and Wales, and towns could endure unemployment rates in excess of 70 per cent – for most Britons, the Thirties was a decade of advance, not decline. So evident was this overall picture that even at the time economists questioned whether the label 'depression' was right. The celebrated Joseph Schumpeter summed it up in 1939 thus:

> [T]he outstanding fact about the English depression is its mildness, which makes it doubtful whether that term is applicable at all.[87]

☛

The New Deal – America's grand plan, sabotaged from within

The popularly held account of the 1930s has it that, facing the economic catastrophe of the Wall Street Crash, Franklin Roosevelt responded with his famous New Deal which powered America's escape from the Great Depression. Warm and reassuring, but not true. This evaluation is largely dismissed by economic historians today. Most now agree that it was the Second World War, not civilian public works, that finally gave the American economy the boost it needed to reverse the Depression years. (Perversely, America came out of the Second World War a stronger economy than it went in.[88]) But leaving that aside, even less familiar to the common story is how the New Deal suffered intense opposition from within the very Americans the plan was aimed to help.

Far from being the universally applauded enterprise that we usually think it was held to be, the New Deal was, in fact, deeply controversial and deeply contested. And much of the effort ended up having to be abandoned because of determined court challenges by vested interests.

The New Deal was, at heart, a grand proposal to spend public funds in direct ways to keep America on the move. In the two hectic years after Roosevelt took office in March 1933, a flurry of programmes exploded out of Washington. There were iconic (and successful) schemes like the Tennessee Valley Authority that still exists today and which helped to regenerate communities in six states through developing hydroelectric power, and technical agencies that provided additional help to those who were not destitute but struggling, like the new Federal Housing Authority that provided insurance for mortgage loans, and the Rural Electrification Administration that funded the extension of the power network to remote towns. A Civilian Conservation Corps was also established aimed at providing socially useful work for 18–25 year olds, and a Federal Emergency Relief Administration provided direct social payments to the poor.

But the highest profile efforts came in schemes to create work for the unemployed and direct financial support for those hardest hit. The twin pillars of the New Deal were the National Industrial Recovery Act and the Agricultural Adjustment Act both passed by Congress during Roosevelt's hectic first hundred days. The former created two agencies, the Public Works Administration to provide grants to states and cities for large scale public construction projects, and the National Recovery Administration to help businesses. The latter helped the hard-pressed farming industry which faced severe problems in selling their produce in the straitened times. The scheme paid farmers compensation payments for adjusting their production by taking land out of use (much like the European Community would do in a later generation to reduce food mountains).

To a modern eye, the programme looks like a bold but necessary response. To the free-market, low government America of the 1930s, this looked like Socialism (and still does to critics today).

The National Recovery Administration (NRA) worked by introducing unprecedented economic planning. It established production controls, maximum hours working and minimum wage provisions, and suspended anti-competition laws that forbade price fixing between companies. To America's business community, the freedom to undercut one's competitor was the hallmark of the free market. The NRA's objective ran in the opposite direction. It sought to foster greater co-operation to keep as many businesses going as possible. Instead of the free-for-all, cut-throat tradition, the NRA wanted to regulate commerce and stabilise prices. It did so by introducing more than a thousand 'fair competition' codes covering hundreds of types of business.[89]

As is America's wont, things headed to court. Companies who objected to the hand of big government got lawyers to find holes in the laws which had understandably been hastily written. When a New York chicken supplier was prosecuted for breaching the industry code by trying to undercut his competitors, the case had powerful backers intent on using it to challenge the Roosevelt Administration's scheme. The argument went all the way to the Supreme Court. The Court unanimously ruled in May 1935 that the extent of the regulatory powers given to the NRA amounted to 'legislation by the executive' and ruled that the constitution did not permit Congress to 'delegate' its legislative authority to the Administration. On a constitutional technicality, the ground was swept away from under one of the central pillars of the New Deal.

The other pillar, the Agricultural Adjustment Act, the 'AAA', hardly fared better. It never recovered in the public eye from the initial criticism that farmers were being paid not to farm. The money that enabled them to do this was obtained by taxing the processors of the agricultural produce, like meatpackers or textile manufacturers. These interests complained that the additional costs were disadvantaging them in international markets. The meatpacking industry, in competition with South America, voiced particular opposition. One giant meatpacker refused to pay the federal government's tax bill claiming the AAA tax was unconstitutional. Once again, the contest reached the Supreme Court. Seven months after the NRA was struck down, the Supreme Court passed judgement in January 1936 on the AAA.

The AAA was on deeply shaky constitutional ground. The US Constitution had no provision allowing the federal government to regulate agriculture, and the taxes were not really taxes for general use but specifically ear-marked for paying to farmers. And there was an 1872 precedent of the Court that had ruled that tax revenues could not be 'appropriated' to aid a private business.

The meatpacking company hired a celebrated lawyer, reputedly for a six figure fee.[90] He struck a theatrically emotional note by bursting into tears before the Court as he pulled at the patriotic heart strings of the judges by declaiming: 'I pray almighty God that not in my time may the land of the regimented be accepted as a worthy substitute for the land of the free.'[91] AAA was duly ruled unconstitutional, and the other main pillar of the New Deal was scuppered.[92]

Both schemes were re-designed and re-enacted in different

form in 1935 and 1938 respectively to avoid the legal obstacles. The NRA became a labour relations organisation promoting harmonious employer-worker co-operation, dropping the aspirations to regulate prices which business had found unacceptably intrusive. The AAA became a farm produce management operation, with government taking farm surpluses into store in good years and providing financial subsidies to farmers in bad ones. They served useful purposes, but were shadows of the original bold vision that Roosevelt argued was needed to meet the economic emergency.

Even the successful Tennessee Valley Authority had to beat a legal challenge. A private power company, aggrieved at what it saw as the usurpation of its business by the government, managed to get a judge to rule in December 1934 that the federal government had no right to engage in generating power. This had the effect, according to senior members of Roosevelt's administration, of negating the entire TVA law. The dispute went all the way to the Supreme Court, which ruled in February 1936 in favour of the government, but only on the narrow ground that the particular dam at issue in the case had been built in pursuit of America's national defence needs – the power it generated went to make military equipment – which was a legitimate activity of the government.[93] Although the Court expressly stated that its ruling was not a judgment on the constitutionality of the TVA as a whole, the benefits of the scheme were by then so clear cut that no one thought better to pursue a wider challenge. And it remains in operation today, serving nine million people now in seven states.

The New Deal was an unprecedented response to an unprecedented crisis. But it tore at the sinews of the American way of life in ways that our simple retrospectives often skate over. The imagery of an America pulling together, with, in Roosevelt's ringing phrase, the only thing feared being 'fear itself' makes a smooth and uncomplicated narrative. But many influential Americans did fear something more than fear itself – the big hand of Washington, and big government. The New Deal took government in America into dozens of new activities that cramped the libertarian norms that were felt to lie in the roots of the country. Despite the enormity of the crisis, the enormity of overturning those norms was larger, and hence Roosevelt faced not just the invisible enemy of economics but the very tangible opposition of political and commercial forces. And in many areas, the latter proved stronger.

But no one likes to remember controversies when looking back contentedly to one's triumph over adversity. Hence we remember the New Deal vaguely: for its soaring inspirational aims, and its social conscience, not the shabby unleashing of self-interest that actually characterised Roosevelt's first two terms and ended up frustrating his grand plan.

☞

Never had it so good?

Of all the decades of the post-war world, the Fifties have been the most consistently misremembered period in our recent history. It is almost impossible to avoid seeing it stylised fondly, in a rich nostalgic glow, coming as it did wedged between the horrors and deprivations of war, and the rebellious Sixties. Its motif is the re-emergence of normality, an age of innocence, simplicity and general well-being, book-ended by instability on either side. It has come to be epitomised in the assertion of Harold Macmillan, Prime Minister of the day, telling a Bedford crowd in 1957 that 'let us be frank about it; most of our people have never had it so good'.

As they say, it's all relative. Coming on the back of two decades, one of great depression, and another of war and austerity, the Fifties were bound to look good to contemporaries. When the mayhem of the Sixties followed, even historians looking back tended to pick out the docile Fifties as an oasis of calm amidst recurring disorder. The tag still sticks to this day, masking a decade that was far from benign and trouble-free. It just goes to prove the truth of the old advice to stand next to a fat person if you want to look thin.

It's often forgotten that the hangover of rationing from the Second World War lasted well into the Fifties. Ration books could not be finally torn up until July 1954 when the last two restrictions – on meat and bacon – were lifted.[94] It had been a painfully slow process. At the start of the decade, a host of staples were still on the ration – petrol, soap, milk, tea, sweets, sugar, cheese and butter. Petrol controls were lifted in May 1950 (but at three shillings a gallon, petrol was at its highest price since 1920).[95] Those on soap and milk later in the year.[96] Tea came off the ration only in October 1952, sweets in February 1953 and sugar the following September. Cheese, butter and fats went only in May 1954 leaving the last two – meat and bacon to go in the summer of 1954 – nine years after the end of the war. It was not a little galling to realise that defeated Germany had abolished its rationing more than four years ahead of Britain.[97]

Britain was also heavily taxed compared with later decades. The standard rate of income tax was a stomping 47½ per cent in 1951,[98] only marginally less than the 50 per cent charged during the war, and was still at 42½ per cent at the time of the 1959 Budget (when it came down to 39 per cent).[99]

Despite the gathering boom in world trade in the 1950s, Britain spectacularly failed to keep up. The country's share of the post-war recovery was pitiful. In 1950, Britain was responsible for producing 25 per cent of the world's manu-factured exports. Only the US exported more. By 1960, it had fallen to 16 per cent. While British exports had increased by 6 per cent between 1950 and 1954, those of the countries about to form the Common Market increased by 76 per cent.[100] In the second half of the decade, while Britain's export growth picked up, by 13 per cent, the Europeans still managed to grow theirs by 63 per cent. The decade was one of Britain unequivocally falling behind – and fast.[101]

It was a decade of chances foregone. Leadership in modern electronics and computing, born from the research pioneered in the war, was rapidly lost to the Americans, and then to Japan (as were the car and motorcycle industries, to Germany and, again, Japan). In just five years, Britain foreclosed on its motor manufacturing. As historian of these times, Corelli Barnett, points out:

> It took just five years for Britain to throw away this commanding position. In 1955 the total of British car exports was lower than in 1950 while West Germany's had quadrupled. In 1956 German car exports overtook British. Britain would never regain her lost lead in this key technology.[102]

By 1954, Germany had also become a bigger shipbuilder than Britain; the following year, Japan roared past too.[103] Other lapses seemed obscenely self-defeating. Barnett also records:

> While Sir Alexander Fleming might have discovered penicillin in the 1920s and professors Florey and Chain might have demonstrated its potential as a cure for bacterial infection in 1940, Britain finished up paying royalties to the American pharmaceutical companies which had developed techniques for mass-producing the antibiotic.[104]

Socially, too, it was a less innocent time than we often prefer to think. We tend to forget the abortions that had to be conducted back street (estimated at 60,000 a year in the Fifties, and not to be legal until 1967). Or the infamous 'pea souper' smogs that regularly afflicted built up areas. The Great Smog that smothered London from the 6th to the 9th of December 1952 killed 12,000 residents in those four days.[105]

It was also the decade of slum clearance, but into the soulless tower blocks that would blight communities up and down the country for decades to follow and seed endless ills and insecurities. The directions laid down by urban planners in the 1950s would scar generations to come.

Immediately after his immortal phrase that day at Bedford, Macmillan uttered words that are less well-known but perhaps let slip a sense that all was not as it seemed:

> Go around the country ... and you will see a state of prosperity such as we have never had in my life time – nor indeed ever in the history of this country. What is beginning to worry some of us is, is it too good to be true? – or perhaps I should say, is it too good to last?[106]

A Freudian slip? Maybe. But in retrospect, Macmillan's initial question turned out to be spot on. On the surface, it may have seemed the best of times, but working away underneath, largely obscured, were the forces that were leading Britain on a sleepwalk to decline.

☞

Origins of selection

One of the most divisive issues in British education policy throughout the 20th century was the 'Eleven Plus', the examination taken by schoolchildren at that age which separated the best performing pupils to go on to a more academic 'grammar school' education and leaving the rest to what was often regarded as a second class, 'secondary modern' schooling. Portrayed by 'progressive' educationalists as an outdated and elitist approach to educating the nation's future, the issue of the Eleven Plus shaped the debate in Britain from the 1960s onwards, with the campaign for its abolition becoming the dividing line between political parties, the more conservative wishing to retain 'selective' education and reformists' arguing for a 'comprehensive' approach.

We tend to assume that the Eleven Plus was the creation of a conservative-oriented philosophy. Many reference accounts state that it was inaugurated by the celebrated 1944 Education Act, the most far-reaching reform of the British education system, brought in by Conservative Education Minister Rab Butler. Certainly, this Act created the so-called tripartite structure of education (grammar, secondary modern and secondary technical – the last never really took off) and the Eleven Plus was instrumental in separating out children at that crucial age into their future streams.

However, the concept of the Eleven Plus dates back far longer than 1944, and derives from a more surprising origin that is (perhaps unsurprisingly) conveniently forgotten by those who argued its heinous effects. The Eleven Plus was first established by none other than social reformer and darling of the left, founder of the Fabian Society and a veritable demi-god in the British social development movement, Sidney Webb.

Webb was responsible for introducing the concept of an eleven plus examination in 1893 for London, a year after he had successfully won election to the London County Council and become chairman of its technical education board. He defined 'technical education' very broadly to include, in the words of his entry in the *Dictionary of National Biography*:

> [A]ll sciences, the arts, foreign languages, modern history, economics, geography, commercial education, domestic economy 'and what not' with the result that the technical education board became a de facto secondary education authority for London.[107]

He once himself wrote that technical education, for him, meant 'all instruction above the level of the elementary school with the exception of Greek and literature'.[108]

He then created the Junior County Scholarship Scheme which used an Eleven Plus examination to select those who would then receive scholarships to the grammar schools. Just over 2,100 scholarships were awarded annually to the successful pupils from the 75,000 London eleven-year-olds.[109] Admittedly, the alternatives for eleven-year-olds in 1893 were school or work, rather than one level of education against another. But it nevertheless will come as a surprise to most to learn that it was a bastion of social progression who introduced the system that in later years would, for many, come to symbolism everything, absolutely everything, that was wrong with the British education system.

☞

In a daze

From the attention that modern medics and law enforcement give to the issue of narcotic drugs, one could be tempted into believing that the battle against dangerous drugs has been a persistent one throughout history. Far from it. Our anxieties are a distinctly modern phenomenon.

While the addictive qualities of opium had been well known since the 18th century, a wide range of mind-changing drugs now prohibited were widely used in 19th century Britain as over-the-counter medicinal tonics sold from high street chemists the length and breadth of the country.

Heroin tablets, synthesised from morphine by the German chemical company Bayer in 1897, were marketed commercially as a cold remedy. Advertising claimed heroin was ten times more effective on colds than codeine. Within a decade, heroin was on sale in Britain in a variety of forms – lozenges, pastilles, and water-soluble salts. Of over 180 clinical studies published around the world in the following six years, nearly all purported to endorse the health-giving qualities of the era's 'heroic' drug.

Cocaine, widely known as a mild stimulant in South America from the chewing of the coca leaf (which contains about 1 per cent cocaine), took off in North American and Europe in the 1860s when it was chemically synthesised. It was used in liquid form as a remedy for toothache and promoted as a temperance drink in preference to alcohol. Cocaine-laced wine was popular from 1863. It was from this that John Pemberton took his inspiration for Coca-Cola – it started as 'Pemberton's French wine coca' before his home city of Atlanta, Georgia, passed prohibition laws in 1886 that forced him to turn his brew into a non-alcoholic version.

For centuries, *Opium* had been cultivated in Britain, and in the 18th century the Royal Society of Arts, supporting the government's agricultural policy, even awarded prizes for the country's most successful growers (farmers in the Fenlands of East Anglia were apparently the most proficient).[110] As late as 1885 a Royal Commission concluded that the drug was no more debilitating than alcohol. It remained legally on sale in Britain until the Dangerous Drugs Act of 1920.

Cannabis was given the official all-clear in 1893 when the Indian Hemp Drug Commission produced a seven-volume, 3,000 page report concluding that the drug had no appreciable medical, psychological or moral effect: 'There is no evidence of any weight regarding the mental and moral injuries from the moderate use of these drugs.' It recommended against banning its use as to do so might drive the Indian poor into worse practices, like alcohol.[111]

References

1   W. H. McNeill, *A World History*, Oxford University Press, 1967
2   *Encyclopaedia Britannica*, 2010 edition
3   Cited in P. Heather, *The Fall of the Roman Empire: A New History*, Macmillan, 2005
4   A. Barbero, *The Day of the Barbarians*, Atlantic Books, 2007
5   Heather, *op. cit.*

6   Heather, *op. cit.*

7   Heather, *op. cit.*

8   Heather, *op. cit.*

9   Heather *op. cit.*

10 Heather *op. cit.*

11 Heather *op. cit.*

12 Heather *op. cit.*

13 Heather *op. cit.*

14 Heather *op. cit.*

15 McKay et al, *op. cit.*

16 At www.bbc.co.uk/radio4/history/sceptred_isle

17 *Bygone Kent*, Vol 7, No 12, 1986

18 H. Jennings, *Pandæmonium: the Coming of the Machine as seen by contemporary observers*, Andre Deutsch, *1985*

19 A. Briggs, *The Age of Improvement, 1783–1867*, Longmans, 1959

20 More, *op. cit.*

21 More, *op. cit.*

22 K. Feiling, *A History of England*, Macmillan, 1950

23 More, *op. cit.*

24 C. Hibbert, *The Illustrated London News Social History of Victorian Britain*, Angus & Robertson, 1975

25 *Ibid.*

26 More, *op. cit*

27 S. Watson, *The Reign of George III, 1760–1815*, Oxford History of England, Oxford University Press, 1960

28 McKay et al, *op. cit.*

29 Feiling, *op. cit.*

30 Feiling *op. cit.*

31 E. L. Woodward, *The Age of Reform, 1815–1870*, Oxford History of England, Oxford University Press, 1938

32 *Ibid.*

33 F. A. Hayek, *Capitalism and the Historians*, University of Chicago Press, 1954, cited in T. E. Woods, *A Myth Shattered: Mises, Hayek and the Industrial Revolution*, Ideas on Liberty, November 2001

34 Watson, *op. cit.*

35   J. Morris, *Pax Britannica*, Faber and Faber, 1968

36   *Ibid.*

37   A. Palmer, *Dictionary of the British Empire & Commonwealth*, John Murray, 1996

38   T. Pakenham, *The Scramble for Africa*, Weidenfeld and Nicolson, 1991

39   *Ibid.*

40   *Ibid.*

41   J. A. Williamson, *A Notebook of Commonwealth History*, Macmillan, 1967

42   *Ibid.*

43   Morris, *op. cit.*

44   J. Morris, *Farewell the Trumpets*, Faber and Faber, 1978

45   P. J. Cain, *Economics: The Metropolitan Context*, in A Porter (ed.), *The Oxford History of the British Empire (Vol III)*, Oxford University Press, 1999

46   *Ibid.*

47   *Ibid.*

48   *Ibid.*

49   *Ibid.*

50   *Ibid.*

51   *Ibid.*

52   Morris, *op. cit.*

53   *Ibid.*

54   J. Bowle, *The Imperial Achievement*, Secker & Warburg, 1974

55   A. Offer, *Costs and Benefits, Prosperity and Security*, in Porter, *op. cit.*

56   *Ibid.*

57   *Ibid.*

58   *Ibid.*

59   M. Sweet, *Inventing the Victorians*, Faber and Faber, 2001

60   M. E. Burstein, English Department, State University of New York College at Brockport, letter to *The Times*, 8 January 2001

61   M. Mason, *The Making of Victorian Sexuality*, Oxford University Press, 1994

62   J. Perkin, *Victorian Women*, John Murray, 1993

63   J. Sutherland, *The Times*, London, 5 June 2007

64 R. Davenport-Hines, *Too Young To Know? The Times*, London, 9 February 1991

65 *Ibid.*

66 A. Hardy, *Queen Victoria Was Amused*, John Murray, 1976

67 *Ibid.*

68 A. Briggs, *The Age of Improvement: 1783–1867*, Longmans, 1960

69 R. C. K. Ensor, *England 1870–1914*, Oxford University Press, 1966

70 S. Mitchell (ed.), *Victorian Britain: An Encyclopaedia*, St James Press, 1988

71 *Ibid.*

72 *Ibid.*

73 Sweet, *op. cit.*

74 F. L. Allen, *The Big Change*, Harper, 1952, cited in R Shenkman & K Reiger, *One-Night Stands with American History*, Quill, 1982

75 J. Harriss (ed), *The Family: A Social history of the 20th Century*, Harrap, 1992

76 *Income, Poverty, and Health, Insurance Coverage in the United States: 2009*, US Census Bureau, 2010 at http://www.census.gov/prod/2010pubs/p60-238.pdf

77 *Ibid.*

78 *Ibid.*

79 C. Panati, *Panati's Parade of Fads, Follies and Manias*, Harper Perennial, 1991

80 J. P. McKay, B. D. Hill & J. Buckler, *A History of Western Society*, 4th ed., Houghton Mifflin, 1991

81 C. More, *The Industrial Age: Economy and Society in Britain 1750–1985*, Longman, 1989

82 *Ibid.*

83 H. J. Dyos & D H Aldcroft, *British Transport*, Leicester University Press, 1969

84 P. Brendon, *The Dark Valley: A Panorama of the 1930s*, Jonathan Cape, 2000

85 T. O. Lloyd, *Empire, Welfare State, Europe: English History 1906–1992*, Oxford University Press, 1970

86 D. Butler & G. Butler, *Twentieth Century British Political Facts*, Macmillan, 2000

87 Cited in P. Brendon, *The Dark Valley: A Panorama of the 1930s*, Jonathan Cape, 2000

88 S. E. Ambrose, *Rise to Globalism*, Penguin, 1976

89 P. Irons, *A People's History of the Supreme Court*, Penguin, 1999

90 T. Morgan, *FDR*, Simon and Schuster, 1985

91 *Ibid.*

92 Irons, *op. cit.*

93 Case summary at: http://supreme.justia.com/us/297/288/index.html

94 *The Times*, 5 July 1954

95 *Chronicle of the 20th Century*, Longman, 1988

96 J. Montgomery, *The Fifties*, George Allen and Unwin, 1965

97 In January 1950. *Encyclopaedia of World History*, Harrap, 1987

98 T. O. Lloyd, *Empire, Welfare State, Europe: English History 1906–1992*, Oxford University Press, 1993

99 Budget speech, Hansard, v603, col 58, 72, 7 April 1959

100 Montgomery, *op. cit.* The original six members of the Common Market, the forerunner of the European Community (and then Union) were Belgium, France, Germany, Italy, Luxembourg and Netherlands.

101 *Ibid.*

102 C. Barnett, *The Verdict of Peace*, Macmillan, 2001

103 *Ibid.*

104 *Ibid.*

105 A. Woodward and R. Penn, *The Wrong Kind of Snow*, Hodder & Stoughton, 2007

106 Report, *The Times*, 22 July 1957

107 *DNB* online entry, at www.oxforddnb.com

108 E. Halévy, *Imperialism and the Rise of Labour (1895–1905)*, Barnes and Noble Inc, 1961

109 P. Robertson, *Shell Book of Firsts*, Ebury Press, 1974

110 M. Booth, *Opium: A History*, Simon & Schuster, 1996

111 R. Porter, *The Greatest Benefit To Mankind*, HarperCollins, 1997

7

Popular Deceptions

Cultures rely on shared beliefs and shared certainties. The older and more certain these feel, the more they shape our current way of life and our attitudes to the past. The older, and more familiar, we think they are the more reverence we give them. And they become the social glue that holds us together. So what happens when our understandings about some of the most cherished mainstays of our culture are revealed to be not all we think they are? Read on.

Christmas

We saw in Chapter 2 how much of our perception of the origins of Christmas is based on false history – we think the Bible tells it to us, but on closer inspection we find our common understanding is the product of centuries of later accretion. Much of the carbuncling of Christmas that has produced our modern celebration is, conversely, less than a hundred and fifty years old, developing mainly in Victorian times. A century or more may be enough to regard the innovations that came from this period as 'traditional', but it remains nevertheless surprising how much of what we take to be customs that are readily assumed to stretch back centuries, turn out to have a much shorter pedigree.

The White Christmas

It would be difficult to get a more stock scene representative of the Christmas season than village houses, country lanes or church towers draped with a covering of snow. One might be forgiven for believing the association of snow with Christmas to be steeped in the long distant past, but that is not the case. In fact, the imagery of snowy Christmastide dates only from the Victorian era, specifically, Charles Dickens. His *A Christmas Carol*, published a week before Christmas in 1843, is responsible for creating the imagery we now take as 'traditional'. He wrote it after trudging around London's streets with a heavy cold, which no doubt explains the rich imagery he created of freezing conditions outside and the alluring warmth of the hearth inside.

The effect was also to re-define the celebration as a family-oriented, pretty-much single day affair (until Victorian times, it had tended to spread across the twelve days between Christmas and Epiphany on 6 January, the traditional date the Magi had made their visit) and offered up the classical images we now cherish of snow-bound streets, frosty windows and roaring hearths.

Dickens was led to the image by his own experience of a freak spate of cold winters in his youth – eight of his first ten Christmases were white as Britain was at the peak of the 'Little Ice Age', the coldest decade since the 1690s. His encapsulation of these London memories into his writing did more than anything to lock into Britons' psyche their totemic yuletide vision. It was far from mirroring the realities of life. Estimates suggest that the 19th century went on to have fewer than twenty white Christmases in all.[1]

The Christmas tree
Not an ancient throwback to pagan traditions, but a relatively modern import from Germany. Prince Albert is often credited with popularising the ritual in Britain when he had one erected for the royal family in 1840, the year he married Victoria (other less prominent Germans had already been following their tradition here for more than a decade – one is first recorded in England in 1829). It was when a reproduction of

the decorated tree for 1848 appeared in the *Illustrated London News* that the fashion for the tree as the centrepiece of the family Christmas took off.[2]

Christmas cards

Another 'tradition' that goes back no further than the early Victorians. The first Christmas card is recorded in 1844, a private initiative by William Dobson, a painter of religious art. He distributed amongst friends lithographs of a sketch symbolising his 'spirit of Christmas'. The practice seems to have taken off quickly, again likely under Prince Albert's influence (Germans had been sending cards at Christmas since the 16th century). One of his equerries, Henry Cole, dashed off the first commercial cards in 1846 – replete with the line 'A merry Christmas and a happy New Year' which pretty much fixed the greeting from then on – and by 1863 the first advertisements are to be found, in the *Illustrated London News*, for Christmas stationery[3]

Santa Claus

The origins of Father Christmas's practice of entering homes on Christmas Eve and being ferried around on a sleigh by flying reindeer dates from 1820s America after Clement Clarke Moore's poem, 'A Visit from St Nicholas' (often rendered also as 'The Night Before Christmas') that appeared in the *Troy Sentinel* in New York in December 1823, a year after he had written it for his children on Christmas Eve, 1822. This set the now classic yuletide scene, mentioning for the first time stockings hanging over the fireplace, a roly-poly St Nicholas, fur-clad (although not specifically in red and white – that would come a century later, care of Coca-Cola), Santa's sleigh, pulled apparently by miniatures ('and eight tiny reindeer') and roof-top delivery of sacks of toys. In just fifty-six lines, Moore had crafted the image of Christmas that would become the staple view of millions of us believing it to hail from centuries before. Moore was famous for nothing else, and he never even copyrighted his most celebrated work.

Carols

And then there are the customs we assume to have respectable origins. According to the Rev. Ian Bradley, editor of the *Penguin Book of Hymns,* some of our most famous Christmas carols may have a darker side to them. In a 1991 article he pointed to 'O come, all ye faithful' whose author John Francis Wade was a Jacobite enthusiast.[4] The carol was written, in Latin, in 1743, two years before Bonnie Prince Charlie's uprising. Bradley asserts that the text is full of Jacobite images, including the thistle and the Stuart cipher. It was not translated into English until a hundred years later. It may well have been a disguised call to arms. It is also a surprise to discover that its famously grandiose tune originated as a piece in a comic Parisian opera.

'Angels from the Realms of Glory' was written not by some mild church hand but by a political agitator, James Montgomery, who had been to jail for his political activities. It first appeared in the radical newspaper he published in Sheffield in 1816.

It also comes as a surprise that some of the tunes that most resonate with ancient Biblical times, like 'Away in a manger', 'O little town of Bethlehem' and 'We three Kings of Orient are' were all actually written in the United States in the second half of the 19th century (1885, 1868 and 1857 respectively).[5]

☞

The unloving origins of St Valentine's Day

A date we assume to have originated for the celebration of lovers is actually one that marks the church's attempt to *curtail* hedonism and unadorned lechery, and the saint who gave his name (how many of us intuitively think Valentine was a she?) to the day has no association in the religious calendar for any attention to loving matters. He just happened to be the saint for the day in question. For it was the day – 14 February – not the saint, that is at the heart of the matter here.

Our modern annual affair is a tame variant of the earlier Roman festival of Lupercalia which ended the series of turn-of-the-year celebrations. It supposedly marked the point when the birds were believed to find their mate for the coming breeding season.[6] The fourteenth, the eve of Lupercalia, was therefore a vital day for selecting one's choice. In pagan times, when the deity honoured was Februa, the goddess of marriage and childbirth, the day became synonymous with debauchery, as young men would draw lots for the favours of the local womenfolk. Original 'valentines' were the slips of paper with the name of the girl chosen. The following day would, if things went to plan, descend into an orgy of sexual abandon.

No one knows precisely when the Christian church authorities stepped in to clean up the day, but the association with Valentine – a doctor who happened to have been martyred on that day in AD 269 – was entirely fortuitous. There were no women saints for the day in question so, bizarrely ever since, the personification of human love and marriage has been a man.

The invention of St Valentine's Day, therefore, had less to do with actively fostering the moods that were stirring at that time of year, and for which we today assume is the underlying purpose. It was primarily about *constraining* the expression of feelings and bringing under control a celebration which had become associated with moral laxity. St Valentine is there to dampen down your spirit of love, not evoke it.

☞

The end of the frost fairs

The freezing up of the river Thames, and the holding of popular winter 'frost fairs' on the frozen waterfront of central London, has been a periodic spectacle down the centuries – until modern times. In the coldest winters, the river provided a solid surface from early December until February, as it did in 1683–4, one of the longest on record. Then, an entire ox was roasted on the ice and the row of shops hawking to visitors stretched from Temple down to Southwark.

The last major frost fair was in 1813, and it has been the popular presumption that the lack of them since has been down to the ever increasing temperatures: global warming. Not so. The real reason for the demise of the fairs was the demolition of the old London Bridge in 1831. This structure, which had stood since 1209, had twenty arches spanning the river, the foot of each arch protected at water level by huge stone 'feet'. The effect of the design was to reduce the width of navigable waterway by 80 per cent, from 900ft (the span of the Thames at this point) to just 194ft.[7] This slowed down the current to such an extent that, when added to the rubbish and detritus that frequently accumulated underneath the arches and the fact that the undredged river was significantly shallower than today, the river easily came to a standstill even in the moderate cold of an English winter.

In 2001, University of East Anglia scientists demonstrated how 'ponding' – the sticking of ice crystals to the upstream part of the bridge pillars – would cause the water flow to reduce dramatically in modestly cold temperatures, giving the perfect conditions for freezing.[8]

Since the replacement of the bridge in 1831 by one that had only five arches (the current one built between 1967 and 1972 has only three), frost fairs have been a distant memory.

☞

Scotch mist

If the English can be said to have got their heritage wrong simply by ignoring their past, the Scots might be said to have done it by actively inventing it. The cultural symbols we intuitively associate with Scottish 'tradition' – tartan and the kilt – are actually a creation of surprisingly recent pedigree (and actually not by Scots at all).

Far from being an ancient style of dress from the Highlands, the kilt was an English invention of 1727.[9] It was created by an immigrant Lancastrian ironworks owner, Thomas Rawlinson, who needed a more practical outfit for his Scottish furnace workers than the actual traditional native dress – the long and flapping cloak-like plaid. The shortened skirt-like result was both safe and comparatively comfortable in the heat of the works. It only took on a national symbolism when the English banned the wearing of them after the Jacobite Rising of 1745 during which they had become associated with the cause of Bonnie Prince Charlie. The irony of the kilt as a symbol of timeless Scottish tradition is not lost on historians, although barely recognised more widely. The kilt does not represent the old way of Scottish life but exactly the opposite – it was created to accommodate, and is a mark of, the transformation of Scotland from the open lands of an agricultural society to the closeted life of the industrial factory.[10]

The tartan has an even more remarkable history. Although it had existed as a style of weave pattern from around the 17th century, the modern concept of different designs delineating Scottish families was a 19th century creation, and based not on Scottish origins but the claims of two fantasist Englishmen, John Sobieski Stolberg Stuart and Charles Edward Stuart. They claimed to be the legitimate descendants of the Jacobite Young Pretender. In fact, they were the English sons of Thomas Allen, a Royal Navy lieutenant and Katherine Manning, the daughter of a Godalming clergyman.[11]

The pair essentially created the modern myth of the tartan

by producing an apparent history of the tradition, *Vestiarium Scoticum* in 1842, which purported to set out the tartans of all the Scottish clans. They claimed it was based on a late 15th century manuscript, but they would never agree to requests to produce the original document. In fact, they made most of them up. They produced a second, larger, volume, *The Costume of the Clans*, in 1844, to further widespread skepticism amongst scholars.

But the theme caught the mood of the times. It was a moment in Scottish history when cultural introspection was on a steep rise. In 1822, George IV had paid the first visit by a reigning monarch to Scotland for 171 years. Sir Walter Scott, novelist and arch cultural fabricator, had been appointed Master of Ceremonies and chose the occasion to accentuate the national image. Together with Colonel David Stewart, with whom he had founded the Celtic Society two years earlier, he prepared a guide to the tartans supposedly belonging to the most important families, and encouraged them to wear them during the royal visit. Scott had the King also clad in a specially created tartan. As one historian puts it, the invention repaired the historic divisions within Scotland between Highlander and Lowlander, and between Scotland as a nation and the English:

> [The King] was warmly greeted by an array of his Scottish subjects, all sporting similar garb and joining in the fun. This was one of the great publicity stunts of British history. At a stroke, it invented a 'national tradition' in which everyone could participate, and most importantly where the dominant Lowlanders could take the Highlanders to their hearts. ...
>
> The fact that Scotland's modern 'Highland Tradition' is entirely spurious is beside the point. It did not matter that the philibeg kilt adopted in 1822 had been created by an English industrialist for the use of his Scottish workers. It did not matter that tartans had never previously been limited

to particular clans. What mattered was that the Scots had found an amusing game which was helping them to sink their differences.[12]

The visit, regarded as a long-awaited affirmation of Scottish national dignity after the recent decades of English suppression, fired a nationalist rebirth, into which the likes of the chancing Allen brothers were easily drawn. Sir Walter Scott had drawings of tartans made by an artist that were said to have existed from time immemorial. These too were fakes[13] and the 'tradition' of Scottish bagpiping also appears to be based on nothing more substantial than the claim of a single individual, Angus MacKay, in 1838 that Scottish piping traditions were taught at a famed Highland school of piping on Skye across three centuries between 1500 and 1800. No other evidence has been found to substantiate the existence of the school, and historians believe it was a hoax by MacKay.[14] Their doubts may have strengthened after MacKay subsequently suffered a mental breakdown in 1854, claimed to have been secretly married to Queen Victoria and had to be institutionalised in a madhouse near Windsor Castle. When he was returned to a Scottish asylum in 1859, he escaped and drowned himself in a river.[15]

These were years when questions were not inclined to be asked when artists and culturists suddenly produced as historical 'fact' facets of a past that the nation earnestly wanted to turn out to be true. The first half of the 19th century saw our modern view of 'old' Scotland rapidly form through an amalgam of invention, charlatanism and wishful thinking. A Scottish national identity was desperately yearned for. If the component parts did not exist as historical truths, few had much interest in spoiling the story merely on that account.

One of Scotland's supposed iconic contributions to popular culture, golf, is more likely a foreign invention. Scotland lays its claim to originating the game to references dating to March 1457, oddly in a resolution of the Scottish Parliament banning it (and football) because of the deleterious social impact the games were having. Researcher Dr Heiner Gillmeister of Bonn University suggested in 2002 that the 'golf' referred to here was not the sedate pastime we think of today but a more aggressive game played by teams with a shepherd's crooks, a forerunner of hockey.[16] Evidence for this comes from an account written in 1460 by a Scottish nobleman from St Andrews who describes a game played with a 'golf-staff' in which a single ball was contested between teams. The first references in Scotland to the game of golf we recognise today seem to date only from the late 1500s.

Gillmeister, along with many other linguists, proposes that 'golf' probably derives from the Dutch 'kolve' or 'kolf', meaning shepherd's crook. Dutch and Flemish paintings from the middle of the 15th century show the game being played on frozen canals with small wooden balls. As evidence of the Low Country origins of the game, Gillmeister pointed to a 1545 Dutch school language textbook, *Tyrocinium linguae latinae*, used to teach Latin by referring to life in everyday Holland, which devotes a whole chapter to describing the game of golf in which players attempt to knock a ball into a small hole.

Another piece of evidence showing the Low Countries to be more advanced in the game, is the decree of King James of 1618 banning the import of Dutch golf balls because of the amount of money leaving the country for their purchase.[17]

As with so many other things, however, it looks like the Chinese probably beat Europe to the first tee. In April 2006, researchers from the prestigious Palace Museum in Beijing announced the findings of a two year study into the origins of the game. Scholars had identified a rule book, *Ball's Rules*, for the game 'hit-ball' dating from 1282, the time of the Mongol Chinese empire, which bore every resemblance to a game we would recognise as golf.[18] Four paintings of the emperor playing the game had been discovered, showing the players using curved sticks and on a course of small holes, each of which is marked by a small flag pole.[19] Professor of Cultural History, Cui Le-quan, told Western reporters, 'If you read *Ball's Rules* and compare that with the rules set by St Andrews in 1754, there is little difference.' The researchers believed that the game travelled to Europe by the Mongol migrations of the 13th and 14th centuries.

☞

The not-so Wild West

Thanks to Hollywood, the abiding image of the American frontier in the late 19th century is fixed in the popular mind as being perennially populated by gunslingers and plagued with lawlessness and shoot-outs every day in the saloon. Names like Tombstone, Deadwood and Dodge City, and their unsavoury characters, epitomise the 'Wild West' we think we know.

But many of our most fervent beliefs about the period are exaggerations, or downright wrong. As one critique eloquently put it, 'more people have died in Hollywood westerns than ever died on the real frontier'.[20] In real life, Dodge City, Kansas, which boomed in the last quarter of the century from being a major hub on the cattle trade routes up from Texas to Chicago, and famous in folklore for its anarchy, actually had just five killings in 1878 – and that was the most deadly year in the town's history. Likewise, the most deaths that Tombstone saw in a year was just five too, and Deadwood's record tally was only four.[21] Records show that even in the most notorious of Kansas cow towns – Abilene, Dodge City, Ellsworth, Wichita, and Caldwell – the violence levels were actually extremely low. Between 1870 and 1885, there were just forty-five murders in these towns.[22]

And the quick-fire draws so beloved of Hollywood were not all that the movies would suggest. Most firearms of the era were so inaccurate that it actually would not matter how quickly a gunman got to his weapon.[23] There is little evidence either that disputes were resolved by the classic shoot-out duel at high noon in the middle of Main Street. The image actually originates only from *after* the high point of the Wild West had passed, appearing it is believed for the first time in Owen Wister's novel *The Virginian*, written in 1902.[24] This achieved popular exposure in Broadway shows, and then twice in film as silent movies before Gary Cooper starred in the iconic Hollywood classic in 1929.

Hollywood is responsible, too, for the persistent image of the Red Indian threat to white settlers. The classic vignette of the outnumbered innocents in their wagon train set upon by savage hordes is perhaps the quintessential image of the period. Yet of the 250,000 pioneers who set out across the West between 1840 and 1860, only 362 died in violent contact with Indians. (For that matter, only 426 died on the Indian side.)[25] More usually, Indians sold food and horses to the travellers, and provided guides in return for useful goods.

The characters who have been burned into our minds as representative of the Wild West turn out to be anything but the wild men we have been brought up with from the movies. **Wyatt Earp**, perhaps the most famous lawman of them all, star of more than two dozen Hollywood films and hero of the shootout at the O.K. Corral, upon closer investigation turns out to be more myth than man. Riding tall in the folklore tales as marshal of Dodge and then Tombstone, scene of the famous shootout, he was in fact never an appointed marshal, and he never ran for the elected office of sheriff. He was only ever a part-time assistant or deputy marshal, as one biographer describes him, more 'a bouncer with a tin star'.[26] He only ever participated in two shoot-outs in his entire life: one was the O.K. Corral, and that lasted less than thirty seconds.

Contrary to the Hollywood image of a righteously-driven upholder of civic peace, his life was a little more complicated. He had had to flee town in 1871 after being charged with horse stealing, and he was caught pocketing police fines in Wichita in 1874.[27] His presence from 1879 in Tombstone actually had little to do with wanting to clean up the town. As an aspiring businessman, he was there to accumulate mining claims and land rights. He also bought a quarter share in the gambling concession of one of the Tombstone saloons. His interest in law and order, such as it was, was strictly a business-related concern.[28]

'**Wild Bill' Hickok**, who kept law and order in Abilene, Kansas, another cattle trail centre, had his reputation enhanced by a glowing account of his exploits published by *Harper's New Monthly* magazine which attributed hundreds of law enforcement killings to him.[29] In fact, historians have concluded he probably killed only five (another says seven). One of them was his deputy, whom he shot by mistake.[30]

William Bonney, '**Billy the Kid'**, was said at the time to have killed a man for every year of his own life (he died four months shy of his twenty-second birthday at the hands of sheriff Pat Garrett in 1881). Historians are now certain that his tally is an exaggeration. The first tales to emerge of The Kid's exploits came from Garrett himself in his celebrated *The Authentic Life of Billy, the Kid*, and some believe that Garrett created the myth, and his killing of the young man, to cover up for the fact that Bonney had managed to escape from his custody. Adherents of the case believe Bonney may have lived on until dying anonymously in Texas in 1950. No grave for Bonney has ever been located. In 2003 the Governor of New Mexico, where he is supposed to have died, announced plans to formally pardon Billy the Kid. For seven years the issue was under consideration before, on the last day of the Governor's

term in December 2010, he announced he was not going to
do so because of the inconclusiveness of the evidence. Such is
the mystique around such things, that as of 2010 the issue was
still under consideration.[31]

Hollywood is also responsible for the stereotypical image
that has come to embody the Wild West but which is simply
untrue. The scene of the pioneering **wagon train** creeping
across the plains, spread out in single file one after the other,
is iconic – and wrong. This was, in fact, the most dangerous formation a group of vulnerable travellers could adopt,
and they didn't. Wagon 'trains' actually travelled side-by-side,
sometimes up to ten miles wide. To do otherwise would be
to leave any part of the elongated chain open to attack by
marauders. It was far more problematic to attack a collection
of wagons spread out laterally. Another obvious consideration
is that to have travelled in a straight line would have ensured
that the dust thrown up by each wagon would blow into every
one following up behind.[32]

And circling the wagons when a train was attacked was
also an invention of Hollywood. The logistics involved in the
manoeuvre would have been far too time-consuming to have
made any difference to their defences. The pioneers did circle
their wagons at night when they rested – but largely to make
a temporary corral to keep the animals enclosed.[33]

Another classic icon of the pioneering West also turns
out to be less enduring than we might think. Famed by
Hollywood as a staple of the period, the **Pony Express**
offered the dramatic mail service delivered by frantically
ridden horses at breakneck pace across the arid terrains. By
stationing horses every seven to twenty miles across the West
(there were 153 changing points), it could transport mail from
St Joseph, Missouri to Sacramento, California in eight to
ten days. This compared with the more dangerous existing
land route that ran through the southern states and which
seemed increasingly insecure with the imminent threat of

the civil war, and the sea route which took twenty-two days and involved sailing to Panama, crossing the isthmus (these were pre-canal days) and then taking another ship up to San Francisco.

Introduced in April 1860, it was actually a failure and lasted only eighteen months. Corruption in the US government prevented the Pony Express company from getting the mail contract from the carrier that used the southern route, despite its clear advantages. Although the civil war, as predicted, did cut off that route a year later, it was the coming of the telegraph that really sounded the death knell. The completion of Western Union's transcontinental link in October 1861 instantaneously transformed communications out to the west and almost as rapidly put paid to the Pony Express.[34]

☞

The age-old kitchen sage?

She was, and remains, the most famous authority on domestic household management of all time. Although entirely unknown by her own name, Isabella Mayson had an influence on almost every single home from the mid-19th century onwards. She was only ever known through her husband, and is remembered to this day simply as Mrs Beeton.

Her husband, Samuel Beeton, was a magazine publisher. In 1852 he had launched the *Englishwoman's Domestic Magazine*, the first periodical aimed primarily at women and a ground-breaking enterprise for the time. For twopence a week he provided a wide range of articles, predictably on gardening, housecare and children, but innovatively too on medical matters, problem pages and dressmaking patterns. These were to become the mainstay of the woman's magazine to this day.

And of course there was cookery. His wife contributed the cooking sections and, over a thirty-month period, ran a part-work entitled the *Book of Household Management*. It proved so successful that they decided to produce it as a self-standing book and in 1861 *Mrs Beeton's Book of Household Management* was published, containing 3,000 recipes as well as learned articles on medical, legal and other household matters.

Over a thousand pages long, it was the most comprehensive work on all things domestic and, for some, remains unrivalled to this day for accuracy and scope. The simplicity of the recipes and the clear instructions on preparation set the standard for every cookery book published since. It was an instant success, selling 60,000 copies in the first year; it has run to sixty editions and has never been out of print.

Flushed with the success, they moved to the Kent countryside where Isabella turned to her next production, a *Dictionary of Everyday Cookery* on which she laboured ceaselessly right up to the last days of her fourth pregnancy in early 1865. Once the child was born she returned immediately to correcting the proofs, too soon however for an infection set in and developed into puerperal fever. She died within days.

More famous through her work than she ever was in life, her image has come down the years as one of the archetypes of the Victorian age. Yet far from the chubby, worldly grandmother of a figure which was suggested by the depth of experience contained in her manual and for which the name Mrs Beeton has come to conjure up, Isabella Beeton was, when she died, just twenty-eight years old.[35]

☞

Victory snatched from obscurity

Probably the most famous ship ever built for the Royal Navy, HMS *Victory*, the flagship of the fleet and Nelson's command for his celebrated battles, and death at Trafalgar, could be assumed to have had the most illustrious of service histories. Far from it.

In fact, in the forty-three years between her construction and withdrawal from the line, she spent less than half of her time actually in service.

She was hardly a new vessel when she performed her most memorable feat at the Battle of Trafalgar in 1805. She was then a ship of forty years' pedigree, but for all her prodigious reputation passing down from history, had actually seen remarkably little action. A month after her launch at Chatham in May 1765, she left for sea trials off Sheerness. After successfully going through her paces she was pronounced satisfactory – then promptly laid up at Chatham for the next thirteen years.

It was common practice then not to commission ships – which meant also having to man them permanently – until they were required for action. (When she was, it took the press gangs three months to find the full complement.) *Victory* did not see her first action until 1778 and it lasted only until 1797 when she returned to the Medway and was found by the up and coming Nelson serving time as a hospital ship. He asked the Admiralty for it to be his new flagship. Just in time, as the Admiralty had had other plans – she was to be totally gutted and converted to a prison hulk.

Nelson won his request in 1800 but it was to be another three years before her rehabilitation was completed. Her bottom had deteriorated so much that it had to be completely re-coppered, an immensely expensive operation. Although finished by 1803, it was the end of June 1805 when *Victory* finally left the Medway under Admiral Nelson for the trip to Trafalgar for her day of glory.

She remained in service afterwards until 1808. In 1816 the Admiralty wanted once again to dispose of her and intended to sell her. It had issued contract invitations to shipbreakers. Public pressure forced a re-think and a special mooring was built at Portsmouth Harbour for her to become the flagship for all commanders of the base. She lay there for well over a century until 1922 when she was moved to her final resting place, where she stands today in No 2 dry dock at Portsmouth.[36]

☞

Titanic myths

One of the abiding characterisations of the *Titanic* disaster, perpetuated by the 1997 multiple Oscar-winning blockbuster, is that class consciousness broke out as the passengers fought for their lives and the lifeboats. In a seminal scene, third class 'steerage' passengers are locked below decks to prevent them from overrunning the better-off. The scene is entirely fictitious, and in fact proportionally more men survived from steerage than from second class as an exhibition mounted by the Public Record Office in April 1998, in the wake of the furore created by the film, revealed. The official casualty figures show that amongst the first class passengers, 34 per cent of men, 97 per cent of women and all five children were saved. In second class, a mere eight per cent of men survived, but 84 per cent of women and all twenty-four children escaped. In third, more men – 12 per cent – were saved than in second, along with 55 per cent of women and 30 per cent of the children.[37] The documents on show included testimony from third class passengers to the official enquiry that denied they had been hampered from getting up on deck. The exhibition suggested that the story of the crew locking doors originated from allegations made by militant union leaders back in Britain, where the docks had been plagued that year with bitter strikes, who claimed that the poor had been sacrificed to save the upper classes.

The wealthiest man aboard, real estate and hotel tycoon John Jacob Astor, worth some £20 million (a multi-billionaire in modern values), died because he was not allowed into a lifeboat until all the women had been able to board.

Another apparent myth about the disaster was that the loss of life was inevitable. A Virginian marine architect analysing the hull of the wreck in 1998 suggested that had the passengers and crew not panicked, they could have stemmed the inflow of water long enough to have stayed afloat until the rescue ships arrived. William Garzke said that most of the gaps caused by the collision with the iceberg were less than an inch wide. Had they stuffed material like clothes and bed sheets into the cracks, it was entirely possible to have staunched the water.[38] Even without any attempts to save her, the ship took two hours and forty minutes to sink. The rescue ship *Carpathia* arrived less than two hours afterwards.

☞

Unexpected origins

The 'hun', the popular British term of denigration for the enemy in the First War World, originated not from the Allies but as a self-imposed moniker by Germans themselves.[39] It arose in the stirring instructions given by Kaiser Wilhelm II to his troops embarking in July 1900 to put down the Chinese Boxer Rising against expatriate Europeans. In a speech described by *The Times* as 'extraordinary', he told his forces to be as ruthless in their mission against China as the Huns:

> No quarter will be given, no prisoners will be taken. Let all who fall into your hands be at your mercy. Just as the Huns a thousand years ago ... gained a reputation in virtue of which they still live in historical tradition, so may the name of Germany become known in such a manner in China that no Chinaman will ever again dare to look askance at a German.[40]

'Wop' was, to begin with, a term of admiration for Italian immigrants into the United States. It derives from the Neapolitan *guappo* meaning 'strong'. It only later became a derogatory slur.[41]

'Ignoramus' is another term of abuse that started with a very respectable meaning, but acquired its current use through one single episode. According to the *Oxford English Dictionary*, the word originally, and properly, relates, to the practice of early juries in the British legal system of indicating their rejection of an indictment by writing 'ignoramus' ('we ignore it') on the back of their verdict paper. The transition appears to have originated from a 1615 Latin play by George Ruggles entitled *Ignoramus* 'written to expose the ignorance and arrogance of the common lawyers'. Ruggles named his chief lawyer character, Ignoramus. According to his *Dictionary of National Biography* entry, the play, which lasted five hours and was performed in front of King James, was Ruggles' solitary contribution to national literature.[42]

The uninformed among British midday diners who tuck into a 'ploughman's lunch' assume they are following an age-old tradition that reaches back to the days of their hard-working country cousins. The hearty snack of bread, cheese, pickled onions and the odd tomato is sold as the kind of fare industrious farmworkers were supplied with for their day's labours. In fact, the whole creation is a marketing invention, dreamt up in the early 1970s as an advertising campaign for the English Country Cheese Council. There is no historic tradition associated with the concoction at all.[43]

Indian curry restaurants in Britain actually pre-date the supposedly archetypal British staple, the fish-and-chip shop – by more than fifty years. The country's first curry house was the elegantly named Hindostanee Coffee House which opened in Portman Square, London in 1809. The site of Britain's first fish-and-chip shop is hotly disputed, but a claim stands for one Joseph Malin who is reputed to have set up shop in Cleveland Street, London in 1860, fifty-one years after the introduction of the Indian.[44]

Chop suey is not a native Chinese dish at all, but was invented in the United States as recently as 1896, by the cook of the Chinese ambassador who is said to have been trying to create a dish that would appeal to both American and Chinese tastes. It derives its name from the Cantonese *shap sui*, which simply means 'bits and pieces', after the chef collected leftovers of pork and chicken and cooked them with bean sprouts and rice.[45]

Fortune cookies are not the ancient Chinese tradition they are often thought to be either. Far from a customary eastern practice, they were invented in Los Angeles in 1918 by the owner of a noodle company as a means to reduce the boredom of customers waiting for their orders. David Jung of the city's 'Hong Kong Noodle Company' initially got a church minister to write Biblical missives for the cookies. Only later did they turn to the fortune telling we are familiar with today.[46]

☞

It is an icon of the orient, but the rickshaw is neither an ancient invention nor even a local one. It was the brainchild of an American Baptist minister, the Rev Jonathan Scobie, who created the contraption in 1869 to transport his disabled wife around Yokohama, Japan. He later built further vehicles to give employment to his converts.[47]

The cash register that reassures shopping customers that they are being charged the right amount for their purchases did not originate for that purpose. Far from being a device to give the buyer an assurance of probity on behalf of the shopkeeper, it was actually invented as an anti-theft machine to give shopkeepers better control over their own staff. James Ritty, a saloon owner from Dayton, Ohio, invented the concept in 1879 after experiencing first hand his bar staff embezzling his establishment. He devised a clock-like machine, said to have been modelled on the counter he saw on an ocean cruise that recorded the revolutions of the ship's propeller, that displayed the price paid for a transaction. Customers thought it was for their benefit. Ritty's objective was otherwise, calling his machine 'Ritty's Incorruptible Cashier'.[48]

After selling just a few dozen machines in five years, he sold out his business in 1884 to John Patterson for just $6,500. Although Patterson immediately had second thoughts and tried to get out of the agreement, Ritty held him to the deal – to his chagrin. Patterson founded the National Cash Register company, redesigned the machine to the more familiar type-writer key style, and had sold 1.2 million of them by 1913.

NCR is still today one of the leading cash transaction machine manufacturers in the world – and it all stems from not being able to trust one's own employees.

The bikini is popularly assumed to have been a modern invention. It hit the headlines in the summer of 1946 by the clever marketing technique of naming it after the Pacific atoll where, four days earlier, an American nuclear test had taken place. French fashion designer Louis Reard launched his 'ulti-mate' swimsuit to the press at the annual Paris fashion show against the backdrop of a new emerging atomic world, and certainly no one had seen anything like it – not, at least, for 2,000 years. Historians have pointed out that the two piece outfits appear to have been worn in Roman times. Depictions have been found in mosaics in Sicily dating from 300 BC, for example, showing women wearing bikinis while doing sports. Seemingly, then, a case of rather old wine in new bottles.[49]

☞

They never said it

We often know – or think we know – the past through the sayings of others. A telling phrase captures the moment and solidifies it for all time, like a fly in amber. Some famous figures are remembered almost entirely on account of a single phrase, and yet it turns out, remembered wrongly. Some instances are well known; others less commonly appreciated.

Marie Antoinette, Queen of France at the time of the Revolution, is remembered in the popular recollection for virtually nothing except her apparently uncaring observation on the starving peasants, '**Let them eat cake**'. It is held to personify how out-of-touch monarchy and people had become. Yet the phrase was never hers. It was written by Jean Jacques Rousseau in his *Confessions* of 1766, when Marie was only an eleven-year-old in Austria. He told the anecdote of an Italian noblewoman of the 1750s who had scoffed at the plight of the poor using the phrase. How it became pinned on Marie Antoinette is lost to history, but she has been saddled with it ever since.[50] The phrase may even have an earlier pedigree. A letter to *The Times* in 1959 claimed that the phrase is found in the Latin letters of John Peckham, Archbishop of Canterbury at the end of the 13th century. [51]

The great 18th century French philosopher Voltaire, is best remembered for a single thought, '**I disapprove of what you say, but will defend to the death your right to say it.**' But the phrase does not appear in print until as late as 1907. It surfaced in a collection of supposed anecdotes about Voltaire written by Evelyn Hall under the pen name of S. G. Tallentyre. Even there, it is clear that it was not intended to be thought a quotation by him. She wrote that, in a controversy over a book, Voltaire had adopted a 'I disapprove of what you say ...' attitude, putting the phrase in quotation marks. 'I did not intend to imply that Voltaire used these words verbatim, and should be much surprised if they are found in any of his works,' she told an enquirer in 1935. Such is the basis for one of the most cherished expressions of political thought in history.[52]

Another post-dated phrase is the Duke of Wellington's supposed assertion that the Battle of Waterloo was '**won on the playing fields of Eton**'. Unfortunately, at the time when Wellington was at Eton, there *were* no playing fields. The phrase only surfaced four years after the Duke's death, in a book about English politics by a French author, Count Charles de Montalembert.[53]

Napoleon is reputed to have originated the phrase about England being **'a nation of shopkeepers'**. Not so. Although he is quoted as referring disparagingly to his enemy while in exile in 1822, the phrase had long been is use, coming first on the scene through the celebrated economist Adam Smith who used the description in his seminal work *Wealth of Nations* published in 1776, when Napoleon was only seven years old. American revolutionary Samuel Adams had also used it that same year, writing specifically of England.[54]

A phrase that is universally known but who's actual origins have never been traced is the warning supposedly uttered by political heavyweight Edmund Burke, that **'The only thing necessary for evil to triumph is for good men to do nothing'**. It does not appear in any of Burke's writings or speeches to Parliament. Yet it is regular trotted out as one of the most potent sayings of the 18th century political enlightenment.[55]

Likewise, one of the most revered of America's founding fathers, Thomas Jefferson, is often cited as the source for telling political advice, that **'Eternal vigilance is the price of liberty'** and **'That government is best that governs least'**. Neither of these lines actually appear in any of Jefferson's writings or speeches.[56]

Abraham Lincoln suffers from a plenitude of false attributions, so esteemed is his reputation amongst Americans. A celebrated ten-point assertion of political philosophy, espoused by amongst others Margaret Thatcher in her winning 1979 election campaign in Britain[57], is entirely bogus. In resonating terms, the passage famously asserts, amongst other messages, **'You cannot bring about prosperity by discouraging thrift. You cannot strengthen the weak by weakening the strong. ... You cannot help the poor by destroying the rich ... You**

cannot help men permanently by doing for them what they could and should do for themselves.' The mantra first surfaced only in 1949 when Ohio Congresswoman Frances Bolton read them into the Congressional Record claiming them to be the words of Lincoln. When investigated by suspicious historians who had never heard of them and could not find them in any of Lincoln's printed papers, they were traced to a campaigning churchman, the Rev. William Boetcker, who had used a genuine Lincoln quotation on a sheet of wartime homilies in lectures to workers, but had filled the back with maxims he had made up. He had declared on the leaflet that those on the back were of his making, 'inspired by Lincoln', but Congresswoman Bolton picked up the phrases by word of mouth from a friend who missed passing on the all important caveat. Even though the quotations have been exposed as myths since the mid 1950s, they still regularly crop up as sayings of Lincoln.[58]

Galileo is most famously remembered, quotation-wise, for a single phrase, **'Yet, it moves'**, supposedly uttered under his breath after being compelled by the Inquisition in 1632 to deny his belief that the Earth moved around the Sun. The phrase only appears more than a century and a quarter later, in a collection of commentaries on Italian authors, *Italian Library*, published in 1757 by critic Giuseppe Baretti.[59]

Another scientist's most famous quote was at least actually said, but it turns out not to be as inspirational as we have come to see it. The only quotation likely to be remembered from Isaac Newton is his protestation of modesty about his achievements when he wrote to fellow scientist Robert Hooke in 1675, **'If I have seen further it is by standing on the shoulders of giants'.** Magnanimous, maybe, but not original. He copied it from the work of another scientist, Richard Burton, in whose *The Anatomy of Melancholy* it had appeared fifty years earlier and with whose work Newton was very familiar.[60] And Burton seems likely to have copied it too. The phrase 'dwarves on the shoulders of giants' has been traced as far back as the philosopher Bernard of Chartres writing in the late 12th century.[61]

Almost the only detail likely to be popularly recalled about motor pioneer Henry Ford's Model T car is that it was available **'in any colour, so long as it's black'**. In fact, for the first five years after its launch in 1908 it was available in four other colours as well as black: red, green, blue and grey.[62] Only later, after he had noticed that the black enamel paint dried quickest did he then restrict the colour scheme in order to keep up the speed of his assembly line.

A perennial favourite for children of the past – when Latin was more common in schools – was the supposed declaration by Imperial conqueror Sir Charles Napier who telegraphed back to London announcing his seizure in 1843 of the Indian province of Sindh by a single word – **Peccavi** – Latin for 'I have sinned'. Clever, indeed. Except is it not true. The honour belongs in fact to a teenage girl, Catherine Winkworth, who remarked to her teacher how Napier could have responded to the criticism he was receiving in Parliament for the action. She sent her joke to *Punch* which printed it as a factual report, leading Napier to be accorded the accolade. It was not corrected until the 1920s, but is still regularly cited as if true.[63]

Another frequent mis-recalling of history is the misattribution of the much remembered reply given by a mountaineer to the question from a press man, 'why do you want to climb Mount Everest?' The reply, **'Because it's there,'** epitomised an air of insouciance that nothing was beyond those who had the courage to try. It is often, and wrongly, attached to Edmund Hillary, the first successful conqueror in 1953. In fact, the quote was uttered by George Leigh Mallory, who attempted the climb in 1924 and disappeared in the attempt (his body was only found in 1999). No one knows for sure whether he got to the top before succumbing. Edmund Hillary's own far less quotable refrain on coming down from the summit was the rather earthy, 'Well, we've knocked the bastard off'.[64]

References

1   Report, *The Times*, London 24 December 2008

2   F. & J. Muir, *A Treasury of Christmas*, Fontana, 1982

3   *Ibid.*

4   *The Times*, London, 21 December 1991

5   www.carols.org.uk

6   A. Jones, *Dictionary of Saints*, Chambers, 1992

7   W. R. Dalzell, *The Shell Guide to the History of London*, W. W. Norton, 1983

8   *Science*, April 2001

9   H. Trevor-Roper, *The Invention of Scotland: Myth and History*, Yale University Press, 2008

10   *Ibid.*

11   *Dictionary of National Biography*, online edition

12   N. Davies, *The Isles: A History*, Macmillan, 1999

13   T. Steel, *Scotland's Story*, Collins, 1984

14   *Ibid.*

15   *Ibid.*

16   Report, *Daily Telegraph*, 20 July 2002

17   J. Rice, *Start of Play*, Prion Books, 1998

18   Report, *The Times*, London, 27 April 2006

19   *Ibid.*

20   R. Shenkman, *Legends, Lies & Cherished Myths of American History*, HarperCollins, 1988

21   *Ibid.*

22   *Myths of the Old West*, at www.unpopulartruth.com/2009/04/myths-of-old-west.html

23   P. Patton, *Made in USA: The Secret Histories of the Things That Made America*, Grove Weidenfeld, 1992

24   J. M. Faragher, in *Past Imperfect: History According to the Movies*, ed. M. C. Carnes, Cassell, 1996

25   J. W. Loewen, *Lies My Teacher Told Me*, Simon & Schuster, 1995

26   C. Tefertiller, *Wyatt Earp: The Life Behind the Legend*, Wiley, 1998

27   D. Wallechinsky and I. Wallace, *The People's Almanac 2*, Bantam Books, 1978

28   Tefertiller, *op.cit.*.

29   *Wild Bill*, Harper's New Monthly Magazine, February 1867

30   D. Wallechinsky and I. Wallace, *The People's Almanac 2*, Bantam Books, 1978

31   Reports, *The Times* 6 June 2003; *Daily Telegraph* 26 July 2010; www.bbc.co.uk, 31 December 2010

32   L. Gregory, *Stupid History*, Andrews McMeel, 2007

33   *Ibid.*

34   D. Wallechinsky and I. Wallace, *The People's Almanac*, Doubleday, 1975

35   *Dictionary of National Biography* at www.oxforddnb.com

36   J. Presnail, *Chatham: The Story of a Dockyard Town and the Birthplace of the British Navy*, Corporation of Chatham, 1952

37   Report, *Daily Telegraph*, 9 April 1998

38   Report, *Daily Telegraph*, 2 December 1998

39   R. Graves & A. Hodge, *The Long Weekend*, Hutchinson, 1985 ed.

40   Report, *The Times*, London, 30 July 1900

41   C. Panati, *Browser's Book of Beginnings*, Houghton Mifflin, 1984

42   www.oed.com; www.oxforddnb.com

43   N. Rees, *Dictionary of Phrase and Fable*, Parragon, 1993

44   M. Sweet, *Inventing the Victorians*, Faber and Faber, 2001

45   R. Hendrickson, *Encyclopaedia of Word and Phrase Origins*, Facts on File, 1987

46   *Ibid.*

47   P. Robertson, *Shell Book of Firsts*, Ebury Press, 1974

48   P. Patton, *Made in USA*, Grove Weidenfeld, 1992

49   www.bestofsicily.com/mag/art55.htm

50   Wallechinsky and Wallace, *The People's Almanac 2*

51   John Ward, *The Times*, 30 April 1959

52   P. F. Boller & J. George, *They Never Said It*, Oxford University Press, 1989

53   *Oxford Dictionary of Quotations, (3rd ed)* Oxford University Press, 1979

54   N. Rees, *Cassell Companion to Quotations*, Cassell, 1997

55 *Ibid.*

56 Boller & George, *op. cit.*

57 And quoted in full on the eve of the election by the Conservative supporting *Daily Express,* 2 May 1979

58 Boller & George, *op. cit.*

59 *Oxford Dictionary of Quotations, (3rd ed)* Oxford University Press, 1979

60 Boller & George, *op. cit.*

61 *Oxford Dictionary of Quotations, op. cit.*

62 D. Wallechinsky, *The 20th Century,* Aurum Press, 1996

63 *Oxford Dictionary of Quotations, op. cit.*

64 F. S. Pepper, *Contemporary Biographical Quotations,* Sphere, 1986